EVE'S
RIB

Mariette Nowak

EVE'S RIB

*A Revolutionary New View
of the Female*

ST. MARTIN'S PRESS · *New York*

Manufactured in the United States of America

Library of Congress Cataloging in Publication Data

Nowak, Mariette.
    Eve's rib.

    1. Sex role.   2. Sex differences.   3.   Sex differences
(Psychology)   I.   Title.
HQ1075.N68   305.3   79-29736
ISBN 0-312-27239-1

To David, without whom this book would not have been written and with whom I've enjoyed being female.

Contents

Introduction

We polish an animal mirror to look for ourselves.

DONNA HARAWAY
(John Hopkins University)

I AM FEMALE. So is half of humankind. So is half of the entire animal kingdom.

What does it mean to be female in the natural world? What are the common concerns, strengths, and problems of the female? How has the female evolved and how does she live? Most intriguing of all, what can the human female learn from her sisters among the other species—from the doe and the vixen, the tigress and the ewe, the lioness and the hen, and above all, from the female primate? What are the roots, the biological bases, of her human existence?

And what can the human male learn? For if there is femininity, there is masculinity; if there is a female role, there is a male role; if there is a lover, there is a beloved. The lives of female and male are, in most species, inextricably bound one with the other. To highlight one is to illuminate the other. As such, although the primary focus in this inquiry will be on the female of the species, we cannot help but gain added perspective concerning the male of the species.

1

I have written this book in the spirit of Konrad Lorenz. Famed scientist and Nobel Prize winner, Lorenz was among the first to realize that a knowledge of animal ways could provide insight into our own human behavior. We are endowed to this day, says Lorenz, with an "enormous animal inheritance."

Since Darwin, of course, we have been aware of the evolution of our bodily characteristics. Medical research, taking advantage of this fact, has long used mice and monkeys as well as other species to work out diagnoses and treatment. The physical responses of these animals resemble our own. Now it is becoming increasingly clear that their behavioral responses, too, often resemble and reflect upon our own. "A biologist . . . must hold," says Robert Hinde of Cambridge University, "that there are continuities between the behaviour of animals and that of man."

It is of utmost importance that we recognize and study these continuities. Our aim, Hinde points out, should not be to explain the human situation directly from animal data, but to abstract principles that might have human applicability. Jane Van Lawick-Goodall, renowned for her work with wild chimpanzees, has stressed much the same thing: "Today we are all aware of the tremendous need for a better understanding of our species, yet only too often the scientist, searching for the biological basis of some human pattern of behavior, is confounded because intellect and culture have conspired to confuse the picture." We cannot afford to neglect any approach, Goodall adds, that might give us a better understanding of our evolution, biology, and social behavior. It is because animals are less complex than we are, less affected by culture, less hindered with inhibitions, less troubled by foresight, less burdened by hindsight—it is because of their very simplicity that animals can help us to clarify our own behavior.

For such reasons, the study of animal behavior has long intrigued me. But what of the female and her role? Even a short time ago, little was said of her. And what was said almost always reinforced the stereotypes attributed to the female in our own species. Despite this dearth of information, I decided to ferret out what I could about the female in the belief that, with the growing interest in animal behavior, more and more data would become available.

To my delight, I found even more information that I had dared to hope for. In the last few years, there has developed a new and growing awareness of the role of the female in the natural world. The reasons for this are several: Not only are there more and more women in the natural sciences, but more male researchers are becoming aware of the past biases in their own work and that of their male colleagues. Together, these scientists have provided a rich and revealing body of information on the female of the species, much of which I will discuss in future pages. And as a result of this new research, many of the stereotyped theories of the past, once accepted as fact, are now being challenged.

The record of bias began early in the natural sciences. In the days of monarchies, the largest member of a honey bee colony was automatically designated as the king. Subsequently, however, his royal majesty was detected in the very unkingly act of laying eggs! In reality, the "king" was none other than a queen.

More recently, there was the question of the Uganda kob. For years the kob, among the most handsome of African antelopes, were thought to live in harems, groups of females headed by rams. Game wardens, hunters, explorers all—and all of them male, no doubt—perpetuated the story. It was a woman, Mrs. Helmut Buechner, who first realized that things were not all as they seemed among kob. Mrs. Buechner's husband was then a professor of zoology at Washington State University and he happened to be carrying out an unrelated research project in the Semliki Flats of Uganda, where kob were common. Taking his wife's cue, Buechner investigated further and discovered a kob world filled, not with harems, but with free-loving females and territorial males.

The rams, it turned out, fight and jockey for position on what is called a stamping ground. There, each on his own territory, the males strut and mince with as much energy as a gyrating Elvis or a disco-dancing Travolta. It's all a big show to impress the females, who nonchalantly amble through the stamping ground making their sexual selections.

Elephant groups were also once thought to be dominated by a single male. Each "herd bull," as he was often called, supposedly watched over and defended a harem of females. In fact, however, an old cow, the matriarch, leads an elephant group of mothers and young. The wandering males only occasionally join them to service a cow in estrus.

Charles Darwin himself was not without bias. He found it "astonishing" that female animals had sufficient taste to make subtle distinctions between males in choosing mates. But there was no other way that Darwin could account for the brighter colors, sweeter voices, and greater ornamentation of males in many species. Nonetheless, he was convinced that males had a decided edge when it came to intelligence.

Darwin notwithstanding, it is interesting to note that the only genius among subhuman primates of whom I am aware happens to be female. Imo, a Japanese monkey, is credited with several food-gathering inventions. Her troop, studied by biologists at the Japanese Monkey Center, was fed sweet potatoes and wheat to supplement their diet. These foods were scattered on a sandy beach near the troop's forest home. At eighteen months, Imo discovered that she could rid the potatoes of sand by washing them in the sea. Later, she came up with a novel way to separate the wheat grains from the sand. Before Imo's discovery, the monkeys laboriously picked out wheat grains from among particles of sand. But Imo, at three years, was seen to toss a handful of mixed sand and wheat into the sea, wait until the sand sank, and then scoop up the wheat. In time, Imo's inventions spread throughout her troop.

Unfortunately, bias can still be a problem today. Ask Dr. Katherine Ralls of the National Zoo. Not long ago, Ralls, a researcher at the zoo and a Harvard graduate, made an interesting discovery about bongos. Rare and beautiful animals, bongos are antelope native to the bamboo forests of Africa, and the National Zoo is fortunate to house the only pair in the country. Ralls noticed that the aging male bongo showed far less interest in mating than the female. To arouse her reluctant partner, the female would often go to great lengths, jumping around, wiggling her rump, and nudging him. Often, says Ralls, "she would prance away and if he wouldn't chase her, she would come back, lick him, nudge him and try to get him to chase her."

Dr. Ralls had to leave the zoo for several days. Her trip precipitated an equally important discovery, albeit a discovery reflecting more on men than on bongos. In Ralls's absence, several male keepers and curators kept an eye on the bongos. When she returned they described the male bongo's activities, but failed to mention anything about the female's behavior. Later, however, a *female* keeper informed Ralls that the female bongo was brazenly soliciting the male while Ralls was away! Obviously, the human male tends to view things from a different point of view than does the human female.

In such ways, often inadvertently, bias has crept into the supposedly objective sciences. My aim in writing this book will be to correct these distortions and present a more balanced view—the true view—of the female of the species and her role in the natural world.

(1) Vive la Femme!

A Virgin conceived, a Virgin bore, and after birth a Virgin still.
St. Augustine

1

THERE OCCURS, IN nature, an extraordinary event not unlike that postulated in some theologies. It is the phenomenon of virgin birth—a female egg bringing forth new life, without benefit of union with a male sperm. Strangely, in the common view, virgin birth has been reserved solely for the goddesses in ancient myths and, more recently, for Christianity's holiest woman, the Virgin Mary, Mother of God. Yet it exists as an everyday reality, termed parthenogenesis in scientific parlance, in a number of species both plant and animal. Moreover, its possible occurrence even among ourselves has been discussed in the medical journals of our day.

A favorite of mine among parthenogenetic animals is *Philodina*, an exquisitely fragile, many-celled miracle in miniature. She is classed with the rotifers, those minute beings whose name refers to their crown of fine hairs beating one after another like a tiny revolving wheel of microscopic dimensions. Magnification of almost any drop of pond water will reveal these curious and abundant beings. Among rotifers, *Philodina*, along with others in her order, is unique. For she is female, always female. Males are entirely unknown in her genus. Yet she flourishes, producing single-handedly generation upon generation of her kind. Prolific as she is, *Philodina* has become by far the best-known rotifer in scientific circles.

In addition to rotifers, a great number of other invertebrates are capable of virgin birth. It also occurs, although far more rarely, in vertebrate groups. Among plants, the phenomenon is even more widespread than among invertebrates. Such a popular strategy in nature's game plan deserves our closer attention.

The most striking, although obvious, feature of parthenogenesis is that in every case nature has seen fit to dispense only with the role of the male of the species. The female has always prevailed, her reproductive role irreplaceable in the natural scheme of things. Among parthenogenetic species, all-female groups like *Philodina*'s are known, as well as those having a preponderance of females. But never, to my knowledge, is the situation reversed. The male, it seems, cannot get on without the female of the species. But *she* can and has, on occasion, flourished with remarkable independence.

Besides *Philodina* and her kind, there are other invertebrates that have entirely female populations. There exists, for example, a species of praying mantis *(Brunneria borealis)* ranging from North Carolina to Texas, among whose members no male has ever been recorded. (Nor, incidentally, have males fared much better among the more common bisexual species of mantids. These females will often eat the males after mating, much as occurs among many spiders.) There are other instances, too, of this penchant for the distaff among invertebrates. We find all-female groups among mites and moths, among worms and wasps, among beetles and insects, and in a number of other disparate groups. Generally speaking, however, such completely unisexual types are relatively rare in the invertebrates. And their occurrence in the more advanced vertebrate groups was totally unheard of until, in a pioneer paper published in 1932, in the midst of the depression days, the

Amazon mollie came to the attention of the scientific world.

It was through the eye-opening research of Laura and Carl Hubbs, then associated with the Museum of Zoology at the University of Michigan, that this unique little fish from the waters of southern Texas and the east coast of Mexico upset biology's staid view of vertebrate capacities. The Hubbses' paper reads rather like a mystery novel, its secrets hidden, however, in the realm of the natural world, in the realm of undeniable reality. They began by investigating three closely related species of mollies. The Amazon mollie, *Poecilia formosa*, they discovered, was "exactly intermediate in all distinctive features" between two other species, *Poecilia latipinna* and *Poecilia sphenops*. They had carefully compared these three species of mollie as to depth of body, placement and size of the dorsal fin, number of dorsal rays, and the vividness of spots. And, in every case, the Amazon mollie was "Ms. In-Between." For instance, where *sphenops* had 9 dorsal rays and *latipinna* had 13, the Amazon mollie usually sported 11 rays. The Hubbses discovered the same thing when they examined fish from the Yucatan Peninsula. The resident Amazon mollie was again intermediate between two other local species of mollie, *Poecilia sphenops* and *Poecilia velifera*. There, the Amazon mollie had 13 dorsal rays, nearly the arithmetic mean between the average number for the local *sphenops* with its 9.5 rays and *verifera*, with 17.5 rays! The mathematical exactitude of the Amazon's intermediate character left little doubt that she was a hybrid form produced by the mating of the two "parent" species of mollie. Nonetheless, the Hubbses sought to verify their hypothesis by mating the parent species, *P. latipinna* and *P. sphenops*, in an aquarium. The twenty-two Amazon mollies produced were living proof of their theory.

Still there remained a greater puzzle to be solved—the Hubbses called it the "outstanding peculiarity" of the Amazon mollie. How was it that she existed over most of her range only as female? Not a single male did they find among the nearly two thousand specimens they painstakingly examined from Mexico and Texas. Only in one population from a river near Vera Cruz in Mexico did they note any males, most of whom were abnormal. Moreover, this was the only place where both parent species were found to be in close proximity.

Wherever the Amazon mollie existed solely as females, it occurred with one—but only one—of its parent species. In Mexico, the Amazon mollie thrived together with *sphenops*, far inland from the coastal range of *latipinna*. In Texas, on the other hand, it abounded in company with *latipinna*, in areas much farther north than those favored by *sphenops*.

The female Amazon mollies, the Hubbses assumed, must mate with *sphenops* males in the Mexican streams and with *latipinna* males in Texas waterways. But here the mystery compounded, for although the two species of males with which the Amazon mollie supposedly mated were very different, the Amazon's young, regardless of location, were always entirely alike—and all females. The Hubbses wondered what peculiar genetic process could account for this strange occurrence.

Back in their laboratories, they once again confirmed their findings in the field. No matter with which species the Amazon mollie mated in their aquaria, the offspring, even as adults, showed absolutely no resemblance to the males involved. And although the Amazons' broods were many and large, not one male appeared among them.

It was obvious, of course, that inheritance in these fish was strictly maternal. Since no male characteristics were ever evident, the eggs must certainly develop without fertilization by sperm— it must be by parthenogenesis, presumed the Hubbses. Yet it was not spontaneous, since unmated females showed no indication of becoming pregnant. This was a form of virgin birth, it appeared, with an incredible twist: the Amazon mollie simply "borrowed" the male's sperm, on a temporary basis, to get her eggs on the road to development. This is what the Hubbses postulated in their initial paper. The fact is now well established. The sperm, in this form of parthenogenesis, soon degenerates, making no genetic contribution to the developing embryo.

This amazing mollie still swims in our southern waters. She still "uses" males in a manner likely to warm the hearts of the original Amazon heroines of Greece. For this must surely be the ultimate debasement for a finned stud—a kind of ichthyic prostitution service providing for the needs of the female fish. To be sure, the males haven't an inkling of the nature of their services. Nor, it seems, have we much understanding of the operation. Michael J. D. White, professor of genetics from the University of Melbourne, has recently written that although well-authenticated instances of this type of parthenogenesis exist in such groups as earthworms, beetles, and various vertebrates, "the phenomenon remains somewhat enigmatic and paradoxical. If the sperm in these cases does not contribute any chromosomes to the egg, what does it contribute?" Researchers are still not sure.

Through the years since the Hubbses' monumental work, about twenty-four additional all-female parthenogenetic species of vertebrates have been discovered. These include several species of fish and salamander, plus about twenty different lizards. For some, like the Amazon mollie, male sperm is required to activate their eggs; while for others, eggs develop spontaneously without need of male assistance.

Nature, though, is a mistress of improvisation and didn't rest here. Like an ingenious composer, to each original theme she adds variation upon colorful variation. So it is no surprise, I suppose, and yet still astonishing to find fish which, like the Amazon mollie, borrow sperm, but with a decided difference: They use the male's sperm not for a short time, but for a lifetime, a generation, after which it is promptly discarded.

These fish, discovered in the waters of northwestern Mexico, are all-female forms of the genus *Poeciliopsis,* originally referred to simply as Cx, Cz, and Fx. R. Jack Schultz of the University of Connecticut first described their peculiar sexual arrangements in the early 1960's. It works this way: A female will mate with a male of a closely related species. The sperm not only stimulates the egg, but actually unites with it. So virgin birth does not really occur and the female offspring shares the characteristics of both parents, just as in typical reproduction.

All seems quite kosher, then, until the time comes when the female offspring matures and produces her own eggs. Normally, in most sexual species, a female passes on to her egg genes from both her parents. But not so with Cx, Cz, and Fx. Their eggs contain only the female's side of the family. The male's genes are lost forever to posterity. Somehow they are simply not transmitted to the egg. In the next mating, of course, an entirely new paternal set of genes becomes available. Sperm and egg unite once again, combining chromosomes, but likewise only for a single generation. Although parthenogenesis does not actually occur, heredity is restricted just as completely to the all-female forms. "Vive la femme!" nature seems to exclaim.

The bizarre ways of these fish still excite ichthyologists, who are now busy investigating the interactions between these *Poeciliopsis* unisexuals and the closely related bisexual species with which they always associate. Through aquaria studies, it was discovered that males have a decided preference for females of their own species rather than for the unisexuals. Yet, among natural populations, there are almost always more unisexual females than bisexual females. No impending extinction for these females! They are obviously thriving despite the discrimination directed their way. Further research revealed that the unisexual females are inseminated by subordinate and immature males who are unable to compete with the dominant males for females of their own species. These low-ranking males must settle for second-best. But it is all the same for the unisexual females—they get their needed sperm and prosper handsomely. Indeed, says one researcher, these females have "the best of two worlds." Being unisexual, each individual is capable of bearing young, a figure double that of bisexual species in which only half the population is so endowed. In addition, among the *Poeciliopsis* unisexuals, each individual also has a share in the genes of the bisexual population, extra genes which give them the same flexibility in meeting environmental demands that every bisexual species enjoys. (The advantages of sexuality will be made clearer at the end of this chapter.) Such is the brilliant modus operandi of these all-female *Poeciliopsis* populations: a way of life evolved slowly but surely through the tireless processes of natural selection.

2

THE COMMON DANDELION must fend for "herself," since the pollen produced by the male part of the flower is generally useless (inviable, as botanists would say). In most plants, pollen is required for seeds to form. Not so with the spunky little dandelion. She doesn't even wait for pollen; instead, she sets about forming her eggs early, even before the flower opens. This is another form of virgin birth, and the dandelion has made the most of her singular situation. Her aggressiveness is, of course, well known, as she invades our lawns and our golf courses without invitation or the least trepidation. And she succeeds so well mainly because of those fluffy white seed-containing fruits she creates, fruits which she can produce even when plucked in her prime, in full flower, and discarded carelessly among the grasses. Undeterred, she simply matures her seed while lying uprooted on the ground.

While the fertility of this brazen beauty may be detested by some, the capacity for virgin birth among other plant species is a boon to humankind. Many of our favorite fruits—bananas, pineapples, Washington navel oranges, as well as some kinds of figs and seedless grapes—all are produced in the same sexless way.

Parthenogenesis has been found in all groups of plants, especially among the composites, one of the most advanced families of flowering plants. It was first discovered about 1898 by a Swedish botanist, Hans Oscar Juel, in his studies of a plant called the everlasting. In dandelions, the female and male components of the flower appear together within each individual flower, but in the everlasting the male and female components occur on separate flowers which themselves are found on separate plants. Juel noted that the female plants of one species of everlasting *(Antennaria alpina)* produced abundant seed despite the rarity of male plants. Moreover, when he did find male plants, their pollen was as useless as the dandelions'.

Among animal groups, as among these flowers, male incapacity can occur. *He* may be too degenerate, or simply too rare. Take the gastrotrichs, tiny animals much like the rotifer in size and shape, but without the rotifer's splendid wheellike crown. Marine gastrotrichs are both male and female, but the male's gonads are incompletely developed and the female, by necessity, usually reproduces without him.

Water bears are minute sausage-shaped creatures, no bigger than the period at the end of this sentence. They live among the sand grains of wet beaches and on the algae, mosses, and other plants bordering both fresh and saltwater bodies. Since water bear males occur far less frequently than do females and may, in fact, be nonexistent within some populations, virgin birth is common. The same situation exists among some crustaceans, including the brine shrimp in the Great Basin area and in the Gulf of California. While brine shrimp may be sexual, among parthenogenetic populations the male of the species is extremely rare.

In other groups, males may be few and sometimes degenerate, but nonetheless functional at critical times in the reproductive cycle. In these cases, we usually find virgin birth dominating through most of the year, followed by a once-a-year sexual binge. *Philodina*'s cousins, belonging to a different order of rotifers, have such an alternating cycle. Through most of the year, females produce only more females. However, these rotifers often live in ponds or streams that dry up by summer's end. Just before this occurs, they will produce a different sort of egg, some of which will hatch into males. Lacking mouths, these degenerate males cannot feed and will live but a few days. In the meantime, though, they will fertilize other eggs that will develop thick, resistant shells and lie dormant through the winter or until environmental conditions once again improve. Then the females will again take over.

A similar reproductive cycle is found among aphids. All through the spring and summer months, all-female adults produce only all-female offspring. Except for this sexual determinism, however, the various generations may be quite versatile. In one species *(Tetraneura ulmi),* for example, some generations live in elm trees, while others live in grass; some generations are winged, some wingless. Still, each individual is female, capable of producing only other females. Then, late in the year, as with rotifers, there is a change. Males, along with females, are produced parthenogenetically. In some species, some females produce only the males, while other females produce just the females. In other species, any female can produce either male or female young. But, whatever the arrangement, it signifies open season for sexual mating, and the resulting fertilized eggs are laid in winter. In the following spring, only females will emerge, ready to start the whole cycle again. Cyclical systems, like those of the aphids and rotifers, have also been described in such groups as roundworms, water fleas, wasps, and beetles.

Bees and most others in the insect order Hymenoptera, however, do it rather differently: Only the males are produced virginally. But like the aphids and rotifers already discussed, life in the
beehive is completely dominated by the female of the species.
The queen bee and all the workers are female. Only when the
queen deigns to produce males (this decision is governed by a
number of environmental and physical factors) do they enter into
the scene. The queen accomplishes all this by regulating the
outflow of the sperm cells that she obtained during her mating
flight. To create her many female cohorts, she releases sperm
before depositing her eggs; to make males, she simply refrains
from fertilizing the eggs. The queen bee, in so doing, controls the
entire sexual structure of her integrated society, a power certain
to be envied by some human onlookers. The males produced,
whether among ants or social bees or wasps, have but one purpose
in life. They are, as Edward O. Wilson states in his book *Sociobiology*, "highly specialized for the single act of insemination."
When they do hang around the nest prior to mating, "males live
a mostly parasitic existence, cared for by the female members of
the colony."

3

IT WAS A few years ago that a good friend of mine announced, in
dismay, her unwanted pregnancy. It apparently had been not only
unplanned, but at least to her, unexplained. "I must have conceived of the Holy Ghost," she laughed rather bitterly, referring
to the New Testament's version of Mary's virginal conception.
We were both, of course, certain then that there must have been
something far more plebeian, a failure perhaps of a birth-control
device or, more likely, of memory, underlying her misfortune.
And so it probably was. Nonetheless, I can never be quite so sure
as I once was. In my investigations of parthenogenesis since that
time, I've discovered that, like the likelihood of life on Mars or
the existence of extrasensory perception, the occurrence of virgin
birth in the human species is regarded as a definite, if remote,
possibility by serious scientists.

Parthenogenesis exists in the higher animals—the birds and mammals—as well as in the other animal groups that I have mentioned. To be sure, as one climbs up the evolutionary ladder virgin birth becomes more and more infrequent. It is a sporadic, accidental thing, and being so singular an event, there are of course no naturally-occurring parthenogenetic populations to examine, and data is scarce.

Not surprisingly, among avian species, the only known reports of parthenogenesis concern domestic birds with whom our long association has resulted in a rich and intimate understanding. In chickens, unfertilized eggs sometimes show short-lived growth. Special strains of chickens have been developed, moreover, which produce a small percentage of live fatherless chicks. But the turkey is the uncontested parthenogenetic champion among poultry. Work with the turkey began in 1952 when Maslow W. Olson, a researcher for the U.S. Department of Agriculture, noted the beginnings of embryonic growth in a surprisingly high proportion, one in six, of unfertilized eggs from a flock of Beltsville Small White Turkeys. By mating hens who had produced the greatest number of parthenogenetic eggs with cocks whose daughters showed the same capabilities, Olson was able to increase substantially the proportion of eggs showing parthenogenetic development. In addition, a great percentage of such eggs reach an advanced stage of development, and from some, live young were hatched.

Over a twenty-year period, Olson produced 1120 fatherless turkeys. They were all males, as expected, since in birds, unlike humans, the male has the two identical sex chromosomes. Even more remarkable, twenty-six of these males have sired offspring. This was accomplished by artifically inseminating female turkeys with their sperm, since none of the fatherless turkeys has ever been observed to mate or to make a serious attempt at mating.

Among mammals, parthenogenesis appears to be far more rare. There have been instances, in such animals as mice, guinea pigs, rabbits, and especially hamsters, of spontaneous development of unfertilized eggs, but the embryos degenerated in the early stages of development. Researchers, using various artificial ways of inducing parthenogenesis, have not had much better luck, although in 1939 a worker named Pincus claimed to have produced normal fatherless rabbits. Unfortunately, Pincus's work is still unconfirmed. The closest thing to virgin birth occurred not long ago at the Jackson Laboratory in Maine. There, scientists fused a parthenogenetic embryo with a normal one and then implanted it in a foster mother. The new embryo was carried to full term and a mouse was born. Produced in part naturally and in part parthenogenetically, this mouse is the best evidence yet that virgin birth may be possible in mammals.

But if a rare viable offspring were produced by virgin birth in a mammal, would it be noticed? Several researchers have asked that very question. To readily observe such an event, the female would have to be kept totally isolated from male intervention. Many breeders of laboratory animals, reportedly, will admit in private to a few unexplained pregnancies in segregated females. Sometimes they pass it off as "mating through the wire" by an escaped animal. However, the geneticist Richard A. Beatty of the University of Edinburgh points out that breeders of both laboratory mammals and pedigree stocks of domestic animals would hesitate to expose such an inexplicable birth since it might well be construed, instead, as a cover-up for an error on their part.

In 1955, Dr. Helen Spurway, then a lecturer in eugenics at the University College in London, broached the subject of virgin birth in humans. Her lecture was discussed in *The Lancet,* one of the most prestigious medical journals in the western world, and led to a scientific examination of some possible cases of the phenomenon.

Parthenogenesis, if it occurs in humans at all, is extremely rare, Dr. Spurway admitted. Suppose, she conjectured, that its frequency were only half that for the birth of sextuplets—a rare event which occurs about once in every three billion pregnancies. The majority of such cases would, most likely, involve women with a recent history of sexual intercourse and would, consequently, pass unnoticed. Among the few remaining cases, what woman could successfully assert the facts of her situation in view of contemporary opinion? Dr. Spurway suggested that such a woman might have more confidence in presenting her claim if she knew that, today, she could be vindicated without reasonable doubt. To begin with, the child produced by virgin birth would be expected to be a girl since, unlike the arrangement among turkeys, in humans it is the female who possesses the two identical sex chromosomes. Blood tests could further help identify the offspring as parthenogenetic, while the culminating proof would be the ability of the mother to accept a skin graft from the child. The reciprocal, Dr. Spurway pointed out, need not be true. The mother would necessarily have all the child's antigens (substances involved in the acceptance or rejection of grafted material), but the child herself may have inherited only some of her mother's antigens. A skin graft from mother to child, therefore, might not be accepted, even by one produced virginally, if the mother's skin contained an antigen foreign to the child.

"Possibly," *The Lancet* concluded its review of Dr. Spurway's talk, "some of the unmarried mothers whose obstinacy is condemned in old books on forensic medicine, or cited as a curiosity by their contemporaries, may have been telling the truth."

Following this provocative discussion, public interest was aroused and a newspaper asked mothers to come forward who genuinely believed they had given birth to a parthenogenetic child. The claims of the nineteen women who presented themselves were carefully examined. Eleven women misunderstood the meaning of virgin birth, thinking that it referred to a conception that occurred while the hymen remained intact, and these were eliminated immediately. Seven cases were dropped since the child possessed either antigens or eye color not shared by the mother. The final case of "Mrs. Alpha and daughter" looked promising. Not only were their blood types identical, but special tests showed further similarities in various blood components. Both also had the ability to taste certain chemicals, an ability that requires identical genes. Following these tests, skin grafting was performed. Unfortunately, the skin graft from daughter to mother was shed in approximately four weeks and that from mother to daughter remained healthy for about six weeks and was then removed. S. Balfour-Lynn, the researcher under whose direction the investigation was carried out, concluded that the significance of the skin grafting results was "obscure." But Beatty, in his review of this work, contends more objectively that a "straightforward interpretation must surely be that the rejection of a graft from daughter to mother means that the daughter possesses antigens not possessed by the mother, and is therefore not parthenogenetic."

The possibility of virgin birth in humans, as in other mammals, consequently remains unresolved. But comparative grounds do lend considerable support to the idea. The geneticist Michael J. D. White suggests that "Some capacity for parthenogenetic development is probably present in all eggs." Among vertebrates, as noted, viable parthenogenetic offspring are found in fish, amphibians, reptiles, and birds; and parthenogenetic embryos occur in mammals, although none have been known to survive outside the laboratory. In view of this evidence, Beatty concludes that, "We would not be altogether surprised if a finding of adult mammalian parthenogenesis were to provide a last link in this already almost complete parallel. In the meantime, the comparative argument can, at least, be regarded as a strong incentive for further research."

4

PHILODINA AND HER sisters abound in our ponds. Dandelions dance en masse in our lawns and waysides. The Amazon mollie multiplies plentifully in our southern waters. Bees and ants thrive in their bustling colonies. Among these and many other species, the female reigns dominant and indispensable, while her male counterpart has become nonexistent, rare, inept, or parasitic. Or else he has become solely a stud whose sperm is used temporarily by the female for purposes of her own.

If the female can so often go it alone, if virgin birth is so successful a reproductive mechanism among some organisms, if the male is not obviously a necessity of life, why then does sexuality exist? Why then did it evolve? A clue can be found in the cyclical rotifers and aphids. Through most of the year, the female of these species reproduce replicas of themselves, replicas sharing their every gene. And this appears to be fine for fair weather times. But when the pond is due to dry up or the cold of winter is approaching, these creatures take to mating.

Certain wasps behave in similar fashion and reproduce either virginally or sexually depending on the season. There are also the water fleas, minute relatives of the lobster that are abundant in all kinds of fresh water. Water fleas produce their summer eggs parthenogenetically, but their winter eggs, laid in the chill of autumn, are produced sexually. These same water fleas, however, when raised indoors with plenty of food and favorable temperatures, have been known to do without sex for four entire years. The females of one species produced, single-handedly, a total of 180 generations during that time! But when aquarium temperatures are reduced, when food is scarce, or when overpopulation occurs, these females once more lay eggs that will hatch into males and begin to mate.

In each of these species—in the cyclical rotifers, aphids, wasps and water fleas—sex comes into play when environmental changes are in the offing. Old patterns may not always do in such uncertain times, past solutions may not always suffice, familiar and identical gene patterns may, indeed, even prove fatal. As our own folk wisdom warns, there is the danger of putting all one's eggs in the same basket.

It is under such circumstances that sexual reproduction is called upon to replace the old unending identity with new diversity. In each act of fertilization, parental genes are reassorted, exchanged, and combined in a series of intricate steps, the end result being a unique, never-before-and-never-again-to-be individual, built upon the past, yet diverging to a degree from its patterns and constraints. A being emerges: new, different, sometimes strange!

The variety of individuals so produced is the stuff of evolution. In time, natural selection will cull from among them the most fit to parent future generations. Sex, in this way, enables each species to better adapt to environmental changes, to expand its range, to take advantage of new food sources, to meet the unpredictable. It's a way, in short, to ensure the group against "future shock." The more variety among its members, the more chances for its future survival.

In contrast, parthenogenesis, at least when it is the sole means of reproduction, is generally considered an evolutionary dead end, a road to extinction. Faced with inevitable change, most such species will eventually go the way of the dinosaur and the dodo bird. Admittedly then, the all-female parthenogenetic population is not nature's preferred order. But it has recently been discovered that the female of the species, at least among mammals, is nevertheless nature's basic theme. She is the original upon which the male is later molded, with appropriate modification. She is the alpha; he, but a beta.

(2) Female Genesis

Nature's first choice is to make Eve.

JOHN MONEY AND PATRICIA TUCKER
Sexual Signatures

1

NO ONE KNOWS just how it first happened or when. Certainly, it was long after life's first molecules appeared in the primeval pools of an infant earth. Likewise, it was long after these molecules coalesced and reordered themselves forming the pristine cells from which all life has since evolved in a kaleidoscopic array of cast and color, form and function. But by half a billion years ago, nature, like some ancient alchemist, had discovered the riches of the sexual encounter and became obsessed with the exponential increase in the options it brought her.

In life's dim beginnings, reproduction was merely a matter of an individual's splitting in two, a way so successful that the amoeba and many another protozoan still multiply today in such manner. But in unknown ways, perhaps forever hidden behind the misty shroud veiling earth's earliest days, there evolved distinctions between species members, distinctions that foreshadowed the sexual differentiation yet to come.

You can see in the paramecium the beginnings of such sexuality. The paramecium is a shoe-shaped protozoan which, at its largest, is just visible to the naked eye. While reproduction for the most part is simply a matter of division, occasionally one paramecium will bind itself to another for a time and exchange genes. At parting, each paramecium will divide twice, forming four new individuals. To you or me, one paramecium of a particular species and variety appears just like the other; their mating, seemingly, a random occurrence upon chance encounter within their watery confines. Things are not, however, quite so simple. In 1937, scientists discovered that these one-celled creatures have a mind of their own: One paramecium will not mate with just any other. There are physiologic differences between individuals that set them off into mating types. In one variety of *Paramecium aurelia*, for instance, mating type I will mate only with mating type II, none other.

Another protozoan, *Volvox*, also deserves our attention. To me one of the loveliest of Lilliputian beings, *Volvox* is a hollow sphere, up to one millimeter in diameter, which whirls about in its liquid medium like a tiny green world unto itself. Forming the surface of this little sphere are thousands of individual cells, interconnected by slender threads. I first marveled at *Volvox*'s fragile beauty when I saw it on a TV film, and since then, first as student, then as teacher, I've had ample opportunity to view this microcosm of evolutionary progress. For *Volvox* is the culmination, in a series of protozoan species, of a trend toward increased sexuality. Whereas among simpler organisms all individual cells can reproduce, in *Volvox* only certain ones take on this role. These reproductive specialists are differentiated even further: For some, simple asexual division is their forte; while others, more advanced, specialize in producing either sperm or egg. These two kinds of gametes, or reproductive cells, moreover, are quite different in size and form and, as such, represent a significant advance over the look-alike gametes of lesser protozoans.

In time, through eons of evolution, such differences resolved themselves into the entities we call male and female. But a question remains: How are these two basic variations produced? How does a male become male? How does a female become female? The odd ways of the sausage-shaped sea worms called *Bonellia* were discovered half a century ago in a classic and much quoted study by F. Baltzer. The free-swimming larvae of these invertebrates have the potential of becoming either male or female. A larva that develops on or very near the female will usually become a minute male, measuring no more than a fraction of an inch in length. Retarded in development, lacking both mouth and anus, the tiny male eventually enters its mother's body and lives as a parasite inside her kidney. There it serves as little more than a sperm-producing machine. Any larva, however, that settles on the sea bottom matures as a female, at least five hundred times larger than the male of the species.

A substance secreted by the female is responsible for this bizarre system of sexual differentiation. By rearing larvae in seawater to which female tissue is added, males are produced. Lacking such extract, the larvae will develop into females. While *Bonellia's* sexual arrangements are, to my knowledge, unique among invertebrates, they foreshadow those of mammalian species, including even ourselves. In both, the female is nature's first form, nature's original creation; something must be added—a secretion among the *Bonellia*, a hormone among mammals—to produce the male. For lack of a scientific label for this phenomenon, I will refer to it simply as the female-base principle. (John Money and Patricia Tucker, in the book *Sexual Signatures,* use the term "Adam principle" to refer to the indispensable supplement required for maleness. This is, however, a misleading term since it is likely to be identified with the Biblical Adam-before-Eve creation.) The female-base principle is, as you'll see, a recurrent feature in human sexual development.

2

ONE EGG AMONG many ripens, then bursts from a mother's ovary and moves along the nearest fallopian tube. Sperm, 2 to 3 million of them, swim toward it in a flood of semen. From among this multitude of competitors, only one will penetrate the egg, creating a single fertilized cell. Such is the genesis of life—yours, mine, and each of the four billion other people who share this earth. The event, of such personal moment, is ironically an extraordinarily fortuitous one, a mere "accident of the night," as Robert Ardrey would have it.

At this time, at conception, chromosomal or genetic sex is set. Among the forty-six chromosomes we receive, half from each parent, there are two so-called sex chromosomes. The male parent supplies either an X or a Y chromosome to pair with the X chromosome always contributed by the female parent. An XX chromosomal pair produces a female, while an XY combination produces a male, the father thus being the party responsible for genetic sex.

Interestingly, for reasons as yet unclear, the X chromosome is far more vigorous than the Y chromosome. Occasionally, chromosomes may be lost (or even gained) amid the complex events surrounding conception. If an X chromosome is lost from an XX pair or a Y chromosome from an XY pair, the fertilized X cell still survives and multiplies, eventually producing a female body, though one lacking fertility. But the loss of an X chromosome from an XY combination is lethal. No human has ever been found with a Y as the sole sex chromosome. (A gain of an extra sex chromosome, incidentally, will cause abnormalities but is not fatal.) The X chromosome, as you can see, is basic and indispensable; the Y chromosome, simply an embellishment upon nature's original theme. The female form is first; the male, a modification. The female-base principle thus makes its debut.

Perhaps this explains the unusual vigor of the female's chromosomal combination, far superior to that of the male. Nature, though, has compensated for this masculine frailty: Based on miscarriage estimates, there are probably as many as 140 XY conceptions for every 100 XX conceptions. Despite this impressive lead, so many XY conceptions fail to develop that, by birth, the ratio of XY to XX combinations has been nearly equalized with approximately 105 boys born for every 100 girls. This ratio remains about the same throughout most of life. For instance, the forty-year-old population in the United States today is about half male and half female. But the greater vulnerability of the male of the species becomes evident again among the elderly: For every

70 men still living after age 65, there are about 100 women. In later life, of course, the male's higher mortality may be due more to environmental factors—such as his greater exposure to occupational hazards and stresses—than to chromosomal differences.

Soon after conception, the fertilized cell begins to divide and multiply rapidly. Cells start to group together, forming the rudimentary structures of the human embryo. Those of sexual potential are, as yet, completely neutral. The gonads might become either testicles or ovaries. In addition, there are two sets of genital ducts, the Wolffian and Müllerian ducts. The Wolffian ducts are named for Kaspar Wolff, an eighteenth-century embryologist who first identified them. They will develop, in the male, into his internal reproductive structures—the seminal vesicles, prostate gland, and sperm ducts. The Müllerian ducts, named after nineteenth-century physiologist Johannes Müller, will in the female develop into the uterus, fallopian tubes, and upper vagina. There is also the genital tubercle, which can adapt itself as either clitoris or penis.

For the first six weeks, the embryo, whether XX or XY, coasts along in sexual ambiguity. But at the end of this time, by some mechanism as yet unknown, the Y chromosome of the male embryo will trigger the gonads into developing as testicles. In the XX embryo, on the other hand, the gonads will yet remain for a time as primitive, all-purpose organs. "Actually the gonad is an ovary, not because it has that structure, but rather because it is not a testis," said J. Gillman of the Carnegie Institution of Washington, and many other researchers concur. Gradually over the second six weeks of the XX individual's life, these gonads, these "presumptive ovaries," as they have been referred to, do indeed develop into true ovaries complete with the lifetime supply of eggs with which a female is normally born.

The primitive gonads, therefore, are basically feminine. In truth, they are nothing other than ovaries in the making. To program them otherwise, to make them male, takes an extra thrust of unknown form emanating from the Y chromosome. So here again the female-base principle is evident.

In the intricate processes leading toward sexual differentiation, the testes are next to act in accordance with this principle. Only several decades ago, in 1947, their role was discovered through the pioneer research of Alfred Jost. In his laboratories at the University of Paris, Jost worked with rabbits, surgically removing the testes or ovaries, respectively, from male and female fetuses. He did this before the rest of the sexual anatomy had differentiated —before the Müllerian or Wolffian structures had developed and before the external sexual features had established themselves. Whatever their genetic sex, whether XX or XY, these castrated fetuses uniformly acquired feminine anatomy. It was perfectly clear: the ovaries are not required for female development. Femininity can occur either with or without them. But for the making of the male, the testes are indispensable. In the concluding words of one of Jost's earliest reports, he suggested that his results with rabbits might prove valid for humans and, if so, could explain certain human abnormalities.

It was two years later, in 1949, that Jost had the opportunity to present a paper to the First Mexican Congress of Gynecology and Obstetrics, held in Mexico City. His brother, Dr. Marc Jost, lived in Mexico City and had shown reprints of Alfred's papers to his colleagues, who subsequently, as organizers of the conference, invited the Parisian scientist to participate. In preparation, Alfred Jost, a physiologist, not a clinician, spent many weeks reviewing the medical literature and was able to explain, on the basis of his rabbit work, various human sexual anomalies of interest to physicians. On his return from Mexico, Jost visited several American experts in the field of sexual differentiation, among whom was Dr. Lawson Wilkins, noted for his work on endocrine disorders of childhood and adolescence. Their first conversation was a long and fruitful one, lasting until late afternoon. Finally Dr. Wilkins concluded, "I'm convinced," and he incorporated Jost's ideas into his book on endocrine disorders published in 1957.

It was by this rather circuitous route that Jost's basic research on sexual differentiation came out of the lab and into the lives of laymen. In the years since, Jost's results have been verified time and again. There have been confirmative experiments with mice and rats, and there have been satisfactory analyses of human sexual disorders. These latter analyses have provided "natural" experiments, where ethical considerations must, of necessity, preclude laboratory experimentation.

The testes, it is now well established, are essential if the male reproductive structures are to take shape. Their role, specifically, is in the production of two important hormones. One, testosterone, causes the Wolffian structures to develop into the seminal vesicles, prostate gland, and sperm ducts of the male. If an XY fetus is deprived of this hormone, it will fail to show anatomic maleness. The fashioning of the female reproductive structures, however, requires no such hormonal push. It is, in fact, because of this that the second male hormone, a special Müllerian-inhibiting hormone, is essential for masculine development. Its role is to prevent the Müllerian structures from achieving their destiny as uterus, fallopian tubes, and upper vagina. Without this hormone, a boy will be born not only with the normal male internal organs, but with female ones as well.

Here, once more, the female-base principle is operative. Unless "something more" is added, this time hormones, fetal development is feminine. The principle is evident, too, in the development of the external genitals. Without any extra hormonal incentive, the genital tubercle and associated structures develop into the female clitoris and vagina. Testosterone, however, must be present for the formation of the penis and scrotum (into which the testicles will later descend.)

It is certainly not surprising, in view of all this, to find the male more vulnerable than the female. The fetus can coast easily along the direct path toward feminine fulfillment. In contrast, the road leading to a masculine destiny is one beset with one fork after another, any of which offers potential hazard should a wrong turn be taken.

One needs only to scan the literature to realize that these facts concerning sexual differentiation are, today, fully accepted. Robert Stoller, professor at the University of California Medical School in Los Angeles, states unequivocally, "The evidence has piled up that in mammalian species at least, the 'resting state' is on the female side and that to make tissues, organs, or organisms male requires an androgen pulse. . . ." John Money and Anke Erhardt, eminent researchers in the field of human sexuality, upon whose work much of this chapter is based, write: "In the total absence of fetal gonadal hormones, the fetus always continues to differentiate the reproductive anatomy of a female."

One can only conclude, as does Dr. Harold Lief in his "Introduction to Sexuality" in the most recent edition of the *Comprehensive Textbook of Psychiatry:* "The primordial fetus is, then, female. If one wishes to be mythically symbolic, one might say that Eve preceded Adam and that the Biblical story is a reflection of ancient male chauvinism."

Not surprisingly, I had arrived at a similar point of view before reading Lief. And I propose that a more accurate, if still fictional, rendering of the Biblical account might go something like this: God looked at Eve and said, "It is not good for her to be alone." And with His almighty genius, He concocted the magic of the Y chromosome and of testosterone. With these, He created a variant upon His original model, a variant called man.

In truth, of course, the two sexes emerged long before humans evolved; even longer before these humans whipped up their strange and apocryphal tale about a first man and his dispensable rib. As it is, *he* can dispense with far less than can the female of the species.

So perhaps while women are begging and bargaining for equal rights, while they're struggling for achievement and recognition in so many fields so long denied them, perhaps they can find consolation, however slight, in contemplating the embryo. Nature, if not culture, has given them the edge. And this shall be their strength.

3

THE GREATEST STRUCTURE ever created by living organisms is not one of the great pyramids or the Suez Canal, not the Grand Coulee Dam or Chicago's Sears Tower, but the Great Barrier Reef stretching more than twelve hundred miles along the east coast of Australia. Remarkable though it is, the reef was built unpretentiously through the slow and relentless accumulation over countless days and decades, over unremembered centuries and millennia, of sponge spicules and worm tubes, of starfish and sea-urchin spines and snail shells, but above all of coral cups and the remains of calcareous algae. This reef is one of the richest and most productive of earth's ecosystems; its abundance of living organisms is rivaled perhaps only by that of the tropical rain forest. Among its many colorful inhabitants, I will mention but one, one whose intriguing ways have bearing on our inquiry.

Labroides dimidiatus is a little scavenger fish that earns its keep by cleaning the mouths and gills of larger fish. Not a loner, this scavenger travels with others of its kind in small groups, each consisting of a number of females led by the biggest and strongest fish among them, who is male. If, however, this leader dies or is killed or simply wanders off, the biggest and strongest of the females takes on his position. With amazing versatility, she assumes not only his role but also his very sex. This new "male" will defend the group's common territory and even, within several weeks, begin to produce sperm to fertilize his harem's eggs. Even so, the new leader can be deposed in short order if a more aggressive member of his species comes swimming by and challenges him successfully. And should this happen, the dethroned male will simply revert to femininity and produce eggs once again.

For over twenty-five years, scientists have been studying sex reversals in animals. Unlike our coral reef scavenger, however, most of these animals have been artifically induced through hormones to switch their sexual identities. Male tadpoles of the clawed frog, for example, can be feminized simply by adding female hormones to their swimming water. For female-to-male reversal, however, this is not enough; testicular tissue from male tadpoles must be grafted into the females in order to complete their masculinization. In a species of killifish, both males and females can be induced to reverse sexes merely by adding the appropriate female or male hormones to their water. These reversals, in both fish and frogs, are so complete that former males are able to lay eggs and former females can produce sperm. In mammals, such as opossums, guinea pigs, hamsters, rabbits, mice, and monkeys, sex hormones can also have far-reaching effects, though not to the extent that the sexually reversed adults are actually fertile.

This hormone research led not only to verification of Alfred

Jost's findings on the anatomical development of the sexes, but also to the incredible, indeed for some, the shocking discovery that the brain itself, and consequently the behavior it directs, is affected by prenatal sex hormones. As Money and Tucker state, "Only a few years ago researchers would have scoffed at the suggestion that there could be any such influence, but today the evidence is unmistakable."

The first clue researchers uncovered involved one of the principal distinctions between females and males: Females ovulate; males do not. A female rat ovulates every 4 to 5 days; a female guinea pig, about every 15 days; a human female, about every 28 days. In each case, ovulation is triggered by a hormone from the pituitary gland.

Through a series of classic experiments, the researcher Carroll A. Pfeiffer showed that the ability of a rat to ovulate as an adult is determined by the absence of testosterone in its early development. Even males will ovulate if their testes, the producers of testosterone, are exchanged for ovaries at an early critical period. But if testosterone is present, neither females nor males will ovulate. Obviously, the female-base principle is applicable once more and testosterone again is the extra agent needed for masculinity.

At first, Pfeiffer thought that testosterone must cause a permanent change in the pituitary gland, the source of the hormone causing ovulation. Once the change took place, he hypothesized, the ovulation hormone was no longer produced. But this was later disproved: Transplanting the pituitary gland of a male rat into a female did not disrupt her female functions, nor did the reverse implantation of a female's pituitary gland into a male produce any changes in his functions. At the same time, however, it was discovered that by stimulating the hypothalamus, a part of the brain lying just above the pituitary gland, ovulation could be induced. Perhaps it was the brain, not the pituitary gland, that was changed by testosterone.

In the course of experiments to learn whether this was true, scientists found that sexual behavior in adult rats could be affected by early treatment with testosterone. Normally when a female rat in estrus is mounted by a male, she arches her back and raises her head and rump. But the behavior of experimental females was quite different. Treated with testosterone shortly after birth, these rats never showed the sexual posture typical of normal females. Equally striking changes in sexual behavior occurred in male rats subjected to early hormonal alteration. If deprived of testosterone by castration within a few days after birth, they would readily display the feminine sexual posture in adulthood when injected with a hormone inducing estrus. In normal adult males, on the other hand, it is next to impossible to elicit female responses through mere treatment with such hormones. Similar changes in sexual behavior were induced, by such methods, in hamsters, guinea pigs, and even beagles.

Since sexual behavior, like all other behavior, is ultimately controlled by the brain, it became clear that testosterone causes sexual changes in the brain at an early critical period of development in the life of a mammal. The brain, consequently, like the gonads, is basically female in its functioning; the female-base principle once again prevails. Without testosterone, whether in the male or female, the brain will retain its female pattern and react to female hormones by producing female sexual behavior and ovulation. With testosterone, in contrast, the brain tissue is made more sensitive to male hormones, less sensitive to female hormones, and female as well as male animals will display predominantly masculine sexual behavior.

But that is not all. In addition to sexual behavior, there are also nonsexual behaviors that seem to be influenced by early hormonal treatment. As always, researchers first examined their favorite, the rat. If a female rat is provided with an activity wheel on which she can run at whim, her running will be cyclic, increasing during the time of ovulation. Males, however, run more or less uniformly from day to day. If castrated early in life and later implanted with ovaries, however, these males will show the same cyclic pattern of running found in females.

In another test in which rats or hamsters are placed in an open field, females prove to be more exploratory and to defecate less often than males. Females also are more adventuresome than males in emerging from an enclosed box into an open arena. But males, at least among mice, are much more aggressive toward intruders: 100 percent of males will attack, while only 20 percent of females will do so.

Of more relevance to the human situation are the reports on how early exposure to sex hormones affects our closest relatives, the other primates. Researchers at the Oregon Regional Primate Center worked with rhesus monkeys and found that females treated prenatally with testosterone were decidedly different from the normal female in a number of social behaviors: They played more boisterously, chased more actively, threatened more frequently, initiated play more consistently, and mounted another female more often and more vigorously.

In this parade of species, the truth gradually confronts us: nature, clearly, cannot be stereotyped. Despite those now who would deny all differences between male and female, despite those who have instead dogmatized that "anatomy is destiny," despite these oscillations of the human cultural pendulum, the natural world, oblivious, goes its way. To the chagrin of the male chauvinist, the female rat is the more exploratory, the more adventuresome of the sexes. And among all mammals, it is female anatomy, physiology, even behavior which is basic, which needs no extra "shot" of testosterone. But to the despair of the ultrafeminist, the typical female mouse or monkey is undeniably less aggressive than her male counterpart. And her brain as well as her body has at least some uniquely feminine features.

Intriguing as all this is, however, neither rat nor hamster, neither mouse nor monkey is human, and with reasonable caution, we might well hesitate to leapfrog freely from these animals to ourselves. There is, fortunately, some human data that may be helpful. In the 1950's, a synthetic hormone, progestin, was sometimes given to pregnant women to prevent miscarriage. Pregnancies were indeed saved, but the hormone had adverse effects on female fetuses, causing masculinization much as testosterone does. Probably because of the time factor, the internal sexual organs of these girls developed normally: The hormone had probably been taken too late to affect this aspect of sexual differentiation. But, in most girls, the external genitals were masculinized to a greater or lesser extent. Usually, this involved nothing more than an enlargement of the clitoris, accompanied sometimes by fusion of the labia; in rare instances, however, the masculinization was so complete that the clitoris looked like a normal penis, and an empty scrotum was present. Postnatal surgery corrected these problems, and the girls needed no further treatment since their ovaries were functional, providing them with the normal composite of female hormones.

Anke Erhardt and John Money have conducted follow-up studies of these girls, comparing them with a control group of girls not exposed to prenatal progestin. This control group was selected to match the test group as closely as possible in age, IQ, socioeconomic background, and race. Some significant differences were found between these two groups of girls. The test girls, those exposed early to progestin, were in a word, tomboys, in comparison with the control group. Everyone agreed to this description —the girls' parents, their playmates, even the girls themselves, some of whom were quite boastful of the fact. It is, of course, not unusual or abnormal or deplorable for a girl to be a tomboy; the control girls themselves sometimes reported tomboy episodes. But the test girls were so consistently, so enthusiastically, so actively tomboyish that the evidence was convincing. These girls, it was reported, "like strenuous physical activity, cavorting about on their bicycles, climbing trees, hiking, and exploring. They join the boys in rough games, including football; they like the competitiveness of it."

There were also other differences between the test girls and the control girls. Although not adverse to dressing up on special occasions, the test girls preferred practical clothes to frills and finery; and this to a significantly greater degree than the matched controls. In addition, the test girls favored cars, trucks, and guns over dolls, which they treated with indifference or neglect.

In counterpoint to these progestin-affected girls are boys who lacked sufficient male hormones during their prenatal development. Usually this happens because their body cells are unable to make full use of these hormones. This problem, called androgen sensitivity, prevails throughout life, since hormonal treatment cannot change the inadequacy of their cell physiology. The behavior of these boys is the mirror image of that of the progestin-affected girls. The boys are quieter than average and less likely to be active in competitive sports.

Just what are the implications of this research? Clearly, it suggests that males are normally more physically active and competitive than females, due to the early effects of hormones. This is also borne out in cultural studies. In the United States, boys of nursery-school age are consistently more physically aggressive than girls are. In six other societies, boys three to six years of age were likewise found to be more aggressive than girls of their age. In the younger children, this difference was most pronounced, indicating a biological basis for the trait.

Nonetheless, these differences between female and male are a matter more of degree than of kind. Animal studies, says Money and Erhardt, show that behavior is "bisexual in potential." Robert Stoller reiterates the same theme: "The higher mammals show degrees of both masculine and feminine behavior in any individual and there is much evidence that there is no such thing as an exclusively masculine or exclusively feminine animal." In monkeys, for example, both females and males engage in boisterous and aggressive play, although males will do so more often. In humans, men are usually the warriors and weapon-makers, but women in some cultures are also actively engaged in these things.

Culture plays a very large role in the expression of human aggression. Margaret Mead gave vivid proof of this in her book, *Sex and Temperament,* in which she contrasted the gentle Arapesh people of New Guinea with their murderous neighbors, the Mundugumor. Mead had set out to study the differences between the sexes in each of these cultures, but she came away in disappointment. Although the two cultures themselves differ immensely from one another, within each, the sexes act very much alike.

In the mountain-dwelling Arapesh, both men and women are expected to be "gentle, responsible, and cooperative, able and willing to subordinate the self to the needs of those who are younger or weaker, and to derive a major satisfaction from doing so." Human nature, the Arapesh believe, is basically peaceful, but people can be taught to be aggressive in the defense of others. When to the wonderment of the Arapesh, some men or women do become violent, the Arapesh resign themselves and try not to provoke these unfortunate souls.

The Mundugumor live in river valleys only about one hundred miles from the Arapesh. Yet they contrast with the Arapesh, said Mead, "in every conceivable way." Until the Australian government put a stop to it, the Mundugumor were fierce cannibals and headhunters who regularly preyed on their swamp-dwelling neighbors. Hostility and distrust are also characteristic of relations between individuals within Mundugumor communities. Both men and women, ideally, are fierce, possessive, and ruthless. "A woman who had the generosity to breast-feed another woman's infant simply did not find another husband when she was widowed," said Mead.

The kinship system of the Mundugumor, moreover, encourages aggressive rivalries between family members. Each individual belongs to a "rope": A boy belongs to his mother's rope and a girl belongs to her father's rope. As a result, families are fragmented. Boys compete with their brothers and fathers; girls, with their sisters and mothers. Bitter conflicts are especially apt to erupt over marriage arrangements, in which each family member is concerned with his own selfish interests in the matter. Even lovemaking is violent in Mundugumor society—partners are expected to scratch and bite and tear each other's clothing apart in their passion.

For each of these two societies, cultural expectations largely determine the extent to which aggression is displayed. Although males are innately more aggressive, little difference between the sexes is apparent among the Arapesh and Mundugumor—surely a dramatic example of the importance culture plays in the expression of human potential.

Nurturance is another trait that may be influenced both by biology and culture. Females are generally considered to be the more nurturant sex—more interested in youngsters and more attentive to their needs. In monkeys, females are often more concerned with young infants than are males. In human society, girls as early as nursery school appear more nurturant than boys, and this difference between the sexes continues through life.

Especially provocative has been the experience of the Israeli kibbutzim. Right from the start, communal care of children was established on every kibbutz. Women would be free of the constant care of their children, free to work in the community at large. But women, it developed, began to have second thoughts on their liberation from motherhood and demanded a more substantial role in raising their youngsters.

On some kibbutzim, women now work only part time for six months to two years after their babies are born. Lesley Hazleton, author of *Israeli Women,* reports that "The children's house, once one of the central institutions of kibbutz life, is fast disappearing as kibbutz after kibbutz takes the decision to have children sleep in their parents' home." Many kibbutzim women refuse to work or study outside the kibbutz, since this would mean that they could not be with their children during the day. These women don't want to miss the "hour of love" during which mothers of young children leave their chores each day to spend time with their children. Significantly, fathers have not asked for this privilege. Nor have they been eager for family housing—which not only tends to undermine the communality of the kibbutz, but is also a very expensive undertaking requiring new and larger housing.

Kibbutzim fathers are not singular in this regard. A study of American fathers with infants a year old found that intimate interaction between father and child averaged an incredibly insignificant thirty-eight seconds a day. Even among older children, father ranks lower than TV in influencing their attitudes, ideas, and values. According to an expert in educational development at a hearing on TV violence, the mother alone supersedes the television set in popularity and influence among our future citizens.

The females' greater aptitude for nurturance may, in part, be due to certain physiological changes associated with birth. Mother rats will care for their newborns instantly, while virgin rats need about a week to do so. The responses of these virgin rats, however, can be stimulated by a substance (probably a hormone) present within the blood of a female rat near the end of her pregnancy.

Despite this apparent biological basis for nurturance in females, the quality in humans is certainly not confined to mothers.

Women without children, as everyone knows, can be strongly nurturant. John Money has found that even women who have a male chromosomal pattern and can never bear children can be as nurturant as normal females. The well-known primate researcher Harry Harlow has made much of his experiences in showing a photograph of an infant monkey to numerous college-age audiences. At women's colleges, the girls (most of them undoubtedly childless) always responded with much audible enthusiasm. Male audiences, in contrast, were completely unresponsive. For women, giving birth obviously just strengthens an already-present trait.

Other than the possible influence of the birth process itself, there is no other evidence for a biological basis for nurturance. If biology cannot sufficiently explain the difference in nurturance between men and women, then what of culture? Harlow's audience reactions could be readily explained from a cultural standpoint. It's fine, after all, for females in our society to ooh and aah over a baby monkey. But what of males? From early on, boys learn not to play with dolls, not to cry, not, in fact, to show much of any emotion. Is it a wonder they don't let on to any feelings about an infant monkey? And even if they actually aren't moved much by the monkey, isn't it possible that their early desensitization might be largely responsible?

One of Harlow's own monkey studies shows that, for monkeys, nurturance is largely a learned behavior. Harlow raised some rhesus monkeys in total isolation, without mothers or other infants of their own age, through the early months of their lives. When these "motherless monkeys," as they were dubbed, later had young of their own, they were completely inadequate as mothers. Many ignored their infants; others became the most cruel and abusive mothers Harlow had ever seen. In monkeys, this suggests, there is no natural and universal instinct for nurturance. Deprived of early social contact, these unfortunate females never learned what it was like to have a good mother and never learned, consequently, how to be one. Other monkey studies have dealt with the nurturance behavior of males. Adult male monkeys, for example, can be induced to care quite effectively for young monkeys by housing adult male-infant pairs together. Nurturance, in conclusion, is not necessarily "natural" to the female, nor is it her exclusive perogative.

Human cultures also illustrate this fact. Anthropologists M. Kay Martin and Barbara Voorhies checked the descriptions of 110 cultures, of which 33 had information about nurturance relative to men and women. In 82 percent of the cultures, the trait was stronger in females than in males. But in a significant 18 percent, no sex differences were evident.

Margaret Mead's gentle Arapesh are an example of a society in which nurturance is well developed in both sexes:

> In Arapesh, both men and women were expected to be succoring and cherishing and equally concerned with the growth of children. Boys helped to feed and grow their small betrothed wives, and husbands and wives together observed the taboos that protected their newborn children. The whole adventure of living centered on making things grow—plants, pigs, and most of all, children. The father's role in conception was essentially a feeding role, for many acts of intercourse were believed to be necessary to build up the baby, which was compounded of father's semen and mother's blood.

Mead also found at least one culture in which nurturance is stronger in males than in females. Among the Manus, islanders living off the coast of New Guinea, only males are assumed to enjoy playing with babies. When Mead gave dolls to the Manus children, the boys, not the girls, pretended the dolls were babies.

The fact that men are less nurturant in American society may merely reflect the dictates of culture. This seems to be the case in Israel, too. Although we think of Israeli women with a gun in one hand and a pair of pliers in the other, the news of late is that male dominance is still gaining in Israel. Not only are women often excluded from "male" occupations, but men are excluded from "women's" work. A young man who wanted to work in an Israeli kindergarten, for example, was turned away. Such work is considered "unmanly."

Fortunately, changes may be in the offing, at least in the United States. Because of the less-rigid sexual stereotypes of our times, American males are beginning at last to become more involved in child-care activities. Jerry Cammarata of New York was the first male teacher in the country to be granted a paternity leave, and millions of men everywhere, with working wives, are necessarily taking greater care of their children. There are Mr. Rogers and Captain Kangaroo, as well as more male kindergarten and elementary school teachers than ever before; and there are also divorced fathers, a few, who are getting custody of their children in preference to the mothers. Equal rights will certainly be of benefit to men as well as to women.

The above examples give ample support to the bisexual view of behavior. As Margaret Mead once said: "Personality traits which we have called masculine or feminine are as lightly linked to sex as are the clothing, the manners, and the form of headdress that a society at a given period assigns to either sex." With the possible exception of physical activity and aggressiveness, more predominant in males as a result of early hormones, Mead remains correct to this day. There are, of course, other areas besides nurturance, physical activity, and aggressiveness in which definite differences between the sexes are evident. Males, for example, show a greater aptitude for mathematics, while females excel in language skills. But whether the differences are due to biology or culture is not yet known.

The point is that we all, each and every one, should be "free to be, you and me," as the title of a wonderfully refreshing children's book proposes. Anatomy certainly is not destiny, as Freud and his ilk have maintained—not unless society so dictates. Freud's pronouncements on the female psyche, based on his cultural bias, are being rejected today—not only by feminists, but by many modern psychiatrists as well.

4

SEXUALITY DOES NOT play the role it was thought to in animal life, as has been revealed in a multitude of animal behavior studies. Nor does it function the way Freud thought it did in human life. By way of explanation for Freud's fallacy, the Dutch ethologist Adriaan Kortlandt has spoken of the growing awareness that the

Freudian dogma was a predictable product of late nineteenth-century society. This same protest crops up time and again in feminist literature and is increasingly being recognized in analytic circles. Unfortunately for us all, Sigmund Freud, despite his genius, was nevertheless a "prisoner of his own culture" as Betty Friedan so ably pointed out. And in a moment I'll show how grossly this distorted his view of women.

But first let me digress to the subject of memories, another instance in which Freudian theories have been put through the wringer of newly acquired data and emerged obsolete. Each such instance helps to dent the sacred cow of Freudianism and, in so doing, reinforces the validity of the feminist protest. Not long ago, at an international symposium sponsored by the Kittay Scientific Foundation, Freud's analysis of childhood memories came up for challenge. Freud had made much of such memories, assuming that the way an adult remembered them was the way they were interpreted by the child. Not so, say many modern psychiatrists: such memories, they've concluded, are actually unreliable guides to past events. These psychiatrists look not to Freud but to the French psychologist Jean Piaget for their answers. Piaget's pioneering research established that children do not think like adults. While adults see logical cause-effect relationships instantly, children are inclined to a more magical and self-centered interpretation of what makes things happen. Dr. George Serban of the New York University Medical School believes that it is the persistence of childlike thinking patterns concerning certain events that causes neurotic illness in adults.

Freud, to his credit, revised his theories many times as he accumulated new data. Undoubtedly, he would have reconsidered his views on childhood memories in the light of Piaget's valuable findings. I believe, too, that Freud would have retracted his propositions regarding female psychology had he had access to the work of Alfred Jost, of John Money and Anke Erhardt, of Robert Stoller, and of others. The contributions of the first three I've already examined in some detail. And now I'll turn to psychoanalyst Robert Stoller, who so persuasively liberates women from Freudian inferiority. Stoller, to be sure, is not some lone voice crying out in the desert; he is joined by many other analysts who together declared their dissent in the *Journal of the American Psychoanalytic Association*'s special 1977 issue on female psychology. Nor are today's analysts the first to take issue with Freud's views on femininity. In the 1920's and 30's, there were Karen Horney and Ernest Jones, and in 1944, Gregory Zilboorg.

Zilboorg argued convincingly and appealingly for the proposition of a primary femininity. Stoller has today furthered this concept, postulating a period of what he calls "protofemininity" as the first stage in the development of both boys and girls. Just as anatomically the human is basically and originally feminine, it is now beginning to appear that even psychologically femininity is first.

But before delving further, here's a quick sketch of Freudian thinking on the matter. According to Freud, an infant boy enjoys the advantage of having a person of the opposite sex—his mother —as his first love object. The boy's main conflict revolves around his father who, as a powerful rival for his mother's affections, is seen by the boy as a threat to his masculinity. Since the most obvious aspect of his maleness is his penis, the boy develops castration anxiety. Nonetheless, if his fears are not excessive, the boy will eventually shift his affections from his mother to other women and will find, in his father, a suitable model for masculinity.

In contrast, "The development of a little girl into a normal woman is more difficult and more complicated," said Freud. An infant girl begins life with a homosexual attachment to her mother which must eventually be relinquished. Noting that she is without a penis, a girl also falls prey to a castration complex, blaming her mother for her apparent castration. Supposedly, every girl longs for a penis and fantasizes about having one. But to achieve mature femininity, according to Freud, she must renounce her wish for a penis and turn to her father for erotic love and gratification.

How does this theory of the development of masculinity and femininity hold up today? Not well, it turns out, for there is evidence that flatly contradicts this Freudian dogma. Most important is the fact that all infants, both boys and girls, spend their early months in intimate, symbiotic association with their mothers. So close is this relationship that psychoanalysts call it a "merging" between mother and child, a merging in which the child experiences himself not yet as an individual but as one with his mother. This means then that the infant, boy or girl, shares for a time in its mother's femaleness and femininity. Stoller calls this early symbiosis the stage of protofemininity. For a boy, this situation can involve hazard: There is the possibility that he might come to identify with the female. But for a girl, such identification will only serve to enhance her femininity. Consequently the boy, not the girl, is now seen to have the more difficult task—for he must separate himself from his mother before he can achieve masculinity.

Stoller presents some well-considered evidence for his theory of protofemininity. Among females, to be sure, few clues will be found, for there is no shift in gender identification to mark the onset of femininity. In males, however, there are several sets of data that back Stoller's view. The first of these concerns male transsexuals who, despite all biological evidence to the contrary, are convinced that they are females. This belief, Stoller's research indicates, is the result of an intense and blissful relationship between mother and son, involving

> skin-to-skin closeness, no frustration of sensual pleasures by his mother (no weaning, toilet training, restriction of masturbation, restriction from playing with and on the mother's body, and so on), no torment, no double bind, no pushing away to provoke separation —and all this continuing uninterrupted for four or five years.

The father of a transsexual, moreover, is generally remote or absent, leaving his son unshielded from his mother's overwhelming closeness. The stage of protofemininity is thus prolonged indefinitely in the case of these unfortunate boys.

Male transsexualism and the circumstances surrounding it are of rare occurrence. Normally, mothers tend to find themselves less comfortable being intimate with their sons than with their daughters. Studies show that infant girls actually receive more physical and visual contact during their early months than do boys. In later months and years, boys may be similarly slighted, anthropologist Ashley Montagu maintains:

> In our culture mothers learn to reject the love of their sons, a love which the sons offer unconditionally but which mothers cannot wholly accept. Unconscious, half-conscious, or conscious anxieties about incest, mother attachments, or fear of making the boy too soft cause many mothers to make the little rejections of their small sons' love which to the child constitute a very real privation and frustration. The father's participation in this process in the form either of an unconscious or of a conscious jealousy of his son's place in the affection of his wife, complicated by the little boy's jealousy of his father, adds to the boy's feeling of privation and frustration and contributes to his store of aggressiveness and hostility.

Obviously, there are special difficulties inherent in a boy's development, difficulties not encountered by girls—quite the reverse of what Freud once postulated.

Another psychological phenomenon supporting the theory of protofemininity is the widespread fear among men of being effeminate and unmanly. As Stoller describes it:

> Once a male has developed a sense of masculinity, achieved in part in the struggle to separate from the symbiosis with his mother and to create for himself a distinct identity (individuation)—an inner vigilance must be established in the boy. Only this vigilance keeps him from the temptation to regress to that Garden of Eden—the blissful, frustrationless, traumaless experiences in the symbiosis with mother. Thus, the boy (and man) is more or less at risk (depending on how well his parents helped him handle the process of separation and individuation) of having the achievement of masculinity weakened or wiped out.

Perhaps this explains why males show sexual anomalies more often than do females. Money estimates that there are at least three or four times as many men as women who are obligative homosexuals, transvestites, and transsexuals. Moreover, a number of sexual anomalies are exclusively masculine: lingerie fetishism, voyeurism, exhibitionism, and necrophilia. The theory of protofemininity may also explain why men are so much more belligerent in defending their masculinity than are women concerning their femininity. It may even explain, as Stoller suggests, "the odd finding that accusations of homosexuality in paranoid psychoses are almost universal in males, although, in females, the accusations far more frequently concern heterosexual misdemeanors."

There is another set of data, too, which seems to be accounted for by Stoller's protofemininity hypothesis. It comes from the study of a very rare group, female transsexuals. These women usually grow up in circumstances the converse of those resulting in male transsexualism: Rather than too much mother and not enough father as experienced by their male counterparts, female transsexuals are the recipients of too much father and too little mother. For these women, the early symbiosis between mother and child is severed due to the mother's severe depression or other illness, while the father actively encourages masculinity in his daughter. In adulthood, female transsexuals prefer to live permanently as "unremarkably masculine men," dressing as men, working with men, having the dreams and fantasies of men.

Such is the substantial evidence with which Stoller backs his claims for protofemininity. Rather than the little girl being a "little man" as Freud maintained, it is beginning to appear that, however devastating this might be to the macho mentality, a little boy in his early months is actually a little woman.

Freud's faith in the primacy of the penis is also today an anachronism, a relic of the Victorian era. It did not seem then, I suppose, like a bad idea. Wherever Freud turned, he was able to muster up evidence. Among mammals, he noted the males' superior strength and size. Among humans, he noted phallic worship in its myriad forms; he recorded the related dreams and anxieties of his clients, and he pointed to the patriarchal family. And then there was the penis itself—so large and visible compared to the unimposing female clitoris. Offered against Freud's arguments, however, we can look to the impressive new research alluded to earlier—the work, especially, of Jost and Money and Erhardt. The first cells, the first tissues and organs, the fetus itself, all are basically feminine unless testosterone is added to initiate the development of the male. As Stoller says, this "new research seems to put Freud's arguments in a most precarious position and since he chose to extend his beliefs from the realm of psychodynamics into morality and other issues, in the last few years, he has been well beaten about the head."

But still one can wonder, for these are embryological, not psychological, facts and the mind might nonetheless regard the penis as primary. Certainly, even today it remains impressive in the human consciousness. But what of the mysteries of the womb, the beauty of the breasts, and the wonder of childbirth? As Karen Horney so eloquently stated:

> I, as a woman, ask in amazement. And what about motherhood? And the blissful consciousness of bearing a new life within oneself? And the ineffable happiness of the increasing expectation of the appearance of this new being? And the joy when it finally makes its appearance and one holds it for the first time in one's arms? And the deep pleasurable feeling of satisfaction in suckling it and the happiness of the whole period when the infant needs her care?

The work of Masters and Johnson has further eroded Freud's credibility. To Freud, the clitoris was only a secondary, inadequate source of pleasure, a vestigial organ from which the female must turn, shifting instead to the more mature pleasures of her vagina and pelvic organs. But Masters and Johnson found no physiological difference between a clitoral orgasm and a so-called vaginal organism. Both, they established, result from the stimulation of the clitoris, either directly through manipulation or indirectly through the friction created during intercourse. In addition, Masters and Johnson found that women with artificial vaginas have orgasms that are physiologically indistinguishable from those of women with natural vaginas. Moreover, Shere Hite, author of *The Hite Report,* notes that, countrary to popular opinion, the great majority of women do not reach orgasm without direct clitoral stimulation.

And so rests the case against Freud, one of history's foremost male chauvinists. Even he himself saw difficulties in his analysis of femininity, becoming less and less sure of his position as the years went by. What is thought to be Freud's last letter, written just before his death, attests to this change of attitude. In the letter, just recently discovered by Dr. Daniel Offer, chairman of the Michael Reese Hospital's psychiatry department, Freud praises his daughter Anna as well as women universally. On May 9, 1938, an eighty-two-year-old Freud, dying of cancer and about to be driven from his homeland Austria by Nazis, wrote of this to his son Ernst: "Anna's useful vigor and optimistic energy have fortunately remained unshaken. Otherwise life would be difficult to carry on at all. In general, women hold up better . . . than do men." For a person who originally thought women less self-sufficient, more psychically rigid and unchangeable than men, and less able to deal with the exigencies of life, this is an about-face indeed.

But this whole approach is wrong to my mind, this constant Freudian predilection for trying to label the "superior" sex. Sure there are differences which cannot be denied. As Stoller says:

> If superiority is measured by body size, phallic dimensions, skill in football, fatherliness, or production of sperm, females are unequivocally inferior; the differences can be measured. Likewise, if superiority is measured by size of bosom, gestational capacity, longevity, resistance to illness, motheringness, or capacity to ovulate, women have the unquestioned edge. In the middle lie innumerable skills at which neither men nor women inherently excel, such as weaving, growing rice, solving problems in psychoanalytic research, running an advertising agency, or bickering. And then there are such imponderables as: Is a woman superior if she can have limitless orgasms or is a man superior if he is completely satisfied after one or five?

There is a children's story of which I am reminded, a story that delightfully pokes fun at the old "ladies first" etiquette which, however limited and phony, gave the female one of her few prerogatives, one of her only claims to superiority. As the story by Shel Silverstein goes, there was a "tender sweet young thing" who took full advantage of her femininity, with a "ladies first" as a reminder to one and all, as she scooted to the front of cafeteria lines as well as jungle safaris and managed to be first at the tropical mangoes. Unfortunately, she and her exploring party were seized by tigers who quickly tied them up and then looked them over for edibility. They found fault with all until they came to the sweet-smelling, delectable little girl. She promptly informed them that she was indeed a tender sweet young thing and a little lady besides and would they please untie her instantly as her dress was getting mussed. "Ladies first, ladies first," she insisted as usual. "And so she was. And mighty tasty, too!" we are told.

Primacy can make for problems, both for the labeler and the labeled. Even Freud, for all his genius, proved to be rash and ridiculous in his claims of male superiority. I, for one, want none of it—neither "ladies first" nor supremacy of the penis. We are, rather, all of a species. Let us walk hand in hand, not one before the other. Let us strive to be a superior species, not half of us a superior sex. Let us, male and female, be equal in dignity and respect, as well as in opportunity and due reward.

(3) Sex and the Subhuman Female

1

IT WAS A black and moonless morning and we waited for dawn. We had driven long the night before, slept but a few hours, then dragged ourselves out of our sleeping bags at three A.M. Forty-five minutes later, we were to meet Larry Crawford, project assistant at the Buena Vista Wildlife Area in central Wisconsin. A bit bleary-eyed, we nonetheless managed to meet Crawford on time, get his directions straight, and follow a fence line by flashlight to get to the blind where we now sat shivering in the chill spring air.

There were three of us, two other naturalists and me. Lynn Remkus, like myself, worked at the Wehr Nature Center in Hales Corners, a Milwaukee suburb. Sue Heinrich was a young student who often helped as a volunteer naturalist at the center. We had come to witness one of the most spectacular spring wildlife events in the Midwest—the courtship of the greater prairie chicken.

Now, though, it all seemed highly improbable, enveloped as we were in the strange black stillness of the predawn marsh. Waiting, we drank coffee from a thermos to warm and wake us, and break-fasted on homemade zucchini bread. Then we heard it for the first time. Seemingly from a great distance came a humming sound, a weird, hollow, three-syllabled "m" sound, repeated over and over. "Like the humming of some psychopathic killer," laughed Lynn. Or was it a sick animal moaning nearby?

The humming continued as, ever so gradually, the sky began to lighten. And yes, there, finally, were the prairie chickens in full regalia before us, beginning to strut and squabble among them-selves. What had been a mere humming before soon swelled to a loud chorus. This, of course, was the "booming" of the male prairie chickens. The sound of a single bird or two is a mere soft hum, as we had first heard, a sound suggested by blowing across the opening of a Coca-Cola bottle. But en masse, the booming of the prairie chickens gains greatly in volume and can be heard up to four miles away when the wind is low.

Only the cocks boom, as a way of advertising their presence to every hen in the vicinity. The more aggressive cocks stake out territories on the booming ground. These they protect by chasing and attacking, if need be, any other male who tries to intrude. When not busy fighting, a male performs his courtship dance. He spreads out his tail, thrusts his head forward, droops his wings, lifts his feather "horns" above his head, and rapidly stomps his feet. All the while, he emits the booming sound from two inflated orange sacs, one on either side of his neck. It is said that the American Indians based some of their dancing on that of the prairie chickens. The resemblance is unmistakable! In addition to his dancing, every so often the cock adds a dash of madness to his act with a "sky-hop." He will suddenly fly a few feet straight up in the air and drop back again, cackling excitedly.

When the hens arrive, the cocks display ever more intensely as they compete with one another for feminine favor. The hens, for their part, wander from territory to territory, browsing among the residents as if they were comparison shopping at a supermarket. Through all this, the stomping and booming and fighting of the cocks reach a crescendo. And to impress their female guests all the more, the cocks will often bow low before them, with wings spread and beak nearly touching the ground. Despite all this attention, however, a hen may lose interest and leave the booming ground. Or she may choose a male who pleases her and signal her readiness for mating by squatting with wings slightly spread, head raised, and neck outstretched. The eager cock, of course, quickly obliges her. After copulation, the female has the peculiar habit of running forward a few feet and then stopping to shake. The cock, on the other hand, simply returns to his booming.

And that is that. But in this simple climax lies millions of years of evolution, evolution created, in a large sense, by and for the female of the species.

It is almost always the female who has the choice, at least the prime choice, when it comes to mating. And there is no doubt about it, she is very choosy. So choosy, in fact, that the word "coy" has been coined by biologists. The female plays hard-to-get, hesitant, cautious, often downright disinterested. But why? Why should she act like this in a catch-as-catch-can world, where predators lurk in waiting, where an opportunity missed may be lost forever? Is she too busy with other affairs? Too concerned with food or finding a nesting site? Too tired? Too old? Too young?

In an attempt to discover the basis for coyness, biologists once hatched female insects in a lab, giving them every opportunity to mate throughout their life span. Food was plentiful; cages were cleaned scrupulously, everything was ideal! The females simply had nothing else to do, and yet still they resisted the males' early advances. The puzzle remained. Yet biologists knew that a behavior so widespread, so fundamental to the very act of reproduction, must have deep-seated value.

Today, scientists think they know the answer. Coyness, according to the new view, has its roots in the relatively large "parental investment" of the female of the species in comparison to that of the male. Sociobiologist Robert L. Trivers has been the eloquent exponent of this idea of parental investment and its ramifications regarding female-male behavior. Not surprisingly, his work has inspired—and been corroborated by—a great deal of new and exciting research.

The female of the species, says Trivers, invests far more in each of her relatively large eggs than does a male in his minute sperm.

This disparity of interests becomes even more apparent in higher vertebrates. Among birds, for example, the egg many constitute up to 25 percent of the female's weight—sometimes more! In mammals, although the egg itself may not be so large, the female must nonetheless generate a placenta, nourish the embryo from her own bloodstream, hazard the risks of pregnancy and birth, and thereafter furnish milk for her newborns—an extraordinary investment in comparison to the male's. Moreover, a male may walk or swim or fly away after copulation, but a female must live with the consequences, for days, months, perhaps even a lifetime. Small wonder she has evolved as the fussy one. A bad decision can botch up her entire reproductive career!

And so she is programmed to act coyly. Often she insists on a chase, perhaps to check out the vigor and perseverance of the male. The female cichlid, for example, will flee from the male. Up and down and around the tank she goes, with the male close at her tail, almost as though she feared him. Yet, with every breathing space, she performs seductive courtship movements to entice the male all the more! Biologist Frank Fraser Darling described a similar courtship among red deer. Approached several times by a stag, the female ran off. But between chases, the female stopped and came to the stag, rubbed her whole length along his ribs, and made as if to mount him. When he turned then to mount her, however, she was off again and running. Finally, she stopped again, and "he mounted and served her."

This kind of interplay can be envisioned as a contest between salesmanship and sales resistance. The male in most species must sell himself, offering every evidence that he is fully fit. Even were he not so, it would pay for him to pretend, for otherwise he might not mate at all. The female, however, would be best off if she could distinguish between the truly fit and the bluff. And so she hesitates, testing and teasing the male into further displays, until she is in a better position to judge his true fitness.

Males, on the other hand, are generally far less discriminating. They have been known to display not only to females of their own species, but also to females of related species, to males of their own and related species, and even, when appropriate partners are not available, to inanimate objects! Take male bullfrogs, for in-

stance. Should you walk through a pond in spring, you may find
a male bullfrog clinging to your boots in the same way that he
clasps a female in mating. The female, however, is much more
discriminating. She needs to be clasped in just the right way by
just the right species of male before she will release her eggs. He
can afford to play fast and loose; she takes far more care, for she
has more at stake. Of course, these behaviors are not consciously
chosen. Rather they are selected, through the long, slow weaning
processes of evolution.

Charles Darwin, though he was astonished at the thought,
was one of the first to suggest the importance of female
choice in animal affairs. Along with competition between
males, female choice was instrumental, said Darwin, in shap-
ing the evolution of sexual differences. Among most animal
species, the male is showier, both visually and behaviorally.
The male peacock has the more splendid tail, and the rooster
has spurs. The stag has antlers and the male lion, a mane.
Male bower birds build bowers and the prairie chicken cocks
dance and boom. The male, Darwin suggested, owes some of
these unique characteristics, particularly his weapons, to his
penchant for peer-group battles. Those males who win out are
more likely to mate and in so doing will produce more offspring, thereby ensuring that their characteristics will live on.
But many other male characteristics, Darwin said, can only be
attributed to female choice. He explained it like this: In selecting particular males with particular characteristics, females
modify males in much the same way that humans modify domestic animals through selective breeding. Today, anthropologist Irven DeVore says much the same thing. "Males," he
maintains, "are a vast breeding experiment run by females."

Despite Darwin's reluctant but persuasive conclusions, the role
of female choice was long dismissed as minor, even nonexistent.
In truth, Darwin had little hard data and, consequently, male
competition got all the publicity. Who has not heard, even from
Bambi, of the battling of stags? The dramatic clashes between
male mountain sheep, fur seals, and bears are likewise notorious.
These male doings are far more visible. And, after all, it sounds
so much better, so much more macho from the male point of

view, to speak of the contests of rival males for the possession of females.

Until recently, then, the importance of female choice—called epigamic selection in the biologist's vernacular—was greatly underestimated. Fortunately, this biased oversight is now being corrected as a result of a variety of field and laboratory observations. We now know that among gorillas, chimpanzees and African wild dogs, females often choose which male or males they care to stay with. We know that female bighorn sheep prefer to mate with large-horned males. We know that domestic ewes, allowed to choose between tethered rams, usually approach the ram with the best mating record.

Surprises came as researchers examined previous misconceptions. One of these researchers was Frank A. Beach, a professor at the University of California. It's been said that credit goes to Beach's wife for the new direction of his studies. Each day, reportedly, Mrs. Beach would take her female beagle Jacky on a long walk in Berkeley's Tilden Park. Each evening, she would tell her husband how Jacky snubbed some male dogs and encouraged others. All the talk of an ardent dog-lover, thought Dr. Beach. He was sure that his wife was reading things into the beagle's behavior, for zoologists "knew" that one male was as good as another to a female animal. So in a series of experiments, Beach set out to prove his wife wrong—and found, instead, that she was absolutely right!

In one of his earlier studies, Beach raised five male and five female beagles from puppyhood and then tested their mating preferences when the females matured and were in heat. There was no doubt about it—the females had minds of their own! The male Broadus was, by far, the most popular with the females; he was always accepted by Peggy, Kate, and Dewey, almost always by Spot and Blanche. Only Peggy, however, liked Eddie. Only Dewey liked Ken—whom Peggy, on the other hand, detested. Uninterested females would let the males know in no uncertain terms when their services weren't wanted. Through snarling, chasing, biting, and threatening, they made sure the males they disliked stayed well away. If a male were somewhat less despicable to a female, he was simply given the cold shoulder. Most remarkable of all, however, was that the preferences of female dogs were shown to be extremely long-lasting. After seven years, Beach repeated one of his experiments using the same dogs. Although the dogs had had no contact with each other throughout the long interval, lo and behold, each female went straight to the same male the second time around!

The basis by which female dogs make their selection has not as yet been deciphered, as far as I know. But among a good many other species, the mystery of just how and why females choose as they do is beginning to unravel. Above all, it is to the advantage of the female to select a mate with good genes. A male who is more showy and vigorous in courtship is likely to be more healthy and fit than his less well-endowed fellows. And so the female can seldom go wrong in choosing the male with the most brilliant colors, with the largest plume, with the thickest mane, or the most vigorous dance. Females, moreover, are capable of incredibly subtle discrimination between suitors. In a certain species of fruit fly, for example, the females prefer outbred to inbred males, because the inbred males can't perform a particular step of the typical courtship as rapidly as the outbred males. A difference simply in timing! This amazing feat on the part of the female fruit fly is another of those wonders that keep nature-watchers in constant awe. Yet, that is not even the whole story. The female's preference is admirably adaptive—she can produce four times as many viable offspring with an outbred male than with an inbred one.

In selecting for good genes, male competition can go hand-in-hand with female choice. This becomes readily obvious in species which, like the prairie chicken, display in an arenalike setting. Only the more vigorous cocks, as mentioned, manage to establish territories on the limited area of a booming ground. These few, moreover, vie among themselves for high-status real estate. A larger sized plot or an interior one makes the most fashionable address. Even before the females arrive, then, the males have obligingly selected among themselves. And the hens wind up in the enviable position of choosing among the crème de la crème!

It is much the same, you will recall, with the Uganda kob. The males select among themselves by fighting to obtain territories, and then the territoried males display eagerly to the females, who stroll casually from territory to territory making their selections.

In their common insistence on good genes, females among the various species can nonetheless be quite versatile in approach. Especially intriguing are those females who prefer the rare or novel male over the "commoners" in their midst, much as some women find foreign men particularly fascinating. Hen peacocks, for example, will choose white mutant males over the wild-type dark form. The mutants, reportedly, are more vigorous and aggressive in courtship than their plebeian competition. Female guppies, likewise, are drawn to the rare male over the run-of-the-mill Charlie.

Guppies, those most popular of aquarium fish, are native to the streams and rivers of tropical South America and the nearby islands of the West Indies. While female guppies are a rather drab olive green, males are extremely variable in color, particularly on their fins, and their kaleidoscopic charms are due, in no small measure, to the female guppy's taste for the new and novel. Such was the conclusion of James A. Farr of the University of West Florida, who recently spent long hours observing the sexual habits of these fish.

Male guppies, Farr found, put their heart and soul into courtship, displaying to the females up to thirteen times every five minutes for hours on end. Their best efforts, however, left the females quite cold. These females seldom, if ever, responded to the familiar males in their group. But should a new male, differently colored, be placed in the aquarium, the females responded within half an hour. An aroused female guppy will wheel around in tight circles, seductively exposing her genitals to the male of her choice. Needless to say, mating soon follows, and among guppies, it is a fairly advanced affair involving internal fertilization. The male will insert his gonopodium—an anal fin modified into a penislike organ—into the female's genital pore and eject his sperm. The female is able to store this sperm for long periods and can produce at least eight broods following a single copulation.

As with most aspects of animal behavior, there is method in the female guppy's madness. By choosing a rare male, she ensures that her offspring will enjoy a maximum amount of genetic diversity, which turns out to be of particular importance to the well-being of this species. Guppies must live with tropical seasonality, and whole populations may be washed out during a rainy season. Fortunately, a single gravid female can easily recolonize a new area. But there is a catch in this, for by doing so, many small populations may be formed during the dry season, populations which necessarily can reproduce only by inbreeding. Over time, of course, inbreeding will lead to degeneration, and so it is extremely adaptive for the female to mate with a new male whenever she has the chance. Moreover, the resulting genetic versatility of guppies has enabled them to thrive in a great variety of aquatic habitats.

While good genes are an important consideration for the female in her selection of a mate, there are often other things she must also keep in mind. In those species in which the raising of young is a demanding two-parent obligation, the female looks to the parental potential of her prospective mates. Among certain nesting birds, for example, the male who can secure or build the best nest wins hands down over his competitors. There are various species of herons, for example, in which males station themselves during the breeding season at old nests, eagerly advertising their valued estates to every passing female. Similarly, the male collared flycatcher of Europe demonstrates his nest hole to nearby females with a special call and a slow, showy flight at its entrance. But it is among the true weaverbirds that males have become most highly specialized in their use of a nest to attract mates.

One of these, the village weaverbird, occurs in almost all of Africa south of the Sahara. The birds are communal nesters and a large number of males will build nest shells in a single tree. When unmated females visit the nest tree, the males hang upside down from their nests, flap their wings, and call out like sidewalk salesmen hawking their wares. It is said to be a truly spectacular sight when all the males simultaneously engage in these nest-advertising displays. The females, typically, hesitate for a long time before approaching the nest of any particular male. Finally, a female weaverbird will make her decision, enter the interior of a nest, and inspect it carefully for as long as twenty minutes or more. She pulls here, pushes there, and tugs and pokes about, as if carrying out a thorough test of a new consumer product. She wants a fresh green nest, made of strong durable materials—excellent criteria for a product that must last at least a full month against the deteriorating forces of a tropical climate. The female may come and go, inspecting a number of nests. Often she takes half a day or more to make her choice, which she indicates, finally, by taking nest materials into the nest.

While the nest itself may be of utmost importance to the female weaverbird, among a number of other species, a female prefers to examine the male's ability to provide for her young. Many times, it is simply a matter of finding a male who is the proprietor of a good territory where food or breeding sites are plentiful. The female pupfish prefers to spawn in a soft sandy substratum and so she is drawn, not so much to certain males in themselves, but to the better spawning sites they command. In at least one species of dragonfly, females are primarily concerned with good egg-laying sites and only secondarily favor males who happen to control territories containing such sites. Among many birds, females are attracted only to males who hold territories, ignoring all others. This is not at all surprising, since a suitable territory can offer a variety of amenities important to avian family life—privacy, an assured food supply, shelter from predators, as well as freedom from competitors. Just how important these are becomes especially clear with red-winged blackbirds. As many as six females may choose to mate with a male who owns an attractive patch of cattail marsh, all of them actively nesting within his territory. At the same time, a male in a nearby but less desirable neighborhood may be able to attract only one female or perhaps none at all.

There are other ways, besides inspecting nests and territories, by which a female may judge her suitor's paternal potential. An important criterion in many species of birds and insects is the courtship feeding of the male. In roadrunners, those cartoon-caricatured birds of our arid Southwest, food caught by the male acts on him like an aphrodisiac. Lizard or snake in beak, he runs off to a female and courts her with ardor—all of which suggests that the female seldom gives a hoot (more correctly, in this case, a coo) to a giftless wooer. By selecting a male who can provide her with food, a female enhances her ability to produce healthy offspring. She is, in effect, selecting a mate who will provide a larger parental investment than is strictly required by male biology.

This has been even more clearly brought out through the painstaking research of Randy Thornhill at the University of Michigan. Thornhill's subject was the hangingfly, an insect that thrives in the lush herb layer of moist eastern American forests. The hangingfly often occurs in tremendous numbers in the warm months of June and July, and being a slow flyer, it is relatively easy to observe. Thornhill, moreover, supplemented his field research with lab work. Thanks to his thoroughness, we now have an amazingly complete understanding of the role of courtship feeding in this species.

Like the male roadrunner, the hangingfly male offers palatable prey to the female as part of his nuptial preliminaries. The female, true to form, is rather fussy about what she will accept. If the prey is too small or distasteful (ladybugs are definitely not her dish), the female will fly away or will copulate for only a short time, too short for an adequate transfer of sperm. If the prey is of respectable size and palatability, however, she will gladly copulate for a full twenty minutes or more, all the while feeding on her nuptial meal. This length of time very nicely corresponds to that needed to provide the female with a maximum amount of sperm and to promote her egg production.

Thornhill discovered another interesting point. An adequate nuptial meal was sufficient to maintain the female for the next three hours or so, during which time she laid her eggs. This, of course, saved her the necessity of hunting for her own prey and increased the energy she could put into egg production. Thornhill also conjectured that a nonhunting female would probably be less likely to be a victim of predation than a hunting female. So this seems to be a very tight, very adaptive system for the hangingfly, a system in which the female's insistence on a mate who will increase his parental investment—by providing her with nourishment for egg-laying—turns out to be best for the species.

Even in those cases where the female does most of the courting, she appears to be very discriminating about the parental qualities of her intended. In phalaropes, which are sandpiperlike birds, the females court, while the males incubate the eggs and care for the young after hatching. Ethologist Niko Tinbergen once observed a female phalarope vigorously courting a male at a pond where he had come to feed. As soon as the male responded, however, by attempting to copulate with her, the female would fly away, acting as coyly as any courted female. For several days, the sequence was repeated over and over again. Tinbergen attributed the behavior simply to the "waxing and waning of an instinct." But, as Trivers points out, "the behavior may have been a test of the male's willingness to brood the female's eggs." As it turned out, the male was already brooding a clutch of eggs. Although the female was apparently unaware of the eggs, she nonetheless was somehow able to sense the male's encumbered circumstances—perhaps through some aspect of his behavior. Tinbergen then decided to destroy the clutch in order to observe a complete reproductive cycle. Remarkably, the female immediately seemed to realize the male's new situation. Within half a day, she mated with him and he subsequently cared for her brood.

The human female also seems to choose her husband with an eye to his ability to provide for the children. In most societies, women tend to marry older, better established men, men who can control more of the resources needed for raising a family. Not long ago, a California study gave good evidence that American women frequently move up the socioeconomic ladder by marrying high-status, well-educated men. Of course, we really don't need a study to tell us this. Prominent men have always had their magnetism for women. Actors often enjoy largely feminine fan clubs. Male singers frequently mesmerize young girls en masse. Male politicians commonly attract cohorts of women to help with their campaigns. And as early as high school, male athletes are exceptionally popular with girls. Interestingly, even unhandsome men, should they be rich and successful, are often able to attract the most beautiful of women as wives and companions. Does this explain, perhaps, the charm of a Henry Kissinger or of the late Aristotle Onassis?

The human female, then, like her lesser sisters, is comparatively selective and men do their best to charm her, in ways not too terribly different from those of their evolutionary fellows. There is the wining and dining, the dancing, the romantic music—the human male's more sophisticated versions of courtship feeding and dancing and singing. There is the display of flashy cars and clothes and high living, the expenditures on gifts and entertainment—all a show of financial resources and the willingness to share them.

Yet, while all these things may well be, the description is considerably oversimplified, and the implications, consequently, are only partially true for humankind. The reason is that men as well as women have their say in mating matters, to a far greater extent than in many animal species. It is true, for example, that women tend to marry up the socioeconomic ladder, but it is the most attractive ones who are especially apt to do so. Obviously, men too have their preferences, such as this predilection for attractive women, and their preferences, along with those of women, together influence marital statistics.

Nor is it only men who display in courtship. Women work equally hard at attracting the attention of the opposite sex. With women, however, personal display is paramount, while economic display, for cultural reasons, is downplayed. Women dress up, make up, and do up their hair; women walk and talk flirtatiously. And they expect to be watched, even whistled at. In our species, in fact, there is actually a reversal of the common pattern among animals, and the female, not the male, tends to be more gazed upon than gazing. All this, again, implies that male choice is operative, and that women, like men, do their best to be chosen.

When you stop to think about it, then, there is a trend toward equal opportunity in mate choice in our species. Both men and women openly express their preferences for partners—at least in this age when marriages are a matter of personal decision, not parental dictate. Charles Darwin himself recognized this "double form of selection," as he put it, for our species. The intriguing thing about all this is that the trend is exactly what would be predicted by Trivers' theory of parental investment for a species in which *both* sexes invest heavily in the care of the young. When both sexes play a substantial role in parenting, then both stand to lose by mismating, and so both sexes tend to be choosy.

For humankind, the extraordinary long and involved care required to raise our infants to maturity has always necessitated shared responsibility on the part of both parents. At first, it is true, the mother bears the heaviest burden, what with her relatively large egg, her nine months of pregnancy, and often, her nursing of the infant after birth. But fathers also take on a share of the parenting, once the infant has arrived. In our culture, the father's economic support has generally been his paramount contribution, but he is of late playing an increasingly active role in the nurturance and care of his offspring. In some societies, he has always done both. This is true, for example, among the Montagnais-Naskapi of eastern Canada, as well as among the Arapesh and Manus mentioned earlier. Men of the Montagnais-Naskapi tribe have traditionally engaged not only in hunting and cooking, but also in childcare. A Jesuit missionary, Paul le Jeune, wrote in the seventeenth century of a man of this tribe who tenderly soothed a sick baby. "Over three centuries later," writes anthropologist Eleanor Leacock who lived with the Montagnais-Naskapi, "I observed the unquestioning patience with which a man sat cradling his sick and fretful infant in his arms, crooning over it for hours."

There are also a good many animal species in which both sexes invest substantially in the care of their young. From burying beetles to the Nile crocodile, from warblers to the wild dogs of Africa, from New World monkeys to such Asian apes as the gibbon and siamang, parenting is a cooperative venture. For them, as for us, both sexes should be more or less equally selective, since both invest heavily in each offspring. Just how selective each sex is in mate choice should, theoretically, be directly proportional to her or his share of parental responsibilities.

The well-known zoologist Nancy Burley decided to test these ideas by carefully studying mate selection in pigeons, a species in which both parents share parental duties. Pigeons pair-bond for life, and males as well as females incubate, brood, feed, and defend their young. Pigeon parenting is not quite a 50-50 proposition, however, for females spend somewhat more time at the nest with the eggs and offspring than do males. The exact contribution of each sex tends to vary among pairs.

Burley gave each of her test birds a choice between two birds

of the opposite sex who differed from each other either in color
or plumage pattern. The choice pair of birds were tethered to nest
boxes at each end of the test enclosure. Since among pigeons both
sexes may initiate courtship, Burley used courting behavior to
determine choice. When the chooser directed 90 percent of its
attentions toward one individual rather than the other, a choice
was considered to have been made.

Just as predicted, Burley discovered that mate selection was a
two-way affair with pigeons. Both male and female pigeons preferred blue mates to red mates. Females, moreover, preferred
mates with checker-patterned plumages over those with a bar
pattern. Males, however, could care less about plumage patterns.
Given a choice between a blue-checkered and a blue-barred female, the male would instead pick out the nest box he preferred.
The nest box then became his center of operation; within it, he
made nest-box calls and nesting postures, and courted whatever
female happened to join him there. This too fits beautifully in
Trivers' theory. The female pigeon, with her preferences for both
the color and plumage pattern of her mate, is rather more selective than the male—just as she should be, given her somewhat
greater parental investment!

With her work on pigeons, Burley clearly shows that greater
equality between the sexes in parental investment is closely associated with greater equality in the mating game. In pigeons, as
in our own species, both sexes choose, both are discriminating,
and in mating, both ideally become true partners rather than
mere paramours. And as we look ever more closely into animal
affairs, we are beginning to find a growing variety of species in
which there is not only more equality in mate choice between the
sexes, but also more equality in courtship. Females may be coy,
but give them an attractive male and they may, in a surprising
number of species, court as actively as the male.

2

THE FEMALE PHALAROPE is a lovely bird. Slender and graceful,
with rufous neck and sometimes underparts, depending on the
species, she outshines the small drab male both in beauty and in

size. She also, as I mentioned, courts the male at mating time.
She will eagerly pursue him on wing or in water, and attempt
to drive away, if she can, all other competition. Actual fighting
between females, though relatively rare, can be fierce. Female
phalaropes have been seen viciously pecking and stabbing each
other with their beaks and at least one observer reports their
fighting like this by the hour.

Female courtship in the animal world is not so rare a phenomenon as it was once thought to be. Now that there are more women
in the natural sciences and more men aware of their past neglect
of the female of the species, a great deal of new data is available
on female courtship. Researchers have even dignified the phenomenon with a new term, a surefire way to call proper attention
to a subject in the scientific community! Not satisfied with the
semantics of "female courtship," they speak now of "procep-
tivity," defined as female initiative in sexual matters.

We have been aware for a long time, of course, of certain
species like the phalarope in which females, being larger and more
colorful than their mates, could hardly be overlooked as they
courted their males. Pipefish and seahorses are the phalarope's
counterparts in the sea, and in these species females court more
actively than do males. Among amphibians, there is the green
poison-arrow frog of Central America. A brightly colored beauty,
the female of this species energetically pursues the male, sometimes even jumping on him. Finally, she disappears with him for
a time beneath leaves, as if the two were involved in some clandes-
tine love affair and this, indeed, is when mating is thought to take
place. Similarly, the female spotted hyena, somewhat larger than
the male, will bite, nip, and harass him into performing when she
is in heat.

But it is not only in species in which the female is the more
conspicuous sex that she does her share of the courting. The
National Zoo's female bongo, who eagerly pursues her aging and
reluctant mate, exemplifies this. Indeed, from fireflies to fish,
from birds to baboons, the female takes a more active role in
courting than we ever imagined.

Firefly courtship, for example, is as fascinating as it is beautiful,
and both sexes play a part. The male of each species flies about

and flashes in a particular pattern. The wingless female on the
ground recognizes the male's "Morse code" and courts him in
turn by flashing back. This attracts him to alight near her and the
two will mate. A person can even mimic the flashing of the female
with a penlight and call in the signaling males. Although each
species of firefly has a distinct pattern, which serves to keep the
species separate, some females will reply to the signals of species
other than their own—and devour the foreign males they trick
into landing!

A male lobster need never worry about such a fate, for a female
lobster is interested solely in sex. She insists on mating every
second year and announces her intentions to a male by sweeping
her antennae across his head. Then, with their claws clicking, the
two lobsters do an awkward dance, after which they embrace and
the male transfers his sperm to the female.

Nor does the average female fish always sit around waiting for
Prince Charming to make the first move. Unfortunately, however, some of the earliest and best-known work on the courtship
behavior of fish, that done on the stickleback by ethologists Niko
Tinbergen and Desmond Morris, seemed to give such an impres-
sion. Stickleback courtship is always initiated by the male, who
seduces the female step-by-step into laying her eggs within a nest
he has built. But things can be quite different with other fish, such
as some of the cichlids. Among certain dwarf cichlids, for example, only the female courts. In a kind of "belly dance," she bends
into a U-shape and then stretches out toward the male to entice
him with the bright red color on her flank. More recently, Dr.
Jeffrey Baylis of the University of Wisconsin took a look at the
Midas and arrow cichlids of Nicaragua, and found that, while
both sexes court, the female is considerably more active than the
male throughout the courtship period. Just before spawning, in
fact, there is a peak of courtship activities due almost entirely to
the female.

Not long ago, Richard Haas of California State University
made a related observation in another South American fish, one
which, for lack of a common name, we must call *Nothobranchius
guentheri*, a name nearly as long in print as the little fish itself.
The male of this species, says Haas, is ready to spawn any time,

and a female hesitates not at all to make the initial approach should a male fail to see her first. In some of our common aquarium fish, females typically take the lead when they are ready to spawn. A female goldfish will vibrate her body to induce the male to follow her. Zebra fish females take a different tack and chase their males, which causes the latter to turn and chase them instead.

It is among mammals, however, that we are now encountering the most surprises concerning the sexual assertiveness of the female. One reason it has taken until now to delve into the matter, explains Frank A. Beach (of the beagle research), is that laboratory experiments were often set up in such a way that female sexuality had little chance to express itself. In a recent study of deer mice, however, the sexes were given equal opportunity. It soon became clear that the females were not going to fit into any passive, sexless stereotype. Traps for deer mice were baited with various odors, including the odors of each sex, and these were set afield to poll the rodents' preferences. The females, it turned out, were captured most often in traps baited with the odor of males and the males, conversely, were captured most frequently in traps baited with the odor of females. Obviously, active mate-seeking is hardly a male prerogative in this species.

The marmot is the western counterpart of the woodchuck, and within days of the female's spring emergence from hibernation, she, too, eagerly seeks out males. Finding a likely prospect, she will investigate his genitals and, often as not, will mount him. This latter behavior is a common feminine ploy among mammals. It is designed to excite a laggard male and to stimulate him into reciprocating, since mating in most mammals requires that the male mount the female from the rear.

Other female rodents are just as sexy. Among Norway rats, a female in estrus will approach males, even if it means crossing an electrified grid to do so. Like most females, however, these rats also like to be chased, and they have gone so far as to specialize in a seductive sort of running. These females will dart and hop along as they race before the male. He seems to find it all most provocative, as copulation records readily prove.

Female ungulates, wild or domestic, are as actively sexual as their sisters among the rodents. When a cow or a sow comes into heat, she will mount the male of her species, just as the female marmot will do. A domestic ewe in estrus will seek out a ram, rub her neck against his body, and nose about beneath his flanks. It is only recently, by the way, that the ewe has been given due credit for her initiative in the sexual affairs of her species. For a long time, it had simply been assumed that the ram was the aggressive one who actively sought out the ewes for mating.

The bighorn ewe of our western mountains can be as sexually preoccupied as her domestic counterpart. She will butt and rub the object of her affections and entice him with coquettish jumps and runs. Like the female bongo the bighorn ewe tries to wheedle the male into mating, no matter how tired and listless he might be. Such behavior was once thought to be rare. New observations, however, suggest that, in high-quality populations, female bighorns court quite frequently.

Female carnivores are no slouches either when it comes to sex. A female mountain lion, naturalists Lorus and Margery Milne report, "screams more insistently than a woman being murdered whenever the mating urge is on her." A female wolf will go to greet the male of her choice and actively court him by pawing at his side. She will also present to him by backing up toward his head with her tail cocked to one side. A female dog presents in the same fashion to a favorite male, sometimes brazenly forcing her vulva to his nose. She may even go so far as to throw her hindquarters against him, literally knocking him sideways!

The most fascinating of the new information on the sexual initiative of the female concerns our closest relatives, the primates. For a long time, we've known that female monkeys and apes often solicit their males. But the new details and descriptions, the new depth of perception and thoroughness of observation, are beginning to provide us with the likes of a "Hite report" on the sexuality of the subhuman female primate.

Most commonly, a female primate will try to tempt a male into mating by presenting to him her sexy bottom, much as the female dog will do. And this, as far as we knew only a short time ago, was nearly the extent of her solicitations. Since then, however, we've learned that the female primate has a far more varied repertoire than this.

In chacma baboons, for instance, a female characteristically displays to the male prior to presenting. Here is a straightforward, no-nonsense approach to sex, as the following description by field researcher G. S. Saayman shows:

> The approach of a soliciting female towards a male baboon was typically unmistakable: the approach was made with a direct and rapid gait, the female fixating the male with eyebrows raised and ears flattened ("eyeface"), sometimes with accompanying lip-smacking. This approach was frequently terminated by a presentation to the male.

The chacma female is also sexually insatiable. When in heat, she will solicit and be mounted by as many as three males within the space of two or three minutes.

The female rhesus monkey is rather more versatile than the chacma in her solicitations. To begin with, she's originated a number of variations on the standard theme of primate presentation. If she is feeling especially sexy, she walks backward as she presents to the male, until her hind end touches his face. Occasionally, perhaps to add zest to her style, she then kicks backward at the male with one of her feet. Other rhesus females are even less subtle: They boldly reach back with one hand and try to pull the male into mounting position.

In addition to such presentations, the female rhesus uses three other gestures as sexual invitations. In the "hand-reach," she rapidly lifts one hand from the floor, extends the arm, and then replaces her hand, sometimes with a violent slap, on the floor farther in front of her. After a second or two, she withdraws the arm, and is apt to repeat the whole sequence four, five times in quick succession. In the "head-duck," the rhesus female rapidly lowers her head, holding it in position for up to several seconds. The "head-bob" is the reverse of the head-duck: the head is rapidly jerked upward and held momentarily in position. The head-duck and head-bob, like the hand-reach, may be rapidly repeated, and all three are performed in close proximity to the male. Though hardly exciting by human standards, these gestures prove to be most provocative to male monkeys—together they initiate a larger number of mounts than do presentations.

In several other monkeys, the presentation typical of the rhesus and the baboon is never seen. The female patas monkey solicits mounting with a characteristic half-run toward the male and then sits with her back toward him uttering peculiar sounds produced by inflating and deflating her cheeks. The female howling monkey has an even more bizarre approach. She rhymically moves her tongue in and out of her mouth as she nears a male, and he'll respond likewise if he is in an amorous mood.

A wild chimpanzee female in estrus will first check out a male's behavior. She catches his gaze and watches for his display of an erect penis. Only if he is properly aroused will she approach and crouch-present, as female chimps do. And he had best be prompt about mounting, for if not she has been known to back forcefully into his swollen organ. Captive females caged with naive males show very complex and individualistic kinds of solicitation. One female, for example, watched for the male's erection and then went through all sorts of maneuvers for his benefit. She would "run up to him, present, back up to him, sway her trunk from side to side, and make short little runs forward and backward," according to researcher A. H. Riesen. Sometimes, too, she'd "fling out her hand at him to get his attention or incite his activity."

Of all subhuman primates, female gorillas are perhaps the most assertive when it comes to sexual matters. A recent report, in fact, suggests that in most cases it is the female who controls mating in these apes. Most typically, the female gorilla solicits copulation by backing into a male and rubbing her genitals against his. Should she want to avoid a particular male, on the other hand, she simply leaves the vicinity and keeps her distance from him. Although males might posture in an impressive manner and approach and touch females, they do not seem to actively solicit copulation. Where mating has been observed, whether in the wild or in captivity, the female has started the action. George Schaller, for example, tells of a wild female gorilla who came up behind a male, "clasped him around the waist and thrust herself against him about twenty times." The male evidently found her charms irresistible, for it wasn't long before the two were copulating. Another observer witnessed a female back forcefully into a male, push him against a wall, and rub her genitals against him by "rhymically raising and lowering her rump with a soft, high-pitched fluttering vocalization." Female gorillas will also lie down near a male and extend a hand in invitation, while seductively moving their rumps up and down. Some females have been seen to lie below a squatting male and take his penis into their mouth, while others simply pull the male down upon them.

This brings us to another interesting aspect of ape behavior. While mating for monkeys and most mammals seems to be a rather monotonous, one-position affair, among apes it is not nearly so stereotyped. Schaller's lusty female gorilla wound up having sex as she sat in the lap of her male. Other gorillas, as well as chimpanzees and orangutans, will sometimes copulate face-to-face rather than in the more ordinary rear-mount position. Gorillas and orangutans, moreover, show numerous variations of these standard positions. They may stand, squat, or kneel. They might lie on their sides or their backs or stomachs. They may caress their partners and they may vocalize, some loudly, others more quietly as they mate.

More important to us than the mechanics of primate copulation, however, is the increasing evidence of female orgasm among these animals. Only yesterday, so to speak, the subhuman primate female, no matter how actively she might solicit copulation, was thought to have been left out in the cold when it came to the pleasures of consummation. The orgasm of the human female, consequently, was considered to be a completely new and evolutionary development—not fully perfected, of course, but a marvelous mechanism nonetheless for maintaining matrimonial pair-bonds. Today we know that the human female's potential was grossly underestimated and women, in fact, are now often viewed as the sexier sex. In a recent Redbook report, an overwhelming 93 percent of the women said they experienced orgasm, two thirds of them most or all of the time, and this was later corroborated by their partners. On top of this good news, the human female has been found to be sexually insatiable—she is capable not only of one but of multiple orgasms!

The nonhuman primate female has also come into her own lately in the literature, now that researchers have begun to notice certain reactions in female monkeys which suggest that they too experience orgasm. The female rhesus monkey shows a clutching reaction during the last phase of copulation when the male is ejaculating. Sexually excited, she turns back to lipsmack, grab, and bite at the male. The female chacma baboon gives a copulation call during each of a series of mounts that culminates in the male's ejaculation. With mouth closed and cheeks inflating, she murmurs "o-o-o-o" and may look back at the male as she does so. Once the male ceases thrusting, the female calls out more rapidly in low-pitched, panting barks and then withdraws from the male with a bound, perhaps running a short way or springing into the branches of a nearby tree or leaping over rocky ledges.

For both monkey and baboon, the reactions are seemingly involuntary, and as such resemble the involuntary contractions characteristic of orgasm. Also, in the female baboon, the reactions are minimal unless there is sufficient thrusting by the male, and they occur not at all unless intromission is achieved. Moreover, adequate stimulation from a fully developed mature male seems necessary for the fullest expression of the female's responses: The reactions occurred less frequently when females were mounted by subadult and juvenile males.

Like the baboon, gorilla and chimpanzee females have characteristic calls during mating. The chimpanzee female gives high-pitched squeaks or screams, and the female gorilla often utters a long sequence of vibrating sounds. The female gorilla also shows special facial expressions. Kati of the Basel Zoo in Switzerland presses her lips together slightly; her cheeks puff up and her eyes close at times. During the final moments of copulation—no doubt as orgasm approaches—there is a rising intensity in these facial expressions. Vocalizations increase rhythmically and grow louder; facial expressions become more urgent, more accentuated.

Quite obviously, then, the orgasm of the human female is not, as some would have it, a revolutionary phenomenon unique to our species. There is a past to the pleasures and passions of women, a long-perfected capacity for sexual enjoyment. Unfortunately, the female's capacities have been repressed, forgotten, and denied by too many in too many cultures in the recent past. Always, however, there were cultures where women were openly sexual, where they not only enjoyed sex without inhibition, but also took an active part in courtship and lovemaking. Some of the ancient cultures in which women held high status were numbered among these. The women of early Egypt, for example, took the initiative in courtship, even going so far as to woo lovers with aphrodisiacs. They chose their own husbands without interference. In classical Sparta, women also enjoyed complete sexual freedom.

Interestingly, even in more current cultures, it is when women enjoy a high place in their society that they are more actively sexual. In the late 1920's, the prominent anthropologist Bronislaw Malinowski studied the sexual life of Melanesians, a culture in which women were highly esteemed and took a leading part in economic and ceremonial activities. Not surprisingly, he found that Melanesian women initiated and responded to sex as freely and openly as did men. Female orgasm, Malinowski noted, was a common and expected feature of lovemaking.

The late Margaret Mead lived among the Tchambuli of New Guinea, another society in which women enjoy a prominent position. Tchambuli women also take the lead in sexual activities and, in fact, are believed to have a far more urgent sexual drive than the men. Consequently, there is much concern among the Tchambuli for young widows suddenly deprived of sex. Listen to Margaret Mead's description of Tchambuli attitudes:

> A young widow is a tremendous liability to a community. No one expects her to remain quiet until her remarriage has been arranged. Has she not a vulva? they ask . . . Are women passive sexless creatures who can be expected to wait upon the dilly-dallying of formal consideration of bride-price? Men, not so urgently sexed, may be expected to submit themselves to the discipline of a due order and precedence.

Tchambuli women also freely select their mates. "No one knows where a woman's choice will fall," wrote Mead, "each youth holds his breath and hopes . . ."

Among the Tuaregs, camel herders of the Sahara, women are

highly privileged and well educated. Descent is traced through the female line (matrilineal descent) and all the portable wealth of the group is owned by women. Here again, the female has a great deal of sexual freedom: Premarital chastity is valued little, married women continue to visit with male friends, and divorce upon demand is a female prerogative. In most matrilineal societies, few restrictions are placed on the sexual affairs of women.

As a final offering from the many-colored quilt of human culture, let's look at the Navajo Indians within our own country. Among the Navajo, women enjoy a high status. Some of the most powerful and important Navajo divinities—Changing Woman, Spider Woman, Salt Woman—are female. The Navajo woman, as bespeaks her highly respected position, is often the instigator in the relationships between the sexes and, reportedly, has control over courting behavior. It is she, for example, who selects her partner at the Squaw Dance, the Navajo's most famous and frequent ceremony, and no young man may refuse her. A sixteen-year-old Navajo high school student was asked about the selection of partners at an Anglo-Saxon type dance. Her words reveal the Navajo attitude on the subject: "Well, sometimes the boys ask the girls, but . . . in Navajo it's always the girl's choice." The girl had just been hit on the head with a rock thrown by a boy who was trying to avoid her attentions. Why didn't she let the boys chase her? It had, she replied, never occurred to her.

Human culture, quite obviously, comes in a potpourri of sexual suppositions and practices, many very different from those of our own. In perusing the anthropologist's notebook, the extent of our human versatility becomes readily apparent. And so it is perhaps only in examining the more simple, ingenuous lives of species closely related to our own that we can get a handle on some of the truly innate aspects of our human circumstances. Since among animals the female is as sexually motivated as the male, sometimes more so, female sexuality, not prudery, must be the more natural way.

In view of this, it is hardly surprising to find that the human female, when given freedom and respect and independence, is also highly interested in sex. This has been so in cultures ancient and modern, prominent and obscure. Today, Western society has belatedly begun to give women the status they deserve, and the growing dimension of female sexuality has caught almost everyone a bit by surprise. Birth-control pills, of course, have helped a great deal by reducing the risk of pregnancy. But I believe it is more than this. It is the female's rising star, her increasing autonomy, her growing prominence. Less restricted by society in her economic and educational opportunities and in the roles she can assume, the female is also less restricted in her sexual life.

As always, along with changes of such magnitude, there are adjustments to be made. A rather staid and traditional young man once informed my husband that a young girl of their acquaintance was far too aggressive when it came to sex. But another young man who had grown up in the more cosmopolitan East was obviously delighted with her outgoing sexuality and the two are now happily married.

There will perhaps always be a certain tension between the sexes. At times, among some cultures and clans and cliques, women will seem to have the upper hand. At other times, men might be so endowed, as they have been recently throughout much of the world. However, this does not mean that aggressive dominance by one or the other is essential to the relations between the sexes. Among many species of animals, the aggressiveness and dominance of one sex toward the other interferes with mating. And it is only when this aggression and dominance are reduced, when the sexes enjoy a greater equality, that mating takes place.

3

JUMPING SPIDERS ARE the tigers of their Lilliputian world. They stalk and pounce on nearly any moving morsel of suitable size, including other jumping spiders. Mating is thus fraught with hazards, especially for the male, who is usually smaller and weaker than his intended mate. Consequently, he takes great pains to show the female that he is indeed one of her kind and not just another prey object. He displays to her, approaching hesitantly in zigzag fashion. He shows off his colors, and in some species, vibrates his legs and body. The female watches at first in a high, braced position, the position of attack. Only when she becomes quieter and more attentive, only after she finally crouches low in a nonaggressive, solicitating posture, will he rush over to her and mate. Then, just as quickly, he beats a hasty retreat.

Among all spiders, we find this mixture of fear and desire and potential aggression in the relations between the sexes. In web-spinners, a male must approach a female via the very web she uses to ensnare her victims. It is with murder in mind that the female of these species ordinarily responds to vibrations of her web, vibrations produced by her struggling prey. The male must make sure his attentions aren't mistaken, so he cautiously plucks the web, in a kind of courting call, to introduce himself. In other spider species, the male locks his fangs with those of the female to keep from being eaten. When mating is done, he lowers a silk line and races off. Certain male spiders, after the manner of the male hangingfly, offer the female a meal of an insect wrapped in silk. Still others, more fearful, tie up the female with a length of silk before mating. Some female spiders, however, are just as proficient at tying up their partners. Moreover, they dine on their unfortunate lovers when the affair is over.

It is the same with many other predator species. Programmed through evolutionary time to capture and kill prey, these animals tend to treat all others of appropriate size, even potential mates, as prey. Their hyper-aggression, ideal as it is for their niche as predators, makes mating a difficult and dangerous proposition.

In this, tigers are a lot like their tiny counterparts, the spiders. The tigress wavers, almost schizophrenically, between loving tenderness and murderous hostility toward the male. She is the first to appear sexually excited. Seeing a male, she rolls on her back and kicks her legs in the air, coaxing and kittenish. When the male approaches, she may slink around him, purring and playfully arching her back. Seductively, she touches his whiskers with her own. But should the tiger respond to her charms too soon, she turns tigress once more, snarling and clawing viciously at him. She has not yet overcome her aggression; mating must wait. Then again she will flirt with the male, and perhaps turn on him once more. Eventually she is ready. Her aggression abated momentarily, she crouches low. In mounting the female, the male himself shows some vestigial aggression. He takes the nape of the female's neck between his teeth, but he does so gently, without piercing her skin. Love, for the tigress, is nevertheless incredibly short-lived. As soon as mating is over, she springs to her feet with lightning speed and turns with fury upon the hapless male. Her fury, in this case, has a physical basis. As the male withdraws his penis, the female's vagina is irritated. Biologically, this is all to the good for it increases the chances of conception. Nonetheless, there is momentary pain for the female. In the small cages of older zoos, where the male could not escape the female's clutches, tigresses have been known to attack their mates so suddenly and viciously after coitus that the males never again attempted to mate with them. Reportedly, tigresses have even gone so far as to kill their erstwhile lovers within seconds after mating.

One of the principle purposes of courtship, says famous ethologist Desmond Morris, is to reduce aggression between potential mates. Infantile behavior, such as the kittenish play of the tigress, is a popular means of doing so. At times, it is the female who, like the tigress, takes on the role of youngster. The female English robin adopts the posture and calls of the young robin, and the male, appropriately enough, feeds her as he would a nestling. Herring gull females are likewise fed by the male during courtship.

At other times, among other species, it is the male who takes on infantile behavior. In certain bowerbirds, for example, the male begs food from the female as would a youngster. Thomas Gilliard of the American Museum of Natural History spent many long hours observing bowerbirds and vividly describes one of his observations of this kind of male behavior: "With its wings outstretched and its tail spread, it crawled tortuously toward the female which perched at the edge of the court and kept moving around its periphery. The male held its head up like a turtle, made gasping movements with its bill and kept up a deep, penetrating 'churr' song."

Male squirrels also court their females by acting like infants. Ordinarily, the female squirrel cares little for the male and will not allow his approach. But when he squeaks plaintively in a childlike manner during courtship, she grows affectionate and readily mates.

Mountain goat males apparently have no choice but to play subordinate in order to attract a female. Canadian biologist Valerius Geist reports that the female is "aggressive as hell, big and exceedingly dangerously armed." She is certainly not someone to fool around with and the male, using the best strategy under the circumstances, goes down on his belly and crawls to the female. Her first reaction is to confront him and chase him away. But he stays on his belly and works hard to be accepted. Eventually, she finds him irresistible and even allows him to be more or less dominant—but only for the two weeks of the year during which she is in heat.

Porcupine males must be equally careful in approaching their well-armed, feisty females. Ever so cautiously, the male will begin to woo his lady love. She usually sits well up in a tree, while he waits patiently a few feet farther down. Like a would-be Caruso, he "sings" to her in a high falsetto voice. From time to time, he hesitantly inches up toward her. If she is in an amorous mood, she will watch him quietly, but should she resent his attentions, her protesting squall can be heard a half mile away. When all goes well, the two sexes finally make body contact and fondle one another quite lovingly. They rub noses together, tenderly touch each other's face and head with forepaws, and lick one another's fur. When the female decides she is ready for mating, she flattens her tail safely against her back and the male mounts her with his forefeet.

In some species, there is so much hostility between individuals that couples must avoid even looking at one another if they are ever to get around to mating. The female red-bellied woodpecker flies over to the male in answer to his drumming, but the two are strangers still and afraid of one another. To ease the tension, the male disappears into the nest hole and hides from sight. The two then strike up a duet, each drumming on opposite sides of the tree trunk. Eventually they become comfortable enough with one another's presence to get together and mate. When black-headed gulls meet during the breeding season, they lower their heads and point their beaks at one another in obvious hostility. This threatening gesture is emphasized all the more by the dark mask that surrounds their weaponlike bills. Should an unmated male and female meet, however, the two birds quickly turn their faces away from one another to show their friendly intentions.

Some recent experiments were designed to determine more precisely whether any correlation exists between sex and aggression. And none was found—the two are basically incompatible, at least in the several species studied. The three-spined stickleback was one of the animals employed in these experiments. Only male sticklebacks are brightly colored during the breeding season and, while females find these nuptial colors most attractive, rival males react to them like a bull to a red flag. In the experiments, each male's aggression was aroused by presenting him with a live rival male for five minutes. Then his sexual responses to a female were tested. In every case, the male's typical courtship activities were greatly reduced, even totally inhibited, by his highly aggressive state of emotion.

In mice, too, no positive relation could be found between sex and aggression. In this case, the idea was to test whether the more aggressive mice were also more sexy. But there was no correlation —those mice who were most eager to start a fight with other males were not necessarily the Don Juans with the females. Female mice, moreover, won't tolerate aggression. In order to mate, the male mouse must actively pursue a female and try to mount her. But if he is at all aggressive in nosing her or grooming her, she can effectively fight him off or escape from him.

Among most species, as with mice, females have the last word, since they cannot be mated without their cooperation. Therefore, rape is extremely rare in the animal world. Valerius Geist, who knows mountain sheep and their ilk better probably than anyone alive, states that copulation in rams, stags, and bucks "can come about only with the female's cooperation." The males of these species simply "are not equipped to physically grab and hold on to the female and copulate with her despite her struggles." Nor can male wolves copulate if the female won't stand or avert her tail for them, says Jerome Woolpy of the Chicago Zoo.

And this is true for most primates, too. Leonard Williams, author of *Man and Monkey*, writes that "The male monkey

cannot in fact mate the female without her invitation and willingness to cooperate. In monkey society, there is no such thing as
rape." Jane Goodall, speaking of the wild chimpanzees at the
Gombe Stream Reserve, reports that although they are promiscuous, "this does not mean that every female will accept every male
that courts her." And she records not a single case of rape in her
fascinating book, *In the Shadow of Man*. About the worst a
female chimp must contend with is being persistently pursued by
a male she dislikes and sometimes being forced to accompany
him. One torrid male went so far as to shake a female out of a
tree. But, says Goodall, "we never saw him actually 'rape' her."
Nonetheless, this male frequently "managed to get his way
through dogged persistence."

Although, by and large, rape does not exist in nonhuman species, it must be noted for the sake of completeness that there have
been a few recent reports of its occurrence—in elephant seals, in
sea lions, in certain ducks and geese, perhaps in a few insects and
frogs, and even in some apes. But the overall incidence remains
negligible. Since nonhuman females are usually successful at fending off unwelcome advances, evolutionary forces have generally
tended to downplay male aggressiveness toward females. The
male who is too rough, too impudent, will have fewer chances to
mate and hence, fewer offspring.

Among humans, however, rape can and does occur with unhappy frequency, as so vividly documented by Susan Brownmiller
in her recent book *Against Our Will*. We human females, unfortunately, cannot easily defend ourselves or escape from the male.
And our cooperation in copulation is not essential as it is among
many other species. In humans, as a result, unlike many animals,
sex and aggression do occur simultaneously—in the act of rape.
Of the two drives, however, Brownmiller found aggression by far
the most important element. "Rape," she concluded after exhaus-
tive research, "is not a crime of irrational, impulsive, uncontrolla-
ble lust, but is a deliberate, hostile, violent act of degradation and
possession on the part of a would-be conqueror, designed to intim-
idate and inspire fear. . . ."

Despite the widespread occurrence of rape among humans,
however, there are several cultures in which it is rare, even nonex-

istent. And it is important for us to try to learn why. Anthropologist James F. Downs reports, for example, that among the Navajo people there is a "remarkably low" incidence of rape. The rate, says Downs, is 9.7 per 100,000 of population, compared with 13.7 of general American rural population. The Navajo rates for murder, manslaughter, and aggravated assault, on the other hand, are a little higher than the rural average, so it is not aggression in itself, but specifically aggression against women that is rare among the Navajo. As you will recall, Navajo women enjoy an important position in their society. Kinship is traced through the female. Female deities reign, women can become practitioners of religious and magical lore, and women take the initiative in courtship. The high status of the Navajo woman could well be a deciding factor in the low incidence of rape among these people.

Margaret Mead studied a number of primitive cultures and discovered that rape occurred in many of them. Among the Arapesh of New Guinea, however, rape is completely unknown, although these people are fully aware that it exists as an unpleasant custom in a nearby community. The Arapesh, as mentioned earlier, are a gentle loving people among whom both sexes are considered equally responsible and equally respected members of society. These egalitarian ideas, along with their distaste for aggression and violence, most certainly can account for the nonexistence of rape.

It is a jump of immense cultural proportions to move from the Arapesh of New Guinea to the people of Sweden, but there is a common tie. For the people of Sweden offer yet another example of a low-rape society. Statistics show that, although Sweden has a population and demographic profile equivalent to that of Michigan, it has only one fifth the number of rape cases. Shari Steiner in *The Female Factor* credits the Swedish moral code for this. "It is based first and foremost," says Steiner, "on equality between the sexes." Neither sex is expected to force itself upon the other —a woman must not insist on sexual attentions, any more than should a man. (Mutual responsibility is also stressed. Proper precautions are to be taken against an unwanted pregnancy, and venereal disease is to be treated at once and sexual activity ceased until the problem can be cleared up.) This points again to the conclusion that where women are respected, where they enjoy a more equal status with men, rape tends to be a relatively rare event. Egalitarian attitudes may also, incidentally, be good for men. Whether for this or other reasons, Swedish men live longer, averaging seventy-two years, than the men of any other country in the world.

The attitude of rapists toward women is quite different from the Swedish way of thinking. Women are viewed by them as weak and vulnerable, says John Feeney, a social worker who deals with sex offenders at Mendota Mental Health Institute in Madison, Wisconsin. "Many of our patients maintain the stereotype that women are solely sex objects, that they were placed on the earth for the sexual gratification of men."

Aggression and the dominance of one sex toward the other, in conclusion, not only interferes with animal mating, it also increases the incidence of rape in humans. Egalitarian attitudes, in contrast, reduce the incidence of rape, as is clearly evident in Sweden, New Guinea, and other places.

More important, the fullest expression of human sexuality is likely to be enhanced when men and women interrelate on a more equal basis, with mutual consideration and gentleness, respect and love. Today may well be the first day of a new millennium, a millennium when equal rights and rewards will be the rule in our private lives and loves, as well as in the public factor. Women are already reportedly enjoying sex far more than did their mothers. And men are, more than ever, eager to please, eager to share the satisfactions of sex with their wives and lovers. We have all discovered, men and women, that sex is more fun, more rich and more wonderful when it is a mutually pleasurable affair.

(4) Reflections of the Homunculus

*We have to look beyond tired old concepts such as dominance . . .
and stereotyped ideas concerning male-female roles.*

JOHN ARCHER
University of Sussex, England

1

THE QUESTION OF dominance is a pervasive one, affecting all
spheres of life. In sex, as we've seen, dominance and aggression
have been downplayed through the simple mathematics of evolution: They interfere with the main purpose at hand—propagation
of the species. But what about dominance in other areas of animal
life? Is the male always the leader of the group, the boss, the one
who runs the show? Is the female always a cowering, submissive
soul so taken up with the tender loving care of her offspring that
she has little interest or aptitude for group affairs? Are the sexes
genetically programmed for such mutually exclusive roles? And
most importantly, are we humans the inheritors of such deep-
rooted traditions?

Needless to say, the answers to these questions are of vital
concern to women today in their quest for equality. Unfortunately, animal behaviorists, in their speculations on these matters,

have been all too quick to draw their conclusions from limited and biased and sometimes chauvinistic observations. The early mistakes, made when ethology was an infant brainchild of first-rate minds, might be forgiven. Mistaken deductions, as I shall show, often arose because too few observers had watched too few animals for too short a time. But today there is little excuse. We should know full well the shaky strength of grandiose generalizations made upon skimpy foundations. Must we still, then, put up with irresponsible speculation regarding some of the most sensitive issues of our day?

Edward O. Wilson, a Harvard scientist, has made the most recent foray into the subject of male dominance over the female. In his otherwise fascinating and brilliant book, *Sociobiology*, Wilson added a subjective final chapter on the biological background of human behavior. There he suggests, among other highly questionable items, that male dominance over females can reliably be concluded to be an inherited human trait, thereby giving scientific respectability to our cultural prejudices.

Not surprisingly, bitter controversy has surrounded Wilson's theories and, as so often happens, there are those who prefer mass execution to selective amputation. Of all critics, sociologists and anthropologists have been most vehemently opposed to Wilson's views. But Margaret Mead, who was, until her recent death, our country's most distinguished anthropologist, rose up as a voice of reason and expressed general support for the validity of exploring the possible genetic elements of culture. Wilson, she knew, is too good to be attacked in totality. Overall, his research is too comprehensive, his analyses too compelling to be dismissed completely. I was also very impressed with much of his work, as any biologist must be. But, as with Freud, we must sift through his work and separate the chaff from the wheat. We must, in Wilson's own words, "discourage the perversion—but not the subject" of sociobiology.

And that we do so is most urgent, for there are reports even now of male backlash against the human female's drive for equality. To cite just one example, documentary filmmaker Jane Farley, who has won more than thirty national and international awards, sees much more polarization now than she did in the fifties when she began her work. "Men are much more afraid of women. . . . Now women have better benefits, but personal relations and attitudes have suffered." That men might refuel their engines of discrimination with the rash speculations of a new science is sufficient cause for our concern.

The situation today is reminiscent of one that existed during much of the eighteenth century. The light microscope was then the scientific toy of the day and the early microscopists toyed with their new discoveries as flippantly as some animal behaviorists do with theirs today. The eighteenth-century scientists were well aware that significant biological contributions were to be made in microscopy and, though the resolving powers of their instruments were limited, their imaginations were not. Throwing scientific discipline aside, these men looked at the human sperm and claimed to see in its head a miniature replica of the human being —the *homunculus*. As other men have since admitted, the *homunculus* was a reflection emanating not from the microscopes in their labs, but from the male chauvinism in their minds. Where none could see clearly, prejudice conjured up its own peculiar substitute for scientific fact.

Similarly today, in the study of human origins, our resolving powers are limited, our ambitions great, our imaginations vivid. Surely it is obvious by now that both biological and cultural factors have had their imput into the making of humankind. We are not yet at the point where we can see precisely how these two are integrated. But naturalists, like nature, seem to abhor a vacuum and so into the void they toss their most tenuous guesswork, knowing full well that while it cannot be proved, neither can it be disproved. They are safe, and they get the attention they so humanly crave and the financial support they require for the long tedious business of amassing hard scientific fact. Reacting in the other extreme are those anthropologists who, finding few irrefutable facts, deny any and all biological contributions to the human personality. For them, too, it is a facile stance—who can prove them wrong? But not being demonstrably wrong does not make one infallibly right.

To give an example, not long ago scientists thought humans were the only primates to hunt cooperatively in small groups. No one had data to prove them wrong—until Jane Goodall and others discovered that chimpanzees and baboons will occasionally join together to catch and eat rabbits, antelope, and other species of monkey. Until recently, too, only humankind was supposedly capable of language. No one could say otherwise. But then a female chimp named Washoe was taught sign language and another, named Sarah, learned to read and write with plastic symbols. The latest celebrity is a female gorilla named Koko. Like Washoe, she has been taught sign language and has become amazingly accomplished. An adolescent of seven years, Koko now has the vocabulary and learning skills of a human child of three or four years, and her IQ has been tested at about 85! An IQ of 100, incidentally, is considered average for humans. (A few male chimpanzees have also been used in language studies, but they have not received as much publicity.)

And so we now know that both our language and our hunting —which seemed so humanly unique only a decade or two ago— have been foreshadowed in our primate past. As we explore ever more closely the supposed dividing line between ourselves and animals, that dividing line grows increasingly blurred. But there is still much more we must learn. Unfortunately, as we look into the hazy images of our past, some of us tend to look so hard and so eagerly that, drugged by desire, we begin to see mirages shaped to our own making. Others of us, hating the haziness and harboring our own illusions, deny all; we see nothing.

2

DOMINANCE RELATIONS HAVE long been overemphasized in primate studies, both by field researchers and by armchair enthusiasts. Like delusions of grandeur clung to by an old aristocracy, they persist in popularity despite the surfacing of new realities that now undermine their importance. But there is a growing discontent among students of primate behavior concerning these old ideas on dominance. Like the imaginary homunculus, the dominance patterns so stressed in early studies are now seen to be reflections often colored by conjecture, dating from a time when facts were few and far between.

The first round of primate studies surely seemed to point to dominance as a major axis of animal society. Most groups, it was reported, appeared to be organized into some sort of linear hierarchy in which adult males usually ranked on top with females and young below them. These studies were, for some time, the only "scopes" with which we could view primate society. Our vision was poor; we did the best we could. But today, there are newer, longer, more varied and more plentiful studies at our disposal. Our vision, while still imperfect, has greatly improved. We can, at last, make out true outlines, forms, and figures. The colors may still be shadowy pastels, razor-sharp edges still beyond us, precision light-years away, but the major features stand out clearly, indubitably. We need only look. And, for many species, dominance is not of great consequence.

Let me defer to the scientists themselves. Ethologist Thelma Rowell, an outspoken critic of the pervasive dominance concept, states that "the concept of dominance has been curiously over-rated as a general governing principle in social behavior." She speculates further as to whether "this could be due to unconscious anthropomorphism: is our own species more than usually bound by hierarchical relationships, at least among males, who have written most about this subject?" Primatologist James Loy echoes her sentiments: "The view that the organization and behavior of a primate group revolve around its dominance network is untenable." Biologist Ashton Barfield has recently said much the same thing: "Now, there is strong evidence that territorial displays and dominance hierarchies are not very important in many mammalian species, particularly in noncaptive animals."

Where then did the earlier studies go wrong? As Barfield has implied, there are significant differences between the behavior of noncaptive animals and that of captive animals. The early emphasis on dominance hierarchies arose mainly from studies of primates confined in spaces many times smaller than their normal ranges in the wild. Competition and aggression are greatly magnified under such crowded conditions. Among certain wild baboons, for example, there is little strong leadership and lots of cooperation between individuals. But put the same species in a cage, and both males and females will form a strict hierarchy in which top positions are won through fierce fighting.

Another flaw in the early studies was the assumption that what was true for one group of animals was true for the entire species. It was an easy mistake to make if you happened to be among the first to study, say, the savannah baboon or the wild rhesus or the vervet or langur or any number of species about which old inferences have now been discarded. Even worse were those behaviorists who took the peculiarities of a single group (and certain domineering, pugnacious baboons were top candidates here) as a springboard for all manner of theories regarding typical animal and even human behavior.

We now know that, contrary to original assumptions, animal behavior and organization is greatly affected by habitat. For example, in addition to the early studies of the more easily observed savannah baboon, studies are now available of the forest baboon. The differences between baboons in these two habitats are quite astounding. The rigid hierarchies, the tyrannical harem bosses, the overall nasty dispositions of the savannah baboon find no counterpart in their forest relations, where life is far more easy and open. Among some forest baboon groups, the classic male hierarchical structure is missing completely, as is male sexual jealousy and competition for females. Nor are baboons alone in the wild diversity of their life-styles. Langurs, macaques, vervet monkeys and others of the more terrestrial (ground-living) primates similarly show wide variability from group to group, influenced sometimes, as with baboons, by habitat; influenced other times by social traditions. Even individual personalities can affect the character of a group.

There are greater variations, as might be expected, between species. The first primates studied—certain baboons and macaques—seemed on the whole a pretty ornery lot. The males among them fought to be first for food and females, they pushed each other around, lorded it over underdogs, worried about superiors, and were generally more competitive than any Wall Street money monger. One of the early writers, Lionel Tiger, in his book *Men in Groups* published in 1969, admitted that "By comparison with other primates both baboons and macaque males are very aggressive and intensely concerned with dominance." Nonetheless, he chose to use these very species to support his contention that the dominance of men over women in human society stems from our primate heritage. Thelma Rowell, in contrast, believes that "if our major research experience had happened to be with primates other than macaques and baboons, the concept of dominance would have achieved little prominence in theories of social organization."

Another early writer, Robert Ardrey, in his popular *The Territorial Imperative,* stated categorically that "In every species of monkey and ape she [the female] is subordinate to all mature males." Yet, even as Ardrey wrote, new and contrasting reports began to trickle in. Among Old World primates, there is the patas monkey, a reddish-brown, long-limbed monkey of Africa. The patas is terrestrial like the savannah baboon. The male patas, like the male baboon, is twice as large as the female. Yet, the patas male shows no signs of dominance; indeed, the female is more aggressive toward the male than vice versa. Gibbons—slender, long-armed apes of tropical Asia—are another case in point. Male and female gibbons differ little in either physical appearance or dominance status, and both sexes share in guarding and leading and organizing their group. There are some species, too, in which females are clearly dominant over males, such as among the vervets and Sykes's monkeys of Africa.

In most New World monkeys, dominance hierarchies were found to be weak, even nonexistent. The titi monkeys of the Amazon forests, for example, live in closely knit family groups in which there is no clear dominance between males and females. Some New World species, moreover, are organized along matriarchal lines. In spider monkeys, males have little to do with the main assemblage of females and young. They wander afar and have, seemingly, neither say-so nor savvy in group affairs. In squirrel monkeys, males are equally if not totally dispensable. During all but the mating season, squirrel monkey males are thin, apathetic, and unsociable. They seldom approach the large group of females and young, whose numbers can swell to the hundred-mark—for good reason, for if they dare, the females will threaten and chase them while the youngsters, good mimics that young primates are, will do likewise. Male offspring will even display, with incorrigible disrespect, the squirrel monkey threat of an erect penis.

The lemurs of Madagascar are probably the most matriarchal of primate species. Alison Jolly, the young woman who has done the major research on this species, points out that for the newborn lemur, "the world is full of mother, and a fringe of less-privileged near-mother females and juveniles." In addition, the female lemur is unequivocably boss. It is she who, at times, will bounce up to any male to snatch his food away, cuffing him over the ear in the process. It is she who threatens and slaps, and perhaps chases him—or any other individual—should she be approached too closely. Generally, however, she is indifferent to her dominance. Neither status-conscious nor power-hungry, she is simply assertive, indicating her annoyance or her needs as the occasion might demand. (Male lemurs, in contrast, seem ever aware of their position in the male hierarchy, either groveling before their betters or swaggering before their inferiors.)

As for those primates most closely related to humans, gorillas and chimpanzees, dominance behavior is very low key. Open aggression is almost nonexistent, for example, among those "gentle giants," the gorillas. Researcher Dian Fossey states that, "After more than 3000 hours of direct observation, I can account for less than five minutes of what might be called 'aggressive' behavior. And even this amounted to protective action or bluff." Though gorilla groups are headed by a top or "alpha" male, group activities may center around a female. Fossey reports on a male-headed group whose pivotal figure was an aged matriarch, Koko. Koko was "an elderly, doddering female with atrophied arms, dried-up breasts, and graying head," but her personality had a

cohesive influence on the five males. Despite her advanced age, which I estimate at about 50 years, she was able to induce play activities and mutual grooming. When she started the grooming—a kind of social behavior involving meticulous hair parting, searching for and plucking particles—the others would do it too. Within a few minutes, there would be an entire chain of intently grooming gorillas.

Chimpanzees, like gorillas, are generally amiable and affectionate souls within their own group. According to Jane Goodall, they have a loose social order, no sexual jealousies, and no permanent leaders. Fighting and aggressive behavior is infrequent between group members, although Goodall has recently found that violence can erupt between warring factions of chimpanzees. As for female-male relations, in the relatively few instances in which there is a confrontation between an individual male and female within a group, the male—by virtue of his greater size and strength—does dominate the female. In most situations, however, females enjoy as much or more social freedom as do males. They mate with whom they will, move freely from one group to another, give and receive more greetings than do males, and enjoy a central position in chimpanzee society.

Taking the broad look at the contrasting life-styles of the many species, one cannot help but conclude, along with John Archer, a biologist at the University of Sussex in England, that "In primates, there are all possible variations of dominance hierarchies and territorial relations: in some cases the female could be said to be dominant over the male, in others the male dominant over the female, and in a third case both sexes form a hierarchy."

The older studies were biased in still other ways, too. Now recognized is the fact that the male of the species often stole the show. Although adult males represent only a small fraction of most primate groups, usually but 10 to 20 percent, they are large and their behavior conspicuous. Consequently, unless observers took care, males received far more attention than they deserved. Unfortunately, too, there was a tendency to extrapolate from the behavior of this noisy minority to that of the entire group.

There was also confusion in earlier studies about the meaning of certain behaviors such as mounting and presenting. In mounting, one animal gets up upon the other from the rear in the typical position for copulation; in presenting, one animal turns its backside toward another, as females often do to solicit male sexual attention. "Mounting," says ethologist Rowell, "has been repeatedly linked to dominance and presenting to submission, in descriptive accounts of monkey and ape behavior." But she and other workers take issue with this view. Mounting, Rowell found, can have many meanings. Sometimes, a rhesus monkey will mount another to enlist its aid, and then both threaten an antagonist. In baboons, mounting is used, along with other kinds of body contact, to reassure others of friendly intentions. Among talapoins, small African monkeys, the male is normally subordinate to the female, and "reciprocal mounting is the common greeting gesture when animals are reunited," according to Rowell.

The gesture of presenting can also have several meanings. Most frequently it has been described as a gesture of submission used as a ploy to keep higher ranking animals from attacking. As a result, submissiveness has been automatically associated with the sexual presenting of females. But presenting can be used in a variety of contexts other than sex and submission. In baboons, it is used both to solicit grooming and as a common courtesy between animals. In talapoins, Rowell describes two distinct types of presenting—one is typically an invitation to copulate, while the other is an invitation to groom the rump.

Another source of error in the past was unexpected—the length of the studies. Who would have thought, in the early days of ethology, that a year might not be enough time to reveal the major aspects of social behavior in any animal group? Today, reports Jane B. Lancaster, a specialist in primate behavior at the University of Oklahoma, some workers discount their first one hundred hours of observation, since it often takes quite that much time to become familiar enough with a group to accurately sample its interactions. George Schaller's classic study of the mountain gorilla was impressive at the time, yet his nine months of field research included only 458 hours of actual observation. Since then, Dian Fossey has put in more than 3000 hours of direct observation of the mountain gorilla. Another researcher, Judith Ann Breuggeman, recently spent fifteen months and catalogued a total of 1600 hours of observation in her study of rhesus monkeys on Cayo Santiago, an island off Puerto Rico. Even more important, Breuggeman's study is a continuation of long-term observations that have been underway on the island for more than twenty years. Neither scientist nor soothsayer need tell us that the new longer studies will be more meaningful, that their descriptions of animal society will be more accurate, that their sampling bias will be much reduced.

The idea that dominance relations took center stage in the drama of primate life was an error compounded, as I have shown, by a number of things. There were the premature generalizations, the overemphasis on males, the shortage of time, the confusion over behavior patterns, and more—all acting synergistically to produce a picture patently false. There was also the idea that the more dominant animal was more successful in sex. Were this so, then dominance would necessarily be a very adaptive and inheritable trait. The more dominant animal would always out-reproduce his lessers.

But it is not at all clear today that dominance and sexual success go hand in hand. Consider the chimpanzees and their essentially promiscuous sexual arrangements. Goodall writes vividly of Old Flo, "bulbous-nosed and ragged-eared," but then the sexiest female chimp along the Gombe Stream. On a single day during her estrous period, she mated in turn with every adult male in the vicinity; even Evered, an adolescent, was not turned down. The more dominant males certainly have no priorities here. Nor does dominance mean much in the sex life of the Japanese monkeys at the Oregon Regional Primate Research Center. Arrowhead, top male at the Center, was quite outdone in the mating game by Big V, one of the lowest-ranking males. Many of the females, it seems, simply refused to stand still long enough to be mated by the dominant Arrowhead. There are also other cases in which females appear to discriminate against overly aggressive and dominant males. Goodall describes Fifi, a young female chimp, who for a long time couldn't bear to mate with an aggressive male named Humphrey.

Many primate studies nonetheless have seemed to show a relationship between sex and dominance. On the other hand, several new ones show none. Furthermore, scientists are now raising many important questions about some of the older studies. For one thing, there is the problem that high-status males mate more openly and conspicuously than those in the lower echelon who tend to be more secretive about it. When one researcher corrected his data to account for this relative "observability," he found little difference between high- and low-ranking males. Only one study, to my knowledge, has determined the exact number of offspring sired by each male of a primate troop. Through extensive blood testing of members of a group of rhesus monkeys, Susan Duvall and her associates found that low-ranking males and even adolescent males fathered just as many offspring as the top-ranking male. Dominance made no difference at all!

For all these reasons and some more technical, there has been much discontent with the concept of dominance as an important explanatory feature of primate society. But even as dominance is gradually being dismissed, new material flowing from three separate ongoing studies points to something quite different as a major axis of animal organization. The studies are those of chimpanzees in Tanzania begun by Jane Goodall in 1960, of rhesus monkeys on the island of Cayo Santiago off Puerto Rico begun in 1956, and of Japanese monkeys begun in 1950 at the Japanese Monkey Center.

A little background is in order on each of these important studies. Goodall began her work, alone, in the forested valley of the Gombe Stream above Lake Tanganyika. Gradually, over many months, the chimps became accustomed to Goodall's presence and she was able to observe and record their ways. Today, the Gombe Stream Reserve has been established and many scientists have joined Goodall in her chimpanzee studies. Rhesus monkeys are the familiar "monkey island" denizens in our zoos. In 1938, anthropologist C. R. Carpenter settled several hundred rhesus monkeys from India on the island of Cayo Santiago. Some research was done in those early days—Carpenter's own studies are often quoted—but it was not until the mid-fifties that a continuing, in-depth research program began. The Japanese monkey is a close cousin of the rhesus monkey, both being in the group called macaques. Since 1950, researchers at the Japanese Monkey Center have kept careful records of the histories of individuals in wild troops located at four different places. These records have been supplemented by more casual studies of Japanese monkeys in several other localities.

Each of these studies, then, was a long-term endeavor during which individuals could be observed not merely for a few months or even years, but throughout their entire life spans. And each of these studies indicated that an essential feature of primate society was the bond between a mother and offspring, leading in time to the matrifocal, or mother-focused, grouping as the basic unit of organization. Indeed, most mammalian societies, from mice to monkeys, are now seen to be matrifocal in make-up. The word *matrifocal* is not to be confused with the word *matriarchy*, which is often used to imply female rule. Although most animal societies are matrifocal, they are not necessarily matriarchal.

In chapter 6, I shall consider the formation of the mother-infant bond, but for now, let's consider its consequences. Several researchers have shown that an infant's attachment to his or her mother does not end with weaning, with adolescence, or even with adulthood. Jane Goodall became increasingly impressed with the depth of this attachment among her chimpanzees. "Who would have thought that a three-year-old chimpanzee might die if he lost his mother? Who would have guessed that at five years of age a child might still be suckling and sleeping with his mother at night? Who would have dreamed that a socially mature male of about eighteen years of age would still spend much time in the company of his old mother?"

Another researcher, Donald Sade, in his observations of rhesus monkeys on Cayo Santiago, found similarly long-lasting attachments between mothers and their offspring. Sade became interested in grooming patterns. Grooming is a major form of relaxation among rhesus monkeys, enjoyable for groomer and "groomee" alike. The groomer meticulously spreads the fur of the other monkey, scrapes gently at the skin, and picks up flakes of loose skin, hair, dirt, dried blood, and fleas if any are present. The monkey being groomed stretches out, lets its limbs go limp, and is very relaxed and placid. Grooming seems to express affection and camaraderie between monkeys, and Sade found that it was the most frequent interaction between individuals. He reports that grooming was fifteen times as popular as mounting behavior, three times as popular as dominance interactions and more than twice as popular as wrestling among his monkeys. It is quite obvious that, of any activity, grooming can tell us most about bonds between individuals.

Genealogical records had been kept for a number of years

before Sade's study and, armed with this knowledge, Sade found that the most important factor in choosing a grooming partner was the close bond between a mother and her offspring. One male, for example, directed 40 percent of his grooming toward his mother. He himself, however, was the recipient of only 9 percent of his mother's grooming, since her attentions were shared with her other younger offspring. Not even the enticements of the mating season, when mating pairs spend considerable time grooming each other, altered the frequency of grooming between mother and offspring.

As Jane Lancaster points out, a rhesus mother, like a human mother, is able to spend less time with her older offspring as younger ones are born. A rhesus female may have, in fact, six or seven living youngsters. But the older offspring soon come to groom each other when the mother is too busy, finding comfort and companionship in their siblings. Thus, the original bond between a mother and her infant extends itself gradually through the years to include subsequent offspring and even several generations of close relations. And so is formed the matrifocal unit so characteristic of primate society. There is, of course, no such thing as a "patrifocal" or father-focused unit among primates, for the simple reason that most primates are promiscuous. Neither monkey nor human observer can readily know just whom the father might be.

While "the matrifocal unit probably exists in all primate societies," says Lancaster, it varies in importance among them. "When the matrifocal group is relatively large, at any one time there are always suitable partners for grooming, resting or feeding, and the individual does not have to look outside the family for a social partner." In such situations, the matrifocal unit becomes very significant.

There are also differences between species that can affect the importance of the matrifocal unit. One interesting study contrasted two closely related monkeys: the bonnet macaque from South India, named for the bonnetlike arrangement of hairs on its crown, and the pigtail macaque from Southeast Asia, named for its short piglike tail. In pigtail macaques, the mother-young bond is very exclusive: mothers jealously guard their young from all others. Bonnet mothers, on the other hand, have a far more relaxed attitude and their young interact with many other females in the group. These differences in mothering can result in significant differences between primate societies. Bonnet macaques are oriented "toward the entire group for grooming, resting and sleeping partners," says Lancaster, whereas pigtails show strong ties between a mother, her offspring, and her daughter's offspring for this kind of companionship.

Close-knit units of individuals related through the female line, such as found in pigtail and rhesus monkeys, are often referred to as genealogies, and they can sometimes become surprisingly prominent in the social life of primates. The Arashiyama troop of Japanese monkeys was, in 1966, headed by three sisters and a brother, whose genealogy included 35 living descendants. All told, there were 16 genealogies, comprised of three or four generations of relatives within this troop of 163 individuals. The genealogy was the hub of social life for its members. Relatives usually groomed each other, ate together, played together, slept together, and traveled together. They even learned from each other faster than from unrelated individuals.

It was through this new vision of the matrifocal roots of primate society that the importance of the female to group stability, organization, and leadership became more and more apparent. The female has resources, it was discovered, through which, in ways sometimes more subtle than the male's but no less effective, she often wields immense influence over group affairs. She can even, as I shall show, modify the behavior of those males who traditionally have been considered most dominant.

To begin with, the female usually provides the group with its identity through time. Males more often come and go, while females with their growing genealogies remain within their original troop. A researcher returning after an absence of several years, reports Lancaster, may recognize her original group only through the adult females. Among rhesus and Japanese monkeys, vervets, baboons, and others, the male is notorious as the wanderer, traveling sometimes alone, sometimes at the periphery of groups, but as often as not simply exchanging one group for another. Females, however, with the exception of the female chimpanzee, change groups only occasionally. And when they do so, the Japanese studies indicate, it can be of far more consequence, for the female is likely to leave with her entire genealogy. Often it is done not so much for the purpose of exchanging groups, but rather to establish a new one.

Through her stability, the female is able to contribute much to her group's well-being. There is, for instance, her lifelong intimacy with her place of birth. A primate society is usually attached to a particular home range or territory, even though individuals themselves may move from one to another. "Terrestrial and semiterrestrial species," says Lancaster, "tend to have large home ranges and to eat a wide variety of scattered and seasonal foods." In times of drought or other disaster, she suggests, the old experienced females, not the wandering males, will most likely be able to lead their group to remaining food and water resources.

Thelma Rowell, in her observations of olive baboons, noted that the old female olive baboons were the true leaders in everyday troop movements, even though not positioned at the front of the group. Rowell would often count heads during group movements, which were usually signaled by adult males moving out a hundred yards or more from the main group. There they would sit facing back toward the group and wait. "We learned," states Rowell, "that there was no point in starting a count until some of the old females rose and started to move after such a male. If they ignored him he returned to the troop after awhile. When they began to move he too would get up and continue along the line he had 'suggested.' " While the males were the indicators, the females were undoubtedly the deciders in troop travels. Although this seems not to be true for all baboons, one wonders how often and how easily such subtle arrangements may have been overlooked. Rowell has also observed a talapoin group in which females usually took the lead in initiating such activities as feeding, grooming, and sleeping.

Females are decision-makers in other areas, too. Judith Ann Breuggeman found that, among her rhesus monkeys on Cayo Santiago, the acceptance of a male into the high-status central core of a troop depended to a large extent on his acceptance by dominant females. And from the forests of northern India has come a report of a rhesus monkey troop which was without an adult male for six months. Led meanwhile by the two eldest adult females, this group remained stable and continued in its typical daily routine. For several months, they repeatedly repulsed attempts by solitary males to join them, and though finally they did accept one, the group maintained its daily routine as before, unaffected by his presence. This is a far cry, incidentally, from the contention of Lionel Tiger and Robin Fox in their book *The Imperial Animal* that the primate group "will persist over time only if a male (and later other males) attaches himself to it and acts as a focus of attention and source of authority."

Female monkeys have also been known to kick out those males who come into their disfavor. X was a Japanese monkey, a subleader in his troop, who disappeared after being attacked by high-ranking females. And in the confined corral at the Oregon Regional Primate Research Center, where female Japanese monkeys cannot actually drive away males as in wild troops, they manage to keep the targets of their wrath in the lower ranks.

Female rhesus and Japanese monkeys are not the only ones to band together at times against males. Langurs, patas and gelada females form similar coalitions. Jane Lancaster has also described in detail such coalitions among vervets, which are greenish-gray, black-faced monkeys of Africa. Female vervets readily joined together to attack even the top three males of their group if these males monopolized prized foods or frightened their infants. The females would run screaming at the offending male, who would turn and flee as fast as he could until he reached the nearest tree or rock. Climbing to the top, he would turn and face his chasers. Threats would be exchanged for a minute or so; then the females would return to the food or infant that was the source of their concern. "After that," Lancaster says, "the male might be free to join them, but now on their terms and not on his."

While such coalitions never affected the rank of the offending male, it did modify his behavior. In particular, vervet males learned to be careful around the "kids," as Lancaster discovered. Several times after an infant screamed through no fault of theirs, every adult male in the vicinity fled in haste. The potential threat of a female coalition was not to be taken lightly.

The primate female, as can be seen, wields considerable sway in primate politics. Although limited sometimes by size and strength and the obligations of motherhood, she has her resources. She pools her power, gathers her coalitions and has her rightful say. Nor does this complete her repertoire. There is also the startling fact that, in a number of species, the female determines the status of her sons and daughters.

It is not really difficult to see how this occurs, explains Lancaster. Among macaques and baboons, juvenile fights occur frequently, especially, as with human children, when play gets too rough. One juvenile will scream, perhaps, and her protective mother will run over and bite the other juvenile, whose mother in turn rushes to the scene. A lower ranking mother will simply snatch up her infant and flee or gesture submissively, while a higher ranking one will threaten and chase the other away. After a few experiences like this, a young monkey learns to act in her mother's ways, fleeing or chasing as rank structure may demand. At the same time, other animals learn that a particular youngster, though weak and insignificant, may have a powerful mother to back her up.

Even adult males may be defended by their mothers. Among the Oregon monkeys, Greater Than, third in the male hierarchy, was sometimes attacked by the two top-ranking males. At those times, his mother, Red Witch, would leap on the backs of the dominant males to distract them while her son escaped. Diversions like this, to deal with the aggressions of powerful males, are common in the female monkey's repertoire. I especially enjoyed the sophistication displayed by Old Female–1, a monkey at Cayo Santiago. On one occasion, she saw her son being attacked by an old male and came running to the rescue on her hind legs, carrying her five-day-old infant. After reaching her son's side, the two of them began to gesture and threaten violently at an empty area away from the old male. Curious, the old male stopped chasing long enough to look in the direction of their threats. But he was not fooled and quickly resumed the chase. Then, again, taking his cue from his mother, the young male began threatening away from his attacker. The old male, no doubt thoroughly perplexed by now, sat down three feet away and peered once more in the

direction of the younger one's threats. Old Female–1 boldly came
up then and sat down between the two males, and her young son
immediately sidled up to her and sat touching and grooming her.
After a short time, she walked away, her son following closely,
while the old male stayed, staring at nothing.

As rhesus and Japanese monkeys mature, the lives of males and
females take different paths. The female will usually remain in the
rank to which she was born—a position just below that of her
mother. The young male, however, may wind up in a rank either
above or below that of his birth, achieving this usually through
fights and other competitive interchanges. But even here family
connections come into play. If born of a high ranking female, he
may be admitted to the central core of dominant males without
engaging in a single serious fight. Even for those males who must
fight for their place in the male hierarchy, the mother's influence
may still carry over. Many fights among monkeys are bluffing
matches, and the sons of higher-ranking females, accustomed to
winning, are likely to be more confident than those of lower
ranking females.

So here again, in unexpected style, the female reveals her power
in primate affairs. As mother and head of her genealogy, she has
a major influence on the entire hierarchical system of her group
—particularly among some of the most social of primates. There
is also the growing realization that the very structure of animal
society—its sexual composition, its mating arrangements, its
forms of female-male bonding—all are determined largely by the
interests of the female. This new development in ethological
thought comes as a fitting denouement to our updated tale of
primate affairs. And it comes, as do so many new ideas, with a new
vocabulary. There is talk of the different evolutionary strategies
of the male and the female.

The male's best strategy, in many circumstances, is to mate
with as many females as possible without paying too high a price
in terms of risky competition with other males. But, for the
female, things are quite different. Her strategy is not simply to
become pregnant as often as she can. That is no problem. Rather,
it is in her interest to raise as many infants to maturity as she can.
And so, as Lancaster states, "males are a resource in her environ-

ment which she may use to further the survival of herself and her offspring."

If there is no need for male protection, if there is little advantage in his helping to "bring up the kids," then a single male may suffice for a group of females. His only role, his only evolutionary purpose, is impregnation. The "harem" then receives a new image: It is designed ultimately for female fulfillment, not male sexual satisfaction. And along with the new image comes a new label. The "uni-male group" is now rapidly replacing the "harem" of the old literature with its chauvinistic implications.

It is true that among a few primates, harems, in the old sense of the word, do exist. Although animal behaviorists have never formally defined the word *harem,* by dictionary definition it refers to a "group of females controlled by one male." Two primate species definitely fall into this category: langurs and hamadryas baboons. Langurs are handsome, black-faced gray monkeys of India that live either in harems having one adult male or in troops with several adult males. Until recently, langurs were considered relatively peaceful and nonaggressive animals among whom threats and fighting were uncommon. According to the latest studies, however, langur life can be much less benign, especially in the harems, where invading males periodically usurp control of the group from the harem leader and murder all the group's infants during the takeover. Although langur females have little choice as to which male takes over, they are otherwise remarkably independent and, within an established troop, there seems to be little overt subjugation or aggression by the harem male toward the females.

The harem organization of the hamadryas baboon of Ethiopia, in contrast, is probably the most "sexist" of all primates. The females are herded by male overlords who not only are twice their size but have large manes of wavy gray hair that make them look all the more impressive. Should a female lag behind or stray too far from the group, the male will bite, slap, or hostilely stare at the female, who responds by running to him.

These species, however, are exceptional. Most uni-male groups, say Dr. Katherine Ralls of the National Zoo, do not fit the dictionary definition of a harem because females are able to move between groups and because male control is lacking. Gelada baboons, for example, live in uni-male groups, just as do hamadryas baboons. Female geladas, however, unlike female hamadryas, can choose which group they prefer to join. Female geladas, moreover, generally take the lead in group movements and are the center of social life within their unit. They can also stray considerable distances from their male without harassment. In fact, when a male does try to herd a wandering female, she generally threatens back and chases the male, sometimes with the aid of her female cohorts.

Patas monkeys also live in uni-male groups. As mentioned earlier, females in this species are more aggressive toward males than males are toward them. Female patas monkeys also "habitually initiate directions and times of group movements," according to primate expert K. R. L. Hall.

Despite these wide discrepancies between female and male roles within harem species (not to mention non-harem species), Lionel Tiger in *Men in Groups* made reference particularly to the hamadryas baboon when he considered the leadership abilities of women. "By analogy," he said, "the leadership structure of hamadryas baboon troops can be seen to be male-dominated." Then, trying to play it safe and yet at the same time pronouncing his sexist conclusions, he states: "While I am not saying there is a necessary connection between baboon patterns and human patterns . . . I am proposing that 'human nature' is such that it is 'unnatural' for females to engage in . . . high politics." Obviously, we could instead take the patas monkey or the gelada baboon or any number of other species and propose quite the opposite!

Where uni-male groups exist, whether traditional "harems" or not, it is usually because such groupings are more adaptive. Uni-male groups, for example, are most common among tree-living monkeys, according to Lancaster. High in the forest canopy, defense against predators must be handled quite differently than in the open savanna. Hunting packs of wild dogs and lions and hyenas prowl the grasslands. But in the forests, predators come singly, stealthily. The leopard pounces suddenly and savagely; the forest eagle-owl swoops down for quick and quiet devastation. In such circumstances, one's best bet is to be forever alert and to stay always on small end branches, which are too weak to support a predator. No great advantage will here accrue to the masculine potential for greater musculature, for larger size, or for more impressive canines. And so, in forest groups, the male's role will be minimal. One male per group may be plenty.

Ultimately, "the number of males in a given troop will depend on what advantage the males are to the reproducing females." Such is the conclusion of J. F. Eisenberg of the Smithsonian Institute, together with his colleagues, in their much-quoted survey of the social structure of primates. In more terrestrial, more open-country species, the male role expands. He is indispensable, not merely for his viable sperm but for his prowess against predators. And he needs help. He needs other males who, while sharing in his protective responsibilities, will share too in the reproductive potential of the group.

There are several well-known exceptions to this general rule for terrestrial species. The patas monkey, the hamadryas baboon, and the gelada baboon are terrestrial species that have, nonetheless, uni-male mating systems. But for these primates, Lancaster suggests, there is a special selective advantage. Food supplies are scarce and of poor quality in their usual arid habitats, so the smaller the foraging unit the better. Extra males are a luxury the group cannot afford.

Certainly, it is high time that the perspective of the female be taken into account. That is not to say that the male's evolutionary strategy need be dismissed. The two are part of the same evolutionary system, but the differences remain. Neither strategy alone gives the complete picture of social behavior among animals. As Lancaster states, "Both are equally valid and we ought to consider both in trying to understand a social system and how it works." It is too bad we had to wait so long to do so.

3

MISCONCEPTIONS ABOUT HAREMS and a neglect of the female point of view have not been confined to primates. Wherever uni-male groups have existed—or even *thought* to have existed— it has been much the same story. And here again, scientists attribute the problem to the superficiality of early investigations. Besides primates, uni-male groups occur mainly in seals and sea lions, and in hoofed animals, the ungulates.

With regard to seals and sea lions, the use of the terms "harem" and "harem master" has been increasingly criticized by field observers. First of all, these so-called harems "result more from the gregariousness of the females than from the efforts of the 'harem master,' " according to R. S. Peterson, whose major work has been with northern fur seals.

> Bulls of several species [says Peterson], chase females that attempt to leave the aggregations within their territories, and in dimorphic species, such as fur seals where the male is much larger than the female, a bull may lift a female and throw her back into his territory. . . . But there are too many females per territory and they are too agile for the bulls. I have watched female fur seals move through five harems in less than one hour.

Another field observer, B. J. Marlow, came to similar conclusions regarding two species of sea lions. In the Australian sea lion, although bulls were very rough in herding cows, there was nonetheless considerable movement of cows. So much so, in fact, that Marlow considers the concept of a harem in this species "meaningless." "The absolute numbers of of cows associated with any bull," Marlow says, "is constantly changing and the individual identity of them is also in a constant state of flux." In Hooker's sea lion, the term harem becomes even less meaningful. Males in this species "do not herd cows and the breeding bulls allow the females to pass from one territory to another without attempting to restrain them in any way." Marlow's vivid description of a breeding area bears little resemblance to a traditional harem:

> In an enormous mass of females all lying together with the most dominant bulls lying in the group and the other breeding bulls lying around the periphery, it is quite impossible to determine which cows belong to which bull at any particular time, and since the cows can pass freely from one group of females to another, the whole

configuration of the association of individual cows and bulls is
continually changing.

As for ungulates, we've already noted some of the mistakes and
prejudices of the past. Most species of antelope were once
thought to live in harems. In past pages, we cleared the record
for the Uganda kob, an antelope which, despite rumors to the
contrary, never did live in harems. The impala, another antelope
of Africa, has been found to live much like the kob: males establish territories through which female groups wander almost at will.
Interestingly, each female impala has a home range of approximately ten male territories.

There are some antelopes, to be sure, that do live in harems.
In zebras, herds of females and their colts are usually controlled
by one male, although females may take on certain leadership
functions. South American vicuñas, small members of the camel
family, also live in harems. Male vicuñas typically chase back
females who stray across the border of their territories. But species
like these that live in classic harems are, once again, exceptions
to the rule.

There has been a wealth of new research on ungulates
within the last ten years that has helped to expose fictitious
harems in a number of species. More important, however, this
research points to the matrifocal grouping as the major feature
of ungulate society, just as it is in the primates. The most elementary type of matrifocal organization is that of the moose—
adult animals get together only to mate, while youngsters live
with their mothers until maturity. More advanced are those
species, including many antelope, where several mother-young
units remain together for long periods. In elephants, the matrifocal tendency is most highly developed and kinship ties are
lifelong. At every level, the role of the males seems to be
related to the needs of the mother-young units, with impregnation and defense being top priorities.

Among some of the more advanced ungulates, matrifocal
bonds play so prominent a part in group life that a matriarchy
develops. In mountain sheep, American bison, red deer, Russian
reindeer, African wildebeests, kudus, and elephants, matriarchy as

a social order reaches its zenith. No volume on the female of the species would be complete without mention of these magnificent mammals with their sophisticated ways, their extraordinary altruism, and their close and long-lived kinship bonds. In all the literature on these animals, there are two studies which, to me, are outstanding in their depth and perception. The first one, published in 1937, is Frank Fraser Darling's classic work on the red deer in the wild highland corries of Scotland. In one day, Darling would walk 30 to 40 miles and climb 8,000 to 10,000 feet in his steadfast quest to know all that he could of these graceful and gregarious animals. The second study concerns the African elephant and was completed but a few years ago. Iain and Oria Douglas-Hamilton lived "among the elephants," as their recent book is entitled. Their tale of elephants reveals a rich communal life among these largest of all land animals, a life full of warmth and familial devotion, and of exceptional tolerance to others of their kind.

Let's first join Darling in an invigorating hike into the Scottish highlands and immerse ourselves in the world of the red deer. Darling was a careful worker. He chose olive-colored clothes to blend in with the landscape and even went so far as to use khaki handkerchiefs, rather than white ones. He carried plenty of them too, he said, "for the nose runs more than normally when moving about the hill." His tools were few, but the best he could buy: binoculars, camera, and most important of all, his telescope, with which he scanned the countryside inch by inch to spot deer in the distance. To keep his vision sharp, he read little at night. And to stalk his prey more easily and quietly, Darling braved bare feet for an entire summer. Prolonged observation, camouflage, and quiet were the essentials of his two-year study. His thorough, dedicated work provided a wonderfully intimate view of the ways of the red deer.

The male and female of this species, Darling discovered, lived lives quite different from one another. For all but a few weeks of the year, during the rutting season, the two sexes keep to their separate ways, grouping together on their separate territories. The stag groups are very loose associations of "egocentric males," as Darling put it. Each male must look out for himself and no true leadership is apparent, although one stag might sometimes be found to bully the rest.

The female groups, which include both females (hinds) and their offspring, are very different. Here leadership is well developed and benevolent, resulting in closely knit groups of great stability and orderliness. So impressed was Darling by these hind groups that he felt that the red deer had reached the highest development of sociality to be found among grazing herds.

Maternal care in the red deer is long by animal standards, the offspring usually remaining with the mother until its third year of life. Since a female bears a calf either every year or in alternate years, she is usually seen with two or three offspring of different ages—"followers" as Darling so aptly called them. It is this lengthy period of dependence among red deer that, Darling believed, gives rise to their highly developed social system.

Each hind group, which might number from five to over two hundred in any one territory, has its own leader. But this large group may be subdivided into smaller units, each with its own leader. Further splitting into individual family groups occurs in times of good weather and in daylight. In all cases, however, when the entire herd is together, the family leaders submit to one leading hind of the herd. This leader is a mature and usually old female. Konrad Lorenz, in his provocative book *On Aggression*, claims that Darling found her to be an "aged female, no longer hampered in her social duties by the obligations of motherhood." Although I have the greatest admiration for Lorenz' work, in this instance, I must defer to Darling himself who stated otherwise. Darling said that the leader usually "had a calf at foot" and, in fact, ceased to be a leader if she were not a regular breeder. Darling believed her leadership over the group was maternal in its origins, and her motherly concern extended to embrace not only her own immediate offspring, but the entire herd as well. This leader is often assisted by a second female who covers the rear position in herd movements.

In reading Darling's masterpiece, one cannot fail to sense his deep admiration for the loving concern, the constant alertness, and the unmistakable altruism displayed by these female leaders. Their leadership, he explains, "is of the mother type and bears no relationship to the masculine egocentric type which enjoys power for power's sake." Always anxious for the herd's welfare, the leading hind raises her head constantly to smell and see and hear, so much so that she has been given the epithet "herself of the long neck." Other hinds take their turns also, but the leader is most alert.

If a potential source of danger is spotted, the deer try to keep it in sight at all times, even as they move in retreat. If they must cross a depression, the rear hind will remain at the crest, watchful and motionless, while the rest of the herd disappears out of sight, there to remain until the lead hind appears once more on a rise beyond the depression and takes up the watch. Only then will the rear hind join her companions. Darling also tells of a leading hind who led her herd to the safety of a rock shelf overlooking a river valley where a woman and her dog were bringing in the cows. On this early spring day, Darling saw that the leader, after bringing her herd to a spot out of sight from the valley below, returned to the edge of the rock shelf. There she remained in watchfulness until cows, dog, and woman had safely disappeared. The hind walked back only then, some three hundred yards, to join her herd.

Of even greater significance was a case where not even hunger deterred a leading hind from her obligatory watchfulness. It was the worst of winter weather and Darling had left maize for the deer, as was his wont. The deer had never grown tame enough to approach the food when he was near, but this time Darling decided to hide not far away. The leader was uneasy, perhaps because she had not seen Darling leave. She allowed the other deer to eat, but she herself remained alert, muzzle raised, some five yards away, although the corn was fast disappearing. Then, after several minutes, she spotted Darling and barked. The other deer ran up to her and all stood looking at the eavesdropper in their midst. Darling describes his chagrin: "They all stood still 25 yards away. The hind barked again and I sat up in full view. They did not move. I got up and walked away rather shamefacedly before their gaze. They knew me well enough not to take precipitate flight." Later, looking through binoculars at a distance, Darling saw the leader at long last approach the maize and begin to eat, followed by the others. "Her behavior," says Darling in understatement, "was not egocentric." He hesitated to call it "conscious altruism," but altruism it was, conscious or not, by the accepted definition today: She risked her own well-being for the sake of the others.

Darling came away from his highland venture with the heady suggestion that the matriarchal system, with its altruistic ways, was a "move towards the development of an ethical system." He was, as it has turned out, far ahead of his time. Animal altruism, if not matriarchy necessarily in itself, is today regarded by many sociobiologists as the key to the evolution of ethics. And matriarchal mammals, it is generally acknowledged, display some of the most altruistic behavior.

But how does one explain altruism in animals? A century ago, Darwin, in a theory now virtually unchallenged, proposed that favorably adapted organisms who are able to survive and out-reproduce others will be successful, while inferior organisms will reproduce less and eventually die out. But how could this account for altruism? Why should one animal come to the aid of another, if it reduces her or his own chances for survival? Why should the leading hind among the red deer set herself up as guard and refrain from eating the maize she needs as sorely as the others during winter's scarcity? Why should dolphins try to lift a harpooned companion to the surface for air when the harpoonist is still near? Why should bees commit suicide for their sisters, which they do each time they sting? (Their barbed stings become so imbedded in the victim that, as the bees pull away, their viscera are torn out and they soon die.) Why does a killdeer spread her wings and feign injury to try to lead you away from her nest, risking her own life in the charade?

Why? Because, sociobiologists say, it enhances her genetic if not her personal survival. Any individual animal shares genes with its sisters and brothers, its sons and daughters, its parents and cousins and nieces and nephews. And in aiding the survival of its kin, the animal ensures that its own genes will also survive. The leading hind watches, the bee stings, and the killdeer puts on her act because they are protecting relatives that share many of their own genes and so increase the chance that some of these genes survive.

With these new ideas, should they be adquately proven, Darwinian theory would be made complete, the last gap—the question of animal altruism—plugged, and the case finally closed. This may, many believe, prove to be the single most important contribution of the new science of sociobiology—the study of the biological basis of all social behavior. Its gene-based explanation for selflessness was anticipated some twenty years ago by British biologist J. B. S. Haldane, who facetiously announced that he would lay down his life for two brothers or eight cousins. Brothers, it seems, share about half of their genes, while cousins share about one eighth, and so the combined genes shared either by Haldane's two brothers or by his eight cousins are equal in number to his own, and their survival thus equivalent to his own personal survival.

Experimental evidence, although limited to social insects, supports the theory of altruism. Worker ants are more closely related to their sisters, with whom they share a full three fourths of their genes, than to their potential offspring, with whom they would share only half of their genes. Fittingly, worker ants spend their time assisting the queen in producing their sisters and have evolved as sterile castes, unable to produce young of their own. These workers are also three times more closely related to their sisters than to their brothers. Sociobiologist Robert Trivers reasoned that, this being so, worker ants should spend three times as much time rearing sisters as rearing brothers. He and his assistant Hope Hare proceeded to study thousands of ants of twenty different species and they found the original hypothesis to be correct. With results indicating a three to one female dominance, their experiment is, at the time of this writing, the strongest evidence yet of a genetic basis for altruism.

Things are considerably more speculative when it comes to human altruism. But generally it's conjectured that our own altruism has its roots in the altruism of animals and has evolved, beyond this, to nongenetic altruism. For we humans help kith and kin, and strangers as well. Our altruism, then, may be rooted, not in our human uniqueness, but in the uniqueness that is life itself.

While some are repugnant to the idea that our selflessness may be, at least in part, innate or instinctual, there are others like anthropologist Melvin J. Konner of Harvard, who believes that this new perspective actually enhances human nature "by showing that altruism, long thought to be a thin cultural veneer, belongs instead to the deepest part of our being, produced by countless aeons of consistent evolution."

The female of the species has had an important role in that evolution. Especially among her matriarchies, animal altruism has flowered. We've already roamed with the red deer and marveled at the maternal concern of the ever-watchful leading hinds. But it is among the elephants that we'll find an altruism more varied and advanced than in almost any other living species.

The elephant is an animal for superlatives. It can weigh up to six tons and it cools this great bulk by using its huge ears both as fans and as radiators. Its droppings alone weigh up to two kilograms (approximately five pounds) a lump. It can drink up to twenty-two gallons of water at a time, an ability which, along with its enormous appetite, can make for weight fluctuations within a given animal of nearly five hundred pounds. The female's seventeen-inch clitoris and the male's sixty-pound penis are largest among terrestrial animals. Even the newborns are enormous. The Douglas-Hamiltons observed an elephant infant which weighed a full 250 pounds.

Iain and Oria Douglas-Hamilton are as remarkable as the elephants they watched. Iain met the vivacious Oria Rocco, "a girl with long dark hair . . . Kenya born and bred," at a party in Nairobi. No stranger to the African bush, Oria was taught to hunt as a young girl by a Masai moran (warrior), who was a friend of her family. Later, in startling contrast, she went to finishing schools in Paris and Rome, joined the existentialist underworld of the Left Bank, and, "driven by a burning restlessness," traveled, learned to speak five languages, did fashion designing, photography, and filming. As she began to succeed in each endeavor, Oria says, "the charm suddenly vanished and I moved on." She could not, however, leave her parents' great highland farm for good, and she eventually returned to run the family's vegetable export business.

Iain had been watching elephants for several years before he met Oria. His earlier days at Oxford had been unimpressive; he was but a marginal student plainly more interested in mountaineering than in zoology. But a summer as a raw research assistant in the Serengeti instilled in him an overwhelming enthusiasm for East Africa and its wildlife. He settled down to his studies, passed his zoology finals, and accepted an offer from his old Serengeti boss to begin a study of elephants. Iain was then able to talk himself into a grant and, once in Africa, learned to fly and take stereoscopic photographs, soon coming to know many of the four hundred to five hundred elephants in Manyara National Park by sight.

The Sunday after they met, Iain flew over to Oria's farm, landing recklessly in a pasture full of holes and long grass. Uninvited but warmly welcome nonetheless, Iain stayed for lunch and convinced Oria to join him in Manyara. Soon the two were working together. Camping beneath unbrella trees and following their elephants by foot and by air, this unique couple have contributed much to science's understanding of the majestic giants of Africa.

The social organization of elephants in Manyara National Park resembles that of the Scottish red deer. Family units of cows and calves consist of ten animals on the average. Most of these units belong to larger kinship groups. Family units might separate for several days but they soon join again and continue to keep company. Cow-calf groups are led, not by fierce bulls as formerly thought, but by large old cows, the matriarchs, as the Douglas-Hamiltons referred to them. As with red deer, these elephant matriarchs are actively reproductive and fearlessly protective.

Male elephants, however, unlike red deer bucks, do not form herds of their own sex. As young bulls begin to mature, they become too "obstreperous and sexy" for their families and are eventually kicked out. These ousted bulls group together only occasionally and never form permanent attachments with individuals of either sex. Their relatively independent and lonely lives are merely peripheral to the matrifocal family units that form the core of elephant society. Indeed, among elephants and many other matriarchal ungulates, males are so superfluous that, except for mating, they play absolutely no part in the main life of the species. Being large animals, elephant cows can defend themselves and their youngsters without male assistance, nor have they need of help in child care. Consequently, the "strategy" of the female elephant involves not even one permanent male per group, but only minutes of male sexual contact on occasion. And such occasions are usually few and far between—once pregnant, a cow does not come into estrus for another three or four years.

The matriarchs then, not the males, are undoubtedly in control of elephantine affairs and for them, the family is all. So enduring are kinship ties that, based on group size, the Douglas-Hamiltons estimated some to have lasted for over a hundred years, possibly much longer. The longevity of these ties are, to my knowledge, unique among animals and are probably related to the elephant's long life of sixty to seventy years, roughly comparable to that of humans. There is also the lengthy matter of maternal nurturing, which lasts at least for the first ten years of life. At birth, an elephant's brain is but a third of its mature weight and, as with the human brain, a prolonged period is required for its learning and enlarging. The very evolution of intelligence seems to hinge on the ever-lengthening amount of time needed for cerebral maturity.

The elephant's gift of time, scores of years of time for living and learning and loving, is singular among land mammals outside of humans. This time has enabled the elephant to reach a pinnacle in animal sociality, creating a communal life outstanding in its intricacy, coherence, and stability. Elephant altruism, moreover, can be rivaled by only two other species, the amiable and egalitarian wild dog of Africa and the congenial and cooperative chimpanzee.

The elephant matriarch is exceptionally altruistic. However risky the situation, she takes the lead in group defense, often launching impassioned charges against dangerous predators, including men. When elephants form their characteristic defensive circles with youngsters tucked between their legs or stowed safely behind their massive bulks, it is again the matriarch who is most courageous. Iain Douglas-Hamilton tells of the time he tried to retrieve a defunct radio collar from a young bull, after tranquilizing him first by dart gun. The surrounding elephants quickly formed an effective defensive circle and shielded the bull from Iain's approach. Dispersing the elephants, Iain slowly drove closer. Finally all the elephants had fled but the matriarch Sarah, who stood with one of her feet resting on the bull's body. Time was running out; the bull would soon die unless Iain injected an antidote to the tranquilizer—which he must do by hand, since he had no darts left. Despite the risk, Iain drove up, leaned from his Land Rover, and gave the injection. At the same time, Sarah thrust her tusks into the radiator, shoved the car backward "like a pram being wheeled by a nurse," and, disregarding a shot in the air to scare her, swung fearlessly at Iain and another passenger before she stalked off.

On other occasions, elephants have tried to raise a darted companion to its feet, much as dolphins attempt to lift an injured member of their school to the surface. Elephants, being so huge, can suffocate under their own weight or overheat dangerously as they lie still in the sun. Elephants also show altruism in caring for offspring, since nursing mothers will usually allow any calf to suckle. Adolescent cows act maternally to the youngsters in their unit; these "aunts" play with the young calves, intervene in their fights, and nudge them awake from naps so they won't be left behind when the group moves on.

Among the many elephants that Oria and Iain Douglas-Hamilton came to know, the tamest, gentlest, and most curious one of all was Virgo, a small one-tusker. Over a hundred of the Manyara elephants came to accept the researchers as harmless and permitted them to approach within several feet. But even after five years of living among these elephants, it was only Virgo that actually came into friendly body contact with them. One evening, just before their departure from Manyara, the Douglas-Hamiltons met Virgo and her family. Oria, holding her three-month-old infant Saba, walked up to Virgo and offered her a gardenia fruit. Only a trunk's length away, Virgo took the fruit and put it in her mouth. Then she moved the tip of her trunk over Saba, smelling her, and Oria wondered if Virgo understood that Saba was her child. The two mothers stood silently then for a long while on that African evening, facing each other with their babies by their sides.

It was a moving moment; an intimate meeting of two mothers, two females, two species, across the countless millennia of separate evolution that lay between them. It was a meeting that seems a fulfillment of our atavistic urge for interspecific communication, of our unquenchable desire to "talk to the animals," to know them and to understand them. It was a meeting that, in its newfound understanding, gives essence to the very theme of this book—for in the elephant, the female finds a most respectable heritage. The elephant matriarch stands like an ancient symbol of feminine intelligence and strength and benevolent leadership. She is our past—and our potential.

4

THE THEMES WE have so far observed reverberate throughout the woods and valleys of the mammalian kingdom. There is, above all, the universality of the mother-young unit as the basic building block of sociality, standing like an ancient monadnock uneroded by time and change and the coming and going of species. Even among the most primitive and solitary of mammals, whose social behavior is limited to mating affairs and maternal care, there is always, like an eternal verity, the relatively prolonged and elaborate interaction between a mother and her offspring. And when bonding between generations occurs, there is its almost inevitable matrilineal focus. Finally, there is the variability in social systems, all largely determined by the evolutionary strategy of the female.

Oxford ethologist and Nobel Prize winner Niko Tinbergen recently advised that "it is equally important to study species such as some primates, that are at the same time related to us and in their social organisation convergent to primitive man, as species such as the lion, the wolf and the spotted hyena, that are less closely related to us but are in their social organisation equally or even more strikingly convergent." And so, in our quest for evolutionary insights into human dilemmas, let us now examine the group-living carnivores. How is it that these animals' predatory ways and consequent life-styles may well parallel our own ancestral arrangements? In particular, how do the females fare among these hunting populations?

The lion pride, like the elephant matriarchy and the primate genealogy, is a long-lasting entity, enduring sometimes for decades. At its core is a sisterhood of several closely related adult females—often actual sisters, or mothers, grandmothers, half-sisters, or cousins—all spending their entire lives together in a fixed territory passed from generation to generation. Cooperation within this sisterhood is superb, superseded, some say, only in the human species.

Very likely the hazards of hunting made cooperative skills an evolutionary mandate. Even for lions, prey animals are not easy to catch and, in fact, most hunting ventures end in failure. Pride lionesses usually hunt together, fanning out to encircle the prey animal and then rushing in upon it from all directions. As might be expected, such cooperative hunting is generally more success-ful than solitary efforts. It is interesting to note that, despite the male lion's formidable reputation, lionesses do most (85–90 per-cent) of the pride's hunting. They are, in fact, better hunters than the males: lionesses can run faster, and their smaller size and lack of manes make them less conspicuous to prey animals.

In addition to their cooperative hunting, lionesses also share in their maternal responsibilities. Just as among African elephants, each nursing mother will permit any cub in the pride to suckle at will. A single cub might nurse from three, four, or even five females to get its fill. "Day care" arrangements are also evident. One lioness often guards the pride's cubs, while the other pride members do the hunting and provide meat for all.

The male lion, in contrast to the lioness, is a comparatively transient and semiparasitic member of the pride. Usually there are several males, often brothers, per pride, and though they do little hunting, they do play a role in maintaining the pride's territory. Invariably young males leave the pride of their birth (only a few females do so) and wander nomadically until they have a chance to join another pride. Their tenure is brief, usually but two or three years, whereupon they are ousted by younger, stronger, or more numerous males, and return to a nomadic exis-tence. It is important to the lionesses and their cubs to have strong, protective males in the group. Intruding males will some-times kill the pride's cubs, and even when this doesn't happen, the lionesses seem to have less success in raising their cubs if there are too many disruptions.

Pride males, by virtue of their superior size and strength, insist on eating first, though the lionesses usually make the kill. In this, they are dominant to the females. But in most other situations, lionesses hold their own. Says George Schaller in his classic book *The Serengeti Lion:*

> In spite of their smaller size, lionesses not only retaliate when males harass them but actually initiate most aggression—frequently with impunity. When a male approached a lioness with small cubs, she rushed him and he trotted off; when a male sniffed the anal area of a female, she clouted him on the head and he moved back five meters; when a male came near a lioness, she hit his face without obvious reason and he merely shook his head and scraped. During an actual chase, the male is usually in pursuit of the female, but as he draws close she whirls around and hits him once or twice, thereby discouraging him from further action.

Female coalitions, similar to those of primates, are also seen: "Several lionesses may attack a male and put him to flight."

Lionesses are also the leaders of the pride. Almost always, it is the females who initiate any activity, the females who lead the group from place to place with the males tagging along, the females who "bring home the bacon," and who care for the youngsters. "Males," says Schaller, "orient much of their activity with respect to the movements of adult lionesses." This goes for sex, too. In Schaller's study, lionesses initiated mating about 60 percent of the time, and they often had the choice when it came to mates.

Hyena females are no slouches either. Though hunting packs always include a majority of males, one or two females take the lead and the males follow. The females are also in sole charge of the cubs—by choice. They raise their babies in a communal den or "nursery pool," from which males, who are often cannibalistic, are usually excluded. Mothers must even stand guard while their youngsters feed on a carcass, for fear that their little ones will be eaten up with the rest of the lunch.

The female hyena needs to be aggressive. Not only must she protect her youngsters, but she nurses them an extraordinary length of time—a total of eighteen months. (Among most carnivores, six weeks is more typical.) Clearly, the growth and health of her cubs depend on the richness of her milk, and every mother must fight for her fill at a clan kill or her babies will starve.

Consequently, for the female hyena, aggressiveness has become her greatest adaption, her best strategy, her modus operandi, and she has capitalized on it to the hilt. She is the undisputed dominant in any female-male encounter. If the sexes should meet, the male moves aside. If his mudhole is her desire, the male makes way. And he'd better, for she is bigger than he. The male, in fact, "always seems to be cringing around the female" according to Hans Kruuk, the Dutch ethologist who spent years studying the ways of the hyena.

As if not to be outdone in any aspect, the female hyena has yet another intriguing feature. She sports a large erectile clitoris that looks, for all the world, like the male's penis. Not only this, but she also has a sham scrotum, masculine in appearance if not function. All this is not mere sexual mimicry or bluff. Surprisingly, the female's elaborate equipment has nothing to do with sex, believes Kruuk. Rather, it is related to the genital displays hyenas perform when they meet one another. Hyenas will sniff one another, each lifting a leg to expose its fully erect genitals. Small cubs and old males, as well as females, are capable of such erections. Following a final good long sniff, the animals move on. This ritual apparently appeases the animosities of these fierce animals, reintegrating them continuously with one another—an important function for this partly solitary and partly social species. The advantage of having a familiar and conspicuous structure as a symbol of an ancient innate truce between clan members has, no doubt, caused its evolution in cubs and females, in whom it has no direct sexual function.

If among hyenas the female reigns supreme, if among lions the female is leader, how is it among the pack-hunting canines—the wolves and wild dogs of Africa? In both these species, separate dominance orders exist for adult females and males. Highest ranking of all are the alpha female and the alpha male. Wolf pups begin to establish their status during play fighting and, while immature, their dominance order crosses sexual lines. At maturity, an alpha female may still dominate most and sometimes all the males of her pack.

Despite the growing body of research on wolves, however, the status of the female wolf remains, on the whole, rather obscure. Many researchers believe that male wolves are invariably the pack leaders. But this has been definitely established, to my knowledge, for only three packs! In his study of the Isle Royale pack, where individual identification was difficult, L. David Mech, our nation's top wolf expert, *presumed* the leader was male because of its larger size. However, while it is true that males on the average are about ten or so pounds larger than females, Mech's own data shows that adult males may occasionally even be smaller than most females. Also, Mech reports that on at least three occasions in winter, a female was seen leading a pack on a hunt. A researcher in Finland, moreover, found that the leader of a wolf pack was *usually female.* About the only thing that seems well established and well accepted is that any female can dominate any male, including the alpha male, when she is caring for her newborn young. All in all, it seems, the case must rest until more evidence becomes available.

Whatever the final resolution, however, the fact is that dominance is not an important phenomenon in wolves. Some semblance of order, some commander in chief plus troops of lesser rank, are important for the pack's hunting success. But a wolf's life is marked far more by cooperation than competition. The pack stalks and chases and ambushes its prey with admirable coordination. The pack leader's rule, while occasionally autocratic, is just as often democratic, and a reluctant pack can prompt a change of plans. In addition, ties between pack members are close and long-lasting, and the feeding and fondling of pups is a group affair. Overall, wolves are a friendly, amiable, tolerant species with a strong aversion to fighting among friends.

The social finesse observed in wolves is even further developed in the African wild dog. The African dog's tightly organized hunts, short and savage, usually end in success, unlike those of wolves and lions and hyenas. Their altruism and mutual concern, moreover, are rarely matched in animal annals. Returning from a hunt, pack members will regurgitate food to the pups, to the mother and to any other adults including the old and the sick and the crippled who remain behind. Even if the prey has been small, unsated pack members will still share what little meat they manage to down. At the kill, juveniles eat first, completely reversing the table etiquette of lions and wolves.

Despite their ferocious hunting feats, the dogs are very easygoing and egalitarian with one another. "Both males and females act as leaders, regurgitate meat for pups, and guard pups while other pack members search for prey," reports Schaller. Apparently, there are separate female and male dominance hierarchies, but status affairs are so subtle, so underplayed, so obviously unimportant that they are easily overlooked by observers. Threats are particularly difficult to detect, while submissive gestures, in surprising contrast, are complex and conspicuous. It is almost, according to one researcher, as if they vie with each other not to be top dog, but to be underdog.

There is also another species whose highly social ways some behaviorists believe may provide insights into our own, and that is the rat. New research reveals that rats, at least among their own, are not really such "rats" after all. Although reputedly aggressive, wild rats seldom seriously fight and males, despite reports to the contrary, rarely kill their infants. Nor is aggression characteristic of relations between the sexes. Instead, females and males interact in an easy and congenial reciprocity, and equal opportunity, even for favored food like chocolate candy, is the rule. Lab experiments also show that rats will readily cooperate with one another to obtain food and are able to learn from each other to avoid poisoned food. So here is another mammalian species that has achieved a degree of sociality far richer, more complex, and more flexible than ever expected, and in which the female, again, is hardly the dominated, submissive soul supposedly so typical of her sex.

As was emphasized earlier, scientists look to animals such as these not to explain the human case directly, but to find certain broad generalizations that might hold true across the species. With this in mind, I have examined the role of the female among those animals whose social organization seems to parallel our own ancestral ways. And her role, in synopsis, is strikingly counter to old notions of feminine frailty and folly and inferiority. The lioness is leader, the female hyena is boss, while among African wild dogs and rats and wolves too, to a large extent, egalitarianism between the sexes has long held sway. What emerges, then, is a portrait of the female of the species at least as versatile and capable, as intelligent and competent, and as important as her male counterpart.

(5) A New Perspective

We hold these truths to be self-evident; that all men and women are created equal.

ELIZABETH CADY STANTON

1

ONCE UPON A time, the human female held high status. She was queen and high priestess, judge, magistrate, governor, warrior, commander in chief, and head of the family. She was business-woman and scribe, real estate agent and moneylender. And this once-upon-a-time was no fairy tale either, but an everyday reality in many of the ancient centers of civilization up through the year 2000 B.C., and in some places even longer.

In Ethiopia of old, women carried arms and were in total charge of public affairs. In early Egypt, the queen was more powerful than the king, and wives wielded more influence than did their husbands. Egyptian women also did the courting, some-times wooing their lovers with intoxicants; the choice of a hus-band, moreover, was theirs alone. A few centuries before Christ, the Greek Herodotus wrote that in Egypt, "Women go in the marketplace, transact affairs and occupy themselves with busi-

121

ness, while the husbands stay home and weave." His contemporary, Sophocles, talked also of how "the men sit at the loom indoors while the wives work abroad for their daily bread." Records found in Egyptian papyri indicate that many women were independently involved in legal matters and business transactions even with their own husbands and fathers. And a female clerk rose from the ranks to become governor, then army chief.

As late as 50 B.C., the historian Diodorus Siculus noted that in Egypt "the husband, by the terms of the marriage agreement, appertains to the wife, and it is stipulated between them that the man shall obey the woman in all things." The reports of Diodorus, however, were dismissed as unreliable by generations of historians —until hundreds of actual marriage contracts were unearthed that proved not only that Diodorus was right, but that he had understated the matter. In these marriage contracts, a man gave over to his wife all his possessions and his wife, in turn, pledged to support her husband, even if she should later decide to divorce him!

In ancient Sumer, women could hold real estate in their own names, lend money, and engage in various other business activities. As a means of recording their many transactions, Sumerian women may well have been first to invent writing, for the earliest examples of written language thus far discovered—over five thousand years old—have been found in a temple in Sumer where priestesses were in charge of finances. In Babylonia, under the law code of Hammurabi, women could hold and manage their own estates, do trading, take legal action, be party to contracts, request divorces, and share in their husband's inheritance. Records dating from the eighth century B.C. show that women also held respected positions as judges and magistrates. A Babylonian mother, moreover, was always represented by a sign meaning "goddess of the house" and a crime against her was punished by banishment from the community.

In Greece, respectable women, both matrons and young girls, spent entire evenings dancing together on the bare hills in spiritual celebrations; husbands disapproved, but preferred not to interfere with religious matters. In classical Sparta, women wrestled naked with their male contemporaries and enjoyed full sexual freedom. Ancient Anatolia, site of today's Turkey, was home to the women warriors, the Amazons, whose queen established the law and relegated domestic duties to men. And on the island of Crete, Minoan women were largely in control of the laws, religion, and customs of society.

How was it that women enjoyed such prestige and power in those ancient days? How was it that their lives contrasted so sharply with those of most women in the centuries since? We do not know, nor perhaps shall we ever know, the full answer. But we do know that, among these civilizations that found women most worthy, there were two outstanding features that resounded time and again among the various groups, like resonant chords embellishing a common theme. One of these was the female's role as the source of all life—only she could bring forth children.

Biological paternity was probably not understood in the very early stages of human existence. Even in our own century, in fact, a few isolated "primitive" peoples are still unaware of the connection between sex and conception. The female, in such groups, gains a great deal of status from her role as the sole parent of the next generation. And lines of descent, naturally, are traced only through the female. This matrilineal kinship system, as it is called, remained widespread even in the more advanced ancient societies, where paternity was undoubtedly understood. In these societies, inheritance as well as descent flowed through the female line: sons, brothers, and husbands gained title and property not in themselves, but through the women to whom they were related. This matrilineal organization, however, did not necessarily mean female control or matriarchy. Although there is strong evidence that the female did reign sometimes both as queen of the land and as head of the household, for the most part the extent to which women may have ruled is still unclear.

The second, and possibly more important feature of note was the prevalence of a supreme female deity. There was Inaana of the ancient Sumerians, Ishtar of the Babylonians, Isis of the Egyptians, and Ashtoreth of the Canaanites. And everywhere the Goddess was revered in countless ways: as creator of the world and queen of heaven, as prophetess and lawgiver, as wise counselor. and inventor of the alphabet, as courageous warrior and as giver

of the gift of agriculture. Words recorded in the city of Thebes
in Egypt about the fourteenth century B.C. tell best, I think, of
the awe and reverence typically accorded the Goddess in those
long ago times:

> In the beginning there was Isis: Oldest of the Old, She was the
> Goddess from whom all Becoming Arose, She was the Great Lady,
> Mistress of the two lands of Egypt, Mistress of Shelter, Mistress
> of Heaven, Mistress of the House of Life, Mistress of the word of
> God. She was the Unique. In all Her great and wonderful works
> She was a wiser magician and more excellent than any other God.

A lesser male god was often associated with the Goddess but
merely as a subsidiary son-lover personage, presented frequently
as a half-size figure standing at her feet.

The Goddess reigned at least seven thousand years, perhaps far
longer. Most of our evidence—the statues, murals, inscriptions,
clay tablets, and papyri—date from about 7000 B.C. to 500 B.C.
But temple caves dedicated to the Goddess have been found in
the Soviet Ukraine, in Spain, and in France, all of them dating
from 30,000 B.C. The Goddess reigned in times alive with the
early achievements and discoveries of humankind. Under her
aegis, agriculture, stock breeding, mathematics, science, architec-
ture, and writing were developed.

All of this is a part of our human heritage that I never learned
as I minored in history in my undergraduate days nor, I am
certain, did any reader. We are indebted for much of the above
information to Merlin Stone, sculptor and art educator, whose
remarkable research took her halfway around the world to librar-
ies, museums, universities, and excavation sites in the United
States, Europe, and the Far East. Simone de Beauvoir, incidentally, also touched upon the subject of the Goddess and the early
high status of women in her important book, *The Second Sex.* But
Stone presents a far more thorough account and cites an impressive array of evidence to support her view. Stone's engrossing
book, *When God Was a Woman,* has been praised as "clear,
conscientious, educative, and prophetic" by John Biram, an associate of the well-known scholar Robert Graves. Meanwhile, "the

archaeological evidence continues to accumulate" regarding the
reign of the Goddess and the early prominence of woman, states
Elizabeth R. Dobell, a writer and student of comparative reli-
gions.

This body of data certainly calls into question the notion that
the male is somehow innately dominant over the female, as Wilson and others have suggested. But a nagging question remains.
How did women, for the most part, lose the power and prestige
they once commanded for thousands of years? Stone reports, with
careful documentation, that the upheaval came when northern
invaders began to overrun the early cultural centers of the Mediterranean world. These invaders were pastoral, patriarchal tribes
who worshipped a warrior god or a supreme father-god, a god who
was always male. And in their religious myths we find the roots
of the male-oriented attitudes that have predominated ever since:
the female is depicted as undisciplined, dumb, and depraved,
while the male is lord and master.

The Goddess, of course, was ousted and the male deity en-
throned in her place to legitimatize the whole affair. But it was
a gradual process and at first, the Goddess was "married off" to
male newcomers like Jupiter and Zeus and then later made sub-
servient to them. Even Christianity could not completely rid itself
of the vestiges of the Goddess. The Christian devotion to Mary,
Mother of God, seems in many ways a replay of the devotion to
the Goddess, mother of all gods.

> Around images of the Madonna and the infant Son in her arms
> [says Dobell], were quickly assimilated an absolutely astonishing
> number of the same symbols and images that once were associated
> with the first Great Mother . . . there are statues that depict Mary
> holding in one hand the entire world and in the other her baby Son,
> while a door in her body opens to reveal God the Father supporting
> the crucified Christ as all the saints look on—all within the womb
> of a virgin, the mother who produced her Son without help from
> mortal man (as did the ancient Goddess) and became the Mother
> of God, as the first Great Mother was the ancestor of all gods.

Nonetheless, as the Goddess gave way to God, men gained control almost everywhere and have stayed in control ever since. In broad perspective, then, history has verified feminist Mary Daly's contention that "if God is male, then the male is God."

All this is not to advocate a return to the time of the Goddess. But women should know their roots and so should men. In the next pages, we will delve further into these roots, examining cultures of more recent historical record. And we will find, among other things, that the invasion by male-oriented cultures has been an ongoing process over many years.

2

THE BALONDA ARE one of the peoples of the Congo. Explorer David Livingstone made their acquaintance when he traveled through the area in 1857. Fortunately for us, Livingstone recorded the event in his book, *Missionary Travels and Researches in South Africa,* and the following is based on his account.

On the sixth of January, Livingstone entered a Balonda village and was taken to the chief. A man and woman "were sitting on skins" writes Livingstone, which were "placed in the middle of a circle, thirty paces in diameter, a little raised above the ordinary level of the ground." Livingstone saluted the man, he says, "in the usual way, by clapping the hands together in their fashion." But the man "pointed to his wife, as much as to say, the honour belongs to her. I saluted her in the same way, and, a mat having been brought, I squatted down in front of them." The woman was Nyamoana, mother of Manenko, the young woman chief. Livingstone wanted to go alone to see Nyamoana's brother, Shinte, the district chief. But Nyamoana insisted that her daughter, Manenko, accompany him. "As neither my men nor myself had much inclination to encounter a scolding . . . we made ready the packages," writes Livingstone. At one point, however, he tried to leave without Malenko as she was not yet ready to go. But the young woman quickly intercepted the explorer,

> seized the luggage, and declared that she would carry it in spite of
> me. My men succumbed sooner to this petticoat government than

I felt inclined to do, and left me no power; and, being unwilling to encounter her tongue, I was moving off to the canoes, when she gave me a kind explanation, and, with her hand on my shoulder, put on a motherly look, saying, 'Now, my little man, just do as the rest have done.' My feelings of annoyance of course vanished, and I went out to try and get some meat.

Despite a cold rain, Manenko walked swiftly to her uncle's village, too fast apparently for Livingstone's men. Chiefs "must always wear the appearance of robust youth, and bear vicissitudes without wincing," Livingstone was informed. Later, when they met Shinte, Livingstone offered the man an ox. This infuriated Manenko, for Livingstone was "her white man," she declared, and the ox belonged to her. Manenko promptly had the ox slaughtered and gave her uncle only one leg. As "Shinte did not seem at all annoyed at the occurrence," observed Livingstone, Manenko obviously had been in the right.

If it were not for this account by David Livingstone, we would not know that originally equal rights were the rule among the Balonda and that women as well as men could be chiefs. Today, reports George P. Murdock in his much-quoted handbook *Africa, Its People and Their Culture History,* political authority is vested only in men.

What happened in those intervening years to skew the power structure in favor of men among the Balonda? The answer lies in colonialism, an invasion in many ways comparable to the earlier invasion of northern patriarchs into the Mediterranean countries. Like the earlier invasion, colonialism imposed its own ideas of male superiority on cultures that were often egalitarian in government and matrilineal in descent.

Says Eleanor Leacock, head of the anthropology department at City College, City University of New York: "Everywhere in Africa that one scrapes the surface one finds ethno-historical data on the authority once shared by women but later lost." M. Kay Martin and Barbara Voorhies, authors of *Female of the Species,* discuss in detail the effect of the European intrusions. Speaking of the ninety foraging societies of Africa, Asia, Australia, and the Americas on which data is available, they state: "Information

. . . on all of these societies was collected by ethnographers well after they had been influenced by technologically more complex peoples. It is important to remember, therefore, that all modern foragers are acculturated to a greater or lesser degree." And in a majority of cases, they say, "change has proceeded in the direction of the ruling culture."

Despite these facts, Edward O. Wilson, who most recently came up with the suggestion of innate male superiority, as recorded in chapter 4, based his bias not only on a distorted view of primate behavior, but also on a survey of living hunter-gatherer societies. Among these groups today, argues Wilson, males often appear to be dominant over females and he infers, from this, that the same condition has prevailed since humankind's earliest hours. It is for this reason that the present chapter exists, a chapter somewhat apart from my primary emphasis on the animal world. It is because all too many animal behaviorists, as well as anthropologists, have extended their mistaken views of male superiority in animals to the world of humans by way of the so-called primitive cultures, as if these cultures have remained static since time immemorial.

Such an approach is increasingly criticized.

To generalize from cross-cultural data gathered almost wholly in the twentieth century [says Leacock], is to ignore changes that have been taking place for anywhere up to five hundred years as a result of involvement, first with European mercantilism, then with full-scale colonialism and imperialism. Indeed, there is almost a kind of racism involved, an assumption that the culture of Third World peoples have virtually stood still until destroyed by the recent mushrooming of urban industrialism. Certainly, one of the most consistent and widely documented changes brought about during the colonial period was a decline in the status of women relative to men.

Now let's see how this happened. Often the original status of women was adversely affected by the European assumption that there had to be a top authority, an assumption that overlooked the egalitarian ways of many early groups. In the Huron Wyandot tribe, for example, men and women both wielded influence but in different areas. Men were in charge of hunting and warfare, while women were in charge of agriculture and land use. A council of men might decide to go to war, but a council of women could effectively veto their decision by refusing to provide them with food supplies. "There was a balance, a give and take," says Leacock, "with each sex controlling the condition of its own labor and controlling what happened to its produce." When the Europeans dealt with the Hurons, however, they assumed the men alone were in authority and dealt only with the men's councils. "The female councils just got relegated to the background," explains Leacock, "and they disappeared from the historical record."

Among the Montagnais-Naskapi of eastern Canada, women and men were also once equals in prestige and autonomy, according to Jesuit missionary, Paul La Jeune, who lived with them in the 1600's. In letters he wrote back to his superiors in France, La Jeune gave a detailed account of these Indians and of his attempts to convert them. In the Naskapi culture, women's work was as important as men's. Women chopped poles for their lodges, while men cleared snow from the ground where the lodge was to be built. Women worked with leather and bark, while men worked mainly with wood in making tools and equipment. Both sexes took part in caribou hunts and helped with the cooking. Although infants were cared for primarily by their mothers, fathers were patient and watchful with small children.

To La Jeune's disgust, Naskapi women enjoyed ribald humor as much as did men. Both sexes, he complained, spoke with "the foul odor of the sewers." But there was little quarreling or fighting between spouses. Each sex, reported La Jeune, carried out its own activities without "meddling" in those of the other.

In those early days, Naskapi women as well as men were shamans—influential religious leaders who communicated with the gods. And women as well as men held special feasts from which the opposite sex was excluded. One Jesuit reportedly was threatened with a knife by a female shaman who resented his interference as she tried to rally her people to war against the Iroquois. (The Iroquois were encroaching on Naskapi territory in order to expand their fur-trapping operations.) Bitter at the loss of their kinsmen, women were far more cruel than men in torturing Iroquois prisoners.

"The women have great power here," said La Jeune, and he urged the Naskapi men to take over: "I told him that he was the master, and that in France women do not rule their husbands." La Jeune also deplored the polygamy he found among the Naskapi, but he had trouble changing their ways: "Since I have been preaching among them that a man should have only one wife, I have not been well received by the women; for, since they are more numerous than the men, if a man can only marry one of them, the others will have to suffer." Appalled at the promiscuity of the women, La Jeune tried to convince the men of the importance of knowing that their children were their own. But the Naskapi retorted: "Thou hast no sense. You French people love only your own children, we love all the children of our tribe."

The Jesuit missionary was also distressed at the autonomy of individuals within the Naskapi tribe, which had no formal chief. "Alas, if someone could stop the wanderings of the Savages and give authority to one of them to rule the others, we could see them converted and civilized in a short time." The Naskapi did, however, have certain "sagamores" or "headmen" who represented the group before outsiders, but the sagamores had no formal authority. As for European-style hierarchies, the Indians had little use for them. "They have reproached me a hundred times," complained La Jeune, "because we fear our Captains, while they laugh at and make sport of theirs." The Naskapi, he went on, "cannot endure in the least those who seem desirous of assuming superiority over the others; they place all virtue in a certain gentleness or apathy."

Despite the Naskapi's resistance to European culture, changes inevitably took place as the missionaries tried to "civilize" the Indians. Chiefs were elected and male converts began to threaten their wives for disobedience. By the time anthropologists visited the Naskapi in this century, other changes could be noted. No longer were there female shamans or separate female feasts. No longer did newlyweds commonly live with the bride's relatives (matrilocal residence). Now, instead, they usually lived with the husband's relatives (patrilocal residence). And, although group life was still loosely structured, there was a definite emphasis on male authority.

As a last example from among native Americans, let's look at the Iroquois of the sixteenth century who, as mentioned, came into conflict with the Naskapi. Iroquois women of the time commanded a great deal of power and influence. They were the gardeners as well as the gatherers of food, while men engaged in hunting and fishing. Both sexes built the longhouses, large buildings where several related women lived with their husbands and their children. As with the Naskapi, matrilocal residence prevailed in the early days.

Descent was also traced through the female line and became a prominent feature of Iroquois life. According to Martin and Voorhies: "Matrilineal kinship penetrated every corner of traditional Iroquois society. One's social identity, real and portable property, and succession to offices and titles flowed exclusively in the maternal line." Women, for example, owned the arable land and had exclusive rights to food crops and to seed. They also had control over their marital situation. Should a husband's behavior prove objectionable, divorce was quite easy. The oldest woman of the longhouse simply asked him to leave and her "eviction notice" evidently was honored.

Iroquois women had power in the public as well as the private sphere. Senior women or matrons nominated and deposed the chiefs of the intertribal council. Here, incidentally, it might be well to distinguish between power and authority. As defined by Martin and Voorhies, "Power refers to the ability to coerce others toward desired ends, whereas authority refers to legitimate or legal power." The Iroquois chiefs, who were male, held positions of authority, but as in many matrilineal societies, women held the power to assign public offices to these men. Iroquois matrons were also very influential in the decision-making of the intertribal council. A special representative acted as their spokesman before the council and, as with the Hurons, women could withhold food to stop their men from going to war. Women also controlled the portable wealth of their communities, such as wampum, quill and feather work, and furs.

In the religious sphere, women and men were equals in both

representation and influence. Half of the sacred leaders, called Keepers of the Faith, were women. These influential "Keepers" were responsible for admonishing wrongdoers and could report serious cases to the council. The murder of a woman, interestingly, demanded twice the compensation for the murder of a man.

Iroquois men were apparently distressed by the white man's lack of respect for their women's views. Listen to "Good Peter," an Iroquois orator who was chosen to negotiate with a governor of one of the colonies:

> Brothers! Our ancestors considered it a great offense to reject the counsels of their women, particularly of the Female Governesses. They were esteemed the mistresses of the soil. Who, said our forefathers, brings us into being? Who cultivates our lands, kindles our fires, and boils our pots, but the women? . . . The Female Governesses beg leave to speak with the freedom allowed to women and agreeable to the spirit of our ancestors.

By the nineteenth century, however, anthropologists reported that "The Indian regarded woman as the inferior, the dependent, and the servant of man, and from nurture and habit, she actually considered herself to be so." How did this drastic change in attitude occur? An important factor was that longhouse life was replaced by nuclear family units in which wives became dependent on wage-earning husbands. With monogamy, explains anthropologist Lewis Morgan, the woman "was now isolated from her gentile kindred, living in the separate and exclusive house of her husband. Her new condition tended to subvert and destroy the power and influence which descent in the female line and the joint-tenement houses had created." There were, of course, many of the other typical results from European intrusion. The double standard, for example, became established and married women were publicly whipped for adultery.

The decline in the status of women among the Hurons, the Naskapi, and the Iroquois were not isolated cases. It is simply that there is better documentation of the decline among these peoples. "Reconstructed bits and pieces from the last five hundred years of North American Indian history," says Leacock, "suggest that parallel developments took place quite widely among previously egalitarian peoples." Nor was this phenomenon restricted to America; wherever European colonialism occurred, it was much the same.

In Africa, it was not only the Balonda of Livingstone's acquaintance who fell victim to European influence. The Ekoi of West Africa are another such society and for them, changes have taken place within our own century. An observer in 1912 reported, "though a woman comes under the influence of her husband on marriage, yet she is his proprietor, and has a right to ask any service." When he first visited the Ekoi, "The chief wife, not the husband, was regarded as the head of the house," but this tradition was "beginning to be influenced by those of white men; especially in places near European centres."

Under colonialism, men were almost always given preference over women: in jobs, education, trade arrangements, ownership rights, indeed, in nearly every sphere of activity outside the domestic area. "The assault on indigenous sex roles occurred along many fronts," say Martin and Voorhies, but it was most effective on the economic level.

> Europeans showed little sympathy for the female farming systems which they found in many of their colonies and in those independent countries where they settled. Their European acceptance that cultivation is naturally a job for men persuaded them to believe that men could become far better farmers than women, if only they would abandon their customary "laziness"

reports prize-winning Danish researcher Ester Boserup. To entice men to farm, colonists instructed them—and only them—in the techniques of cultivating cash crops. Women continued to provide their families with staples, but they inevitably lost their former status. Men did the new, prestigious, wealth-producing farming, while women represented the "old drudgery." Virtually the same status changes occurred in those cases where men—and primarily men, again—were recruited for wage labor. "As subjects of the earliest educational efforts, and the primary links to desired foreign material items, men soon assume a social position superior to that of women," conclude Martin and Voorhies.

The bias against women perpetrated by colonialism has been supplemented, in scientific journals, by the bias of anthropologists themselves. Sometimes it may have been inadvertent because most field workers in anthropology happened to be men. Explain Martin and Voorhies: "The most important ethnographic data-gathering technique, participant-observation, is often practical or permissible only with informants of the same sex as the investigator. The cultural world of half the target population is thus left unrecorded." Leacock says much the same thing: "Anthropologists have on the whole been men who interview other men, and assume that the data collected is thereby sufficient for understanding a society." Others have been less kind. A group of women anthropologists complained not long ago: "A lot of essential questions have never been asked—the result of male anthropologists' chewing the fat with male informants has been a view of women that proceeds almost directly from male norms."

Woman and her activities have been consistently treated as peripheral to society as a whole. Often a description of what women do and what their value is to the group is relegated to a few sentences, a few paragraphs, or perhaps a chapter in an anthropological text, says Leacock. The built-in bias implicit in many studies is perhaps no better illustrated than in slick generalizations referring to, as one author put it, "The normal importance of men."

Examples abound of the inevitable distortions that follow such thinking. One anthropologist, for example, wrote rather lyrically: "If I were to make a symbolic painting about a 'Kung as a man and a father and head of a family I would show him carrying the whole family on his shoulders and in his arms, as well as the tools for their living." Actually, however, 'Kung women play a more important economic role in their society than do men, according to Leacock. As gatherers of vegetable materials, women "provide the overwhelming majority of food supplies." Meat, which the men provide through their hunting, constitutes a much smaller proportion of the diet. Moreover, meat is not restricted to an individual family unit, as implied in the statement above, but is shared with the entire group.

Robert Cohen, an anthropologist at Northwestern University, has come up with another "fact" that seems to be unsupported by field data. As an example of male authority in hunter-gatherer societies, he cites male-led communal hunts of the Mbuti pygmies in the Congo. However, Colin Turnbull, who actually saw the Mbuti hunts, describes the involvements of both women and men in the hunts and he found no evidence of leadership direction by men. On the contrary, he states, "all decisions concerning the hunt are made by joint discussion, in which women take part." Another observer of a Mbuti hunt did notice two elderly leaders. One was a man and one was a woman.

The bias of anthropologists has not only affected what they say; it has also affected what is said to them. Anthropologist R. S. Rattray had worked among the Ashanti people of Dahomey in western Africa in the early part of this century. When he returned some years later he found, to his surprise, that the Queen Mother had once outranked the King. He asked his informers why he had not been told this before. "The white man never asked us this," they would always say, "We supposed the European considered women of no account and we know you do not recognize them as we have always done."

Now let's take a closer look at contemporary hunter-gatherer societies. It was these societies in particular, you will recall, that Edward O. Wilson cited to support his contention that male dominance over females is part of our evolutionary heritage. Wilson has not been alone in this. Hunter-gatherer groups have been consistently utilized in evolutionary theory, and the emphasis has always been on Man, the Hunter. Indeed, a symposium under that title was held in 1966. The male of the species is generally portrayed as the hunter-provider, upon whom a woman and her children are completely dependent. Moreover, the male's cooperative hunting efforts are proposed as the vanguard of all manner of evolutionary advance—intellectual development, tool-making, food-sharing, even art.

This description, however, simply does not square with the facts, protest many anthropologists today. Men, it is true, generally do the hunting, but women make a substantial contribution with their gathering activities. Ironically, it was at the Man, the Hunter symposium that the significance of gathering first became apparent. Most of the hunting-gathering peoples of Africa, Asia, Australia, and North America, it turned out, depend primarily on plants gathered by women for their food needs. Since then, Martin and Voorhies examined ninety extant hunter-gatherer societies and found that gathering is the dominant food-getting technique in 58 percent of them. Over two thirds of the sample groups, in fact, depend on products of the hunt for only 30–40 percent of their diet. Obviously, most such groups ought to be called "gatherer-hunters," as anthropologists Adrienne Zihlman and Nancy Tanner of the University of California, Santa Cruz, have suggested. I shall do the same hereafter.

Much has also been made of the supposed male-oriented residence and descent patterns of modern gatherer-hunters. Man, the Hunter advocates have argued that the logical pattern among cooperative hunters would be for related males to live together. Here, again, Martin and Voorhies have examined their ninety sample societies and come up with some interesting information. They found that, on face value, the data does suggest a male emphasis, since patrilocal residence is most strongly represented among the ninety societies. However, nearly half of these societies designated as patrilocal offer matrilocal residence as an alternative. When these societies are combined with those designated as matrilocal, we find that fifty-eight of the ninety sample societies, nearly 65 percent, offer matrilocal residence as a viable option! This is "all the more striking," say Martin and Voorhies, in view of the influence of Western culture. Western influence also seems to have affected descent patterns. The most common pattern among the sample groups is bilateral descent (descent reckoned through both parents) which is, of course, the standard pattern of the Western world.

On the basis of these facts, Martin and Voorhies conclude "that there is no consistent or universal pattern of male orientation in the kinship structure of foraging societies." (These anthropologists often use the term "foraging societies" in place of "gatherer-hunter societies.") Nor did they find any relation between kinship structure and the status of women. "Patrilineal descent among foragers, for example, does not indicate the subjugation of women." Martin has found, rather, that the residence and descent patterns are simply those most adaptive for the given culture's political stability.

One of the most important findings of Martin and Voorhies concerns the egalitarian relationships between women and men. "Our most accurate generalization about the relative status of men and women in foraging societies as a whole is that the worlds of the sexes are separate but equal." Males, they state, typically hunt and fish and maintain order and harmony, while women are responsible for gathering and for child care. But

> it is not the *tasks* assigned to the sexes that are ranked, but rather the relative proficiency with which they are performed. High status may attach itself to the successful hunter, the skilled gatherer, the bearer of many children, the healer of the sick, or the spiritual medium. As such, both women and men have the potential for greatness, for special talent, for charisma, for respect in the daily life of the community, and for wisdom in old age.

Another anthropologist, Leacock, has also stressed the egalitarianism between the sexes in most gatherer-hunter societies. In short, Edward O. Wilson and his ilk must look elsewhere than among gatherer-hunters to support their male-dominance theories.

3

EARLIER, I SPOKE of those ancient societies in which women enjoyed high status. Despite the widespread encroachment of colonialism into almost every area on earth, there still remain societies today where women are held in high regard. These societies deserve our closer attention.

Let's begin with the Tiwi, gatherer-hunters who live on Melville Island, off the coast of northern Australia. Although there has been a relatively long history of contact with Western culture, little inland penetration occurred and the Tiwis have been able to retain much of their traditional life-style. Among the Tiwi, the usual division of labor found in gatherer-hunter groups does not exist. Rather, men generally oversee the food resources of sea and air, while women take charge of those on land, whether plant or animal. Hunting and gathering, therefore, are practiced by both women and men, each in their respective areas.

Tiwi women hunt by stalking and clubbing land animals such as opossums and bandicoots. Not only is the Tiwi woman a hunter, she is also a toolmaker. The stone axes she makes are used to club prey animals to death, to strip bark for containers, and to gather certain plant materials. Even young girls, seven or eight years old, have been known to make rafts with which to gather foods in a swamp. Women's hunting and collecting provide the major food supply for their group, according to anthropologist Jane Goodale (this is not Jane Goodall, the chimpanzee expert), who published her field study of the Tiwi in 1971. "Men's hunting," she noted, "required considerable skill and strength, but the birds, bats, fish, crocodiles, dugongs, and turtles they contributed to the household were luxury items rather than staples." Here, in short, is a society where women are not only the main producers, but hunters and toolmakers as well. Quite enough, surely, to make Man, the Hunter devotees blush in chagrin!

Both matrilineal and patrilineal kinship systems are recognized by the Tiwi. Landholding rights are inherited from one's father, while social relationships are inherited through one's mother. The latter, the matrilineal descent system, is by far the most important, for it defines each person's position in the group as well as their respective rights and duties regarding others.

The Tiwi also practice polygyny. Nonetheless, women are apparently able to manipulate their marital affairs as much as men. As Martin and Voorhies put it, women enjoy a "fluctuating inventory of husbands." An older Tiwi woman, moreover, frequently commands a great deal of power and respect, much of which can be attributed to her position as head of a matrilineage.

To sum up, Tiwi women show none of the dependency and inferiority so often attributed to the female in gatherer-hunter societies. She is, on the contrary, a woman of her own who is able to function on her own. Unfortunately, the Western world is making new inroads into the Tiwi culture. Goodale has reported that the power of old women is gradually being eroded: the government has refused to recognize women as heads of households, and the official discouragement of polygyny is eliminating the influential position of head wife.

Now let's turn to a culture where women have more control than do men. The Tchambuli of New Guinea, as mentioned in chapter 3, are a society in which women's sexual needs are considered more urgent than men's and where women freely choose their husbands. Tchambuli women are just as independent and enterprising in other aspects of their lives. They are in charge of the fishing, farming, and manufacturing of trade items upon which their community's economy depends. Women also manage all the valuables and raise their children in houses apart from the men. Margaret Mead, who lived among the Tchambuli, described these women as cheerful, cooperative, and friendly.

Tchambuli men, in contrast, are the artists and musicians of their community and live together in ceremonial clan houses down by the lake. They apparently are the more emotional sex, given to cattiness, petty jealousy, quarreling, and tantrums, according to Mead.

The relationship between Tchambuli women and men is, in essence, a mirror image of that characteristic of our own culture. A Tchambuli man, says Mead, looks to his female relatives "as a solid group upon whom he depends for support, for food, for affection." Women, on the other hand, treat men "with kindly tolerance and appreciation." As a consequence, although Tchambuli society is legally a patrilineal one, men are dependent on women both for their material and emotional well-being.

Men are also considered more emotional than women among the Mescalero Indians of our southwestern states. "Men cry because they are *extremely* emotional . . . Men are always children . . . A woman is not like that. A woman is practical," said a Mescalero man who was anthropologist Clair Farrer's primary consultant when she lived with them. Farrer describes the Mescalero as a "predominately matrilineal, matrilocal, matrifocal . . . group." Nonetheless, the relationship between women and men, unlike that in Tchambuli society, is basically egalitarian, says Farrer. Men and women, for example, have an equal voice at tribal meetings.

There are a number of other societies with a decidedly matrifocal emphasis in which women enjoy prominence both in the home and in society at large. Among the Javanese of Indonesia, for example, the mother-young bond is very strong and persistent, and women have more authority and influence within the family than do men. Outside the home, both sexes function on a relatively equal basis. Women, as well as men, can attain prestigious positions in religious and political affairs. Women can also find employment in agriculture, in trade, and in civil service jobs, like teaching, as easily as can men. In small-scale agricultural trade, in fact, Javanese women actually outpace men.

The Atjeh are another matrifocal ethnic group of Indonesia. Among these people, husbands come to live in houses owned by their wives. The Indonesian word for *wife*, in fact, means "the one who owns the house." Although men technically own the land, women carry out most of the agricultural work and control the main produce, which is rice.

A husband's chief responsibility is to provide money, not rice (which women can obtain for themselves). To do so, he must find work outside his village. Many Atjehnese men, for example, have small firms in Sumatra's larger cities. Because men are away from home much of the time, they occupy a peripheral position with respect to their families. Anthropologist Nancy Tanner reports that men are "only minimally involved in family decision making; they do not control the family purse strings, nor are they active participants in child rearing." Another researcher says bluntly that men, whether rich or poor, "are powerless in their families."

If a man does try to interfere in his wife's domain, it can sometimes have unhappy results. One enraged wife kicked her husband, stabbed at him, and tried to slash him with a cleaver, as a result of a disagreement over household matters. He, in turn, hit her. After the fight, she moved his mattress out of the bedroom. Every time she remembered how he had hit her, moreover, she would attack him anew and he would stand there and take it. Although the details of this fight may have been exaggerated by neighbors, a field worker noted that this was the kind of predicament that "villagers imagine a man confronts if he does not provide what his wife wants."

Among the Atjehnese, in conclusion, women are the dominant figures in their homes, as well as in their communities, where the rice they grow provides the mainstay of village agricultural economy. Tanner also reports the interesting fact that husbands and fathers don't even enter into a woman's vision of the hereafter. Women think of paradise as a place "where they are reunited with their children and mothers."

The Minangkabau, another ethnic group in Indonesia, have been eminently successful in many areas of national life. Says Tanner, who lived among them for several years, "They are entrepreneurs par excellence and have made contributions . . . in fields as diverse as literature, politics, religion, business and education far in excess of their small numbers."

Like Javanese and Atjehnese women, Minangkabau women have important economic roles. They do most of the agricultural work, and many carry on home industries such as weaving and embroidery. Many also sell their agricultural produce and craft items in the marketplaces of larger cities. In addition, women may work as teachers, clerks, judges, and shopkeepers. Minangkabau men work in a wide variety of fields, thereby providing financial support for their families. They also act as their families' political, ritual, and legal representatives.

Related Minangkabau women—mothers, grandmothers, great-grandmothers, and sisters—often live together in a common household. In most homes, in fact, there are more adult women than men, which puts women "in a strong position" when it comes to family affairs. The senior woman, or women, of the household, in particular, plays an important part in family decision-making. "Her position [on a family matter] often prevails," says Tanner. "In addition to the respect the men have for her views, she also controls the rice necessary for any ceremony."

Minangkabau women, consequently, are the central figures in the home and their centrality is enforced by cultural tradition. "The mother," says Tanner, "is considered a source of wisdom." Reminiscent of the Goddess of ancient cultures, moreover, is the Minangkabau's mythical queen mother—Bundo Kandueng. "Her importance," says Tanner, "is celebrated in women's ceremonial dress, in weddings, parades, etc. Even a local bus was named Bundo Kandueng."

Turning to Africa, we also find matrifocal cultures where women are important and respected members of society. One such African group, the Ibo, live in eastern Nigeria. Although the Ibo are patrilineal, the basic social unit consists of a mother and her children. The mother-child bond is very strong and long-lasting, and mothers are considered the founders of patrilineal segments. The wealth of these founding mothers is often referred to by subsequent generations, and her property is divided among the children when she dies.

Customarily, brothers live together in the same village with their wives and children, and sometimes other relatives. A rich man—or woman—may have several wives. Victor Chikenzie Uchendu, a native Ibo and an anthropologist, has described his own home situation. Uchendu's mother, who was a successful trader, needed household help "and so she 'married' one wife after another." Such a "marriage" involves paying a bride-price in exchange for rights in the labor of a woman.

Women grow garden crops near their homes and control the local markets where these crops are sold. Men, in contrast, generally handle long-distance marketing. In one region of Nigeria, Ibo women have highly organized their trading activities. A queen and her counselors regulate trading: they determine what may be sold, by whom, and for what price. Violators may be taken to court.

In addition to their economic activities, women have other important functions in Ibo society. Since married women have kin outside their villages, for example, they often act as intermediaries between different villages. Women also have organizations through which they keep in contact with the female friends and relatives they lived with before their marriages. The importance of women in the economic and social life of the community is reflected in religious and cultural traditions. There are female deities and women may become specialists in rituals associated with the Ibo religion. In sum, Ibo women enjoy relative equality with men in their communities.

Another African culture in which women have high status are

the Yoruba of southwestern Nigeria. Peggy Sanday, an anthropologist from the University of Pennsylvania, states that "Yoruba women are perhaps the most independent in Africa." Here, too, women have institutionalized their work as market traders. Trade guilds "regulate the conditions and standards of the craft and protect the interest of members." The trade guilds are also powerful politically. "Such organizations in many African societies," says Sanday, "are examples of the very real authority exercised by women in African political systems."

One of the most unusual of African cultural groups are the Tuareg camel herders of the Sahara. Tuareg men do the herding, but women own all the livestock and other movable property. Negro serfs and slaves do most of the household chores, which allows women to devote themselves to music and poetry. While only a third of Tuareg men can read and write, all women can do so.

Nominally the Tuaregs are Muslim, yet women enjoy freedoms seldom allowed their sex in Muslim societies. They are not secluded nor do they wear veils. Although formal leadership is in the hands of men, women can openly express their opinions on public issues. Premarital sex is common, married women maintain friendships with men other than their husbands, and divorce upon demand of the wife is traditional. "The shock of early Arab travelers at this state of affairs is understandable," says one anthropologist, and it was "aggravated by the fact that the men were veiled and the women were not."

South America also has cultures where women are highly regarded. The well-known anthropologist Colin Turnbull recently reported on such a culture in Surinam, South America. Women in the farming and fishing villages of this country, says Turnbull, are "physically strong and occupy prestigious positions. Both wealth and status are inherited in the female line."

Italy is also viewed as a case in point by some. According to Shari Steiner, a foreign correspondent and 1971 winner of the Guida Monaci International Journalism Prize, Italian men are relegated to second sex status. In social situations, men are more frequently ill at ease, stuttering or twitching or nervously adjusting their penises; and in a crisis, it is a woman who always takes

charge. Ernst Bernhardt, a noted German psychologist, calls the
Italian woman the Great Mediterranean Mamma, and her matriarchy has a long and rich history. Mamma is head of the family
in a culture where the family is all and she is in full control of the
cassa or till, "counting out the money in every family-owned shop
in the country." And her status is just as evident in the churches,
where Mamma is both Mother Church and Madonna. In Rome,
alone, there are forty-four churches dedicated to Maria, but less
than a half dozen to Christ.

Obviously, both today and in the past, there have been great
variations in the relative status of the two sexes. In view of this,
we could use one of Wilson's own arguments to dispute his
position on male dominance. In an article in the *New Scientist,*
Wilson criticizes those who suggest that humans share a general
aggressive instinct with animals. He states:

> But if we look closely at a number of species we see that aggression
> occurs in a myriad of forms and is subject to rapid evolution—there
> is no general instinct. For instance, we commonly find one species
> of bird or mammal to be highly territorial, employing elaborate,
> aggressive displays and attacks, while a second, closely related spe-
> cies shows no territorial behavior. *If aggression were a deeply rooted
> instinct such differences would not arise* [my emphasis].

Applying this argument to the status of the female, we need
only note the immense variations within our own species, a single
species, as well as throughout the animal world. To paraphrase
Wilson, if male dominance were a deeply rooted instinct, such
differences would not arise.

4

THE PERCEPTIVE READER will already have noticed it. Tiwi women
are the main food producers for their families; Tchambuli women
are the fishermen, farmers, and manufacturers of their communities; Javanese women are traders, farmers, and teachers; Atjehnese
women grow rice, the mainstay of their village economy; Minangkabau women are farmers, traders, shopkeepers, and judges; Ibo
women are gardeners and traders; Yoruba women are market

traders par excellence; Tuareg women own the livestock and movable property; and Italian women control the *cassa*. Wherever women have economic control over their lives, they enjoy a status equal or superior to that of men. Based on their survey of human societies, Martin and Voorhies came to a similar conclusion: "Power attaches itself," they found, "to those who control the distribution of food or wealth, irrespective of sex."

M. Kay Martin and Barbara Voorhies, authors of *Female of the Species*, have written what I consider one of the most eminently rational books on the history of the human female and her role in society. In it, they trace the status of the female through the various stages in cultural evolution. These stages are related to the economy of the culture and evolve from foraging to horticulture or herding, to agriculture, and finally to industry.

In foraging or gatherer-hunter societies, as noted, women are the primary food producers and the sexes generally have equal status. Horticultural societies are those which farm with hand tools, and in them women still assume the primary economic role as food producers. But in these, as well as in herding societies, there is a tremendous variation in the status of women. Usually women have the highest status in matrilineal societies and a more "variable and uncertain" status in patrilineal societies, according to Martin and Voorhies. The status of the female in the latter is associated primarily with the degree of economic control she is able to maintain. Whether a society is patrilineal or matrilineal depends not so much on any power play between the sexes, suggest Martin and Voorhies, but on which system is the most advantageous way of living in a certain environment. Patrilineal systems seem to be better adapted to survive in places where there is intense competition over the resources of the land. Defense of resources, in such cases, generally falls to the male.

In agricultural societies, women's status plummets most drastically. Agricultural societies are those in which farming requires irrigation or plowing, and in these the productive role of women is usurped by men. Here again, however, there is no need "to propose a theory of sexist or class conspiracy," say Martin and Voorhies. The changes are simply advantageous to society as a whole. Men, being stronger and not hampered in mobility by nursing infants, are the sex best suited for agricultural work. Plowing and the digging and maintenance of irrigation systems is physically demanding and often requires work at a substantial distance from home. Nonetheless, the results are devastating for women. They soon become relegated to the house and, as Martin and Voorhies state, "Entirely new mythologies appear to redefine the innate aptitudes of the sexes . . ." The male, in his new productive role, naturally gains prominence both within his family and in the greater society. The female, in contrast, loses status and becomes the dependent and subordinate sex. Her mobility and sexual activities are restricted, and her legal and political rights denied. Child-rearing and housework, in the end, are her only prerogatives.

Things pick up again for women in industrial society and Martin and Voorhies have high hopes for the future. The advantage of male strength is not so important in the world of the factory and office. Generally, whenever jobs are open to women in industrial societies, women work. And whenever they work, advances are made toward their legal and social equality. This is precisely our situation today, as any reader of a newspaper knows.

Although much remains to be accomplished, women's drive for equality has made many gains over the last few years. Women are obtaining jobs in fields once denied them and their numbers in the professions have risen dramatically. Since 1970, the proportion of women physicians rose from 9 to 13 percent, the proportion of women bank officials and financial managers from 18 to 25 percent, the proportion of women lawyers from 5 to about 9 percent. The future looks even more promising as women swell the ranks of our nation's law, medical, and business schools, some of them all-male bastions only a short time ago.

In politics, too, women are making headway, both on the state and on the local scene. The number of women in state legislatures has virtually doubled. Ninety cities with populations of more than ten thousand have women mayors. And in Minneapolis, almost half (six of thirteen members) of the city council are women.

Women's new independence is having telling effects, not only in society at large, but within the home as well. Isabell Sawhill, an economist at the Urban Institute in Washington, reports that women employed full time have more power at home than women working part time or not at all. And women with prestigious jobs or with an income greater than their husband's have the most power. "As more women move into the labor force and contribute a larger fraction to the total family income, they will acquire new rights as wives and improve the bargaining position within the marriages," says Sawhill. "The wife who had to ask her husband's permission to buy a new dress will have freedom to make her own decision about these matters, in addition to the higher status which generally accrues to income earning adults."

Another survey, by Suzanne McCall of East Texas State University in Commerce, reveals that the more income a working wife makes, the happier her husband is. Not only does working improve a woman's relative status in the family, it also allows her husband to be freer about buying things, about changing jobs, about early retirement, and about going back to school.

But regardless of whether women have economic clout or not, whether they enjoy high status or low, women along with their children have always constituted the basic unit of society. Say anthropologists Tanner and Zihlman, "Among contemporary human groups, this unit remains important: it is the basic organizational form that is relied upon when other more complex or extended structures become ineffective." It is this aspect of the female role to which I will now turn.

(6) The Bond

*To every thing there is a season, and a time to every purpose under
the heaven.*

Ecclesiastes 3:1

1

THE EVENT IS often painful, undoubtedly messy, always intense.
It is supremely creative, yet commonplace; immensely personal,
but with worldwide implications. It may be welcomed or feared,
planned or accidental, joyful or tragic. Its beginnings occurred
months ago, often in loving and quiet embrace. It ends with the
abruptness of harsh infantile cries rejecting the new realities. It
is all these and more, its meaning and manner uniquely individual,
for all its universality. It is the birth of a child.

For nine long months before, the child lay in uterine warmth
and comfort, succored via the umbilical cord. Now the cord is
severed, the biological union at end. But in nature's wisdom this
marks not an end but merely a transition, a transition reminiscent
of the physicist's matter-energy transformations. For what was
primarily a physical temporal bond will soon be replaced in most
cases by an even stronger, albeit invisible, bond—the psychologi-

148

cal attachment between mother and child—a bond of far more energy and endurance, of far more wonder and remark, than the passing umbilical cord. It is a bond that is as primitive as it is modern, a bond that is the focal point of both human and mammalian societies.

Let's look now more closely at the makings of this extraordinary bond. Our search will begin first, as always, among those simpler souls who came before us, whose secrets and successes, perfected through a long evolutionary journey, constitute our heritage. Close psychological bonds between a mother and her offspring can be seen in many animal species. Often these bonds appear to form during a certain limited period of time, a critical period, following birth. Just as with the now-or-never importance of timing in sexual differentiation, bonding must often occur within the first few hours of birth if it is to "take." Events during this special time influence not only the immediate relationship between a mother and her offspring, but can have far-reaching effects on the young animal's future social life.

Konrad Lorenz, the famed ethologist and Nobel Prize winner, was the first to give the phenomenon a name. He chose the German term *Prägung,* which was later translated as *imprinting.* While the term imprinting is usually restricted to Lorenz' concept of unique and rapid learning that takes place within a relatively short period, it has also been used by Cambridge's eminent ethologist, Robert Hinde, to mean simply "the learning of the parental characteristics" by young animals. Here, I will use the term itself only in its original classical sense; such "Lorenzian" imprinting will be emphasized. Yet, I do not plan to exclude from this discussion any related processes involved in infant-mother attachment that are implied in Hinde's broader definition. Whether these other processes involve classical imprinting is not always known with precision; but that they affect the bond between mother and offspring is reason enough for our interest.

Lorenz worked primarily with ducks and geese, finding, as did several scientists before him, that if newly hatched young were exposed to him, rather than their mothers, they would regard him as their mother and pay no attention to their real mother. In Lorenz's delightful book, *King Solomon's Ring,* we laugh at the embarrassing and uncomfortable moments brought upon him by his young admirers. He found that mallards, for instance, are imprinted to the quacking, not the sight, of the mother. So Lorenz, their adopted parent, was forced to squat low and quack for hours on end—all to the horrification of tourists who chanced to see him, a bearded man, dragging himself as if demented through a meadow constantly calling, "Quahg, gegegegeg, Quahg, gegegegeg," and peering endlessly over his shoulder. The tourists, unfortunately, could not see the ducklings following him in the tall meadow grasses. Even worse was the importuning of the male jackdaw who fell in love with Lorenz and insisted on feeding him "finely minced worm, generously mixed with jackdaw saliva." And if Lorenz refused to accept these goodies by mouth, the jackdaw would instead fill his ears with the warm mashed worm. Early imprinting, Lorenz confirmed in such unsavory ways, can often affect later sexual preferences.

The phenomenon of imprinting was noted long before Lorenz, however. Among the Greeks, Pliny the Elder wrote in A.D. 27 of a goose that followed his friend Lacydes faithfully. In the seventh century, wild eider ducklings were undoubtedly imprinted on St. Cuthbert, the protector of birds and other wildlife. According to the monk Reginald, who wrote of Cuthbert's life some centuries later, the saint lived on one of the Farne Islands off the coast of England. So attached were the birds to Cuthbert that they fled to him when they were endangered or attacked and "submitted to him as if they were his slaves."

Later, in the sixteenth century, Sir Thomas More described imprinting in artificially incubated eggs in his classic, *Utopia:* "They rear a very large number of chicks by an amazing device. For the hens do not sit on the eggs. Instead they keep a great number of eggs warm with an even heat and so hatch them. As soon as the chicks come out of the eggs, they follow the men and recognize them as if they were their mothers."

Around the turn of this century, there appeared a number of sporadic reports on imprinting, most of which involved the attachment of young birds to their human caretakers. In addition to geese, ducks and chicks, a great variety of other species were observed to form such attachments: pheasants, partridges, plovers, moorhens, terns, doves, pigeons, eagle owls, corncrakes, even South American rheas. A pattern was beginning to emerge among these early reports. There was a definite limited time in the young bird's first days during which imprinting could take place. Beyond this time, fear set in and imprinting was impossible.

One of the first to discover this was a Britisher named Douglas Spalding, who published his findings in 1873. Spalding put hoods over chicks immediately after they hatched to prevent them from seeing. If he removed the hoods within the first three days, the chicks would quickly follow him. But if the hoods were removed after three days, the chicks exhibited extreme fear. It was such a striking reversal of behavior that Spalding was convinced that it was a change within the animal itself, a change that could not be due to the effect of experience. In 1908, John Watson, the famous founder of behaviorism, discovered the same thing among noddy and sooty terns. During their first day after hatching, the terns would follow readily and identify him as their parent. But thereafter it was impossible for the terns to form such an attachment. Their critical period was of even shorter duration than that of Spalding's chicks.

Since those early days, and especially within the last few decades since Lorenz's original reference to the phenomenon, much has been learned about imprinting. Eckhard Hess of the University of Chicago, perhaps more than any other researcher, has, in the words of his old friend Konrad Lorenz, put imprinting "on the map." Much of what is known today of imprinting, particularly among birds, is due to Hess's more than twenty-five years of research on the subject. His findings, plus those of others working with higher animals, have amply confirmed the occurrence of critical periods for imprinting.

But aside from these critical periods with their tightly bound time limits, scientists have found evidence of other periods of special sensitivity, periods having less precise parameters than those of imprinting. Nevertheless, during these "sensitive" periods an animal, plant, or amazingly even a bit of living tissue may possess peculiar potentialities which, unless taken advantage of there and then, may be lost forever.

2

AT THE TURN of the century, a botanist named Hugo De Vries discovered a remarkable thing about a particular variety of poppy. In its first weeks, this poppy is able to turn its pollen-producing parts, the stamens, into extra pistils within which seeds later develop. Under good conditions, many extra pistils are formed and many more seeds can potentially be produced—a way no doubt for the plant to take advantage of an ideal environment. But the poppy's flexibility does not last forever. After the seventh week, the poppy has made a final "decision" regarding the number of pistils and nothing can be done to change it.

Similar short-lived periods of sensitivity are also evident in embryonic tissue. At first, such tissue is wide open to all possibilities and can react with versatility to various cues from its environment. For example, if embryonic neural tissue is transplanted onto a prospective skin area during this sensitive period, the tissue will develop as if it were actually skin tissue (and vice versa). After this sensitive period, however, embryonic neural tissue will develop only as nervous tissue, no matter where it is relocated. Eventually the tissue becomes, as it were, set in its ways and external conditions can no longer affect it; scientifically speaking, differentiation has occurred. This process of differentiation, preceded by a period of special sensitivity to environmental cues, is basic to the development of all but the simplest of living things. The early sensitivity allows for flexibility in "deciding," in effect, the best way in which to specialize; in differentiation, the specialization takes effect.

Charles Stockard did extensive research in the early part of this century on congenital defects, subjecting sea minnow eggs to a variety of environmental insults: low temperature, reduced oxygen, and toxic chemicals. He was able to prove that all congenital defects that were not hereditary, could be blamed on the arrested development of the embryo. Each particular defect, he noted, could be produced by stopping development at a particular "critical" stage.

While the biologists were examining their data on sensitive periods, behaviorists were discovering similar patterns in the human species. The American psychologist, William James, was one of the first of these. Among his many observations, James noted that the human baby, like the young calf, must have the opportunity to suck within its first days, or it will lose its instinct to do so:

> The instinct of sucking is ripe in all mammals at birth . . . But the instinct itself is transient, in the sense that if, for any reason, the child be fed by spoon during the first few days of life and not put to the breast, it may be no easy matter after that to make it suck at all. So of calves. If the mother die, or be dry, or refuse to let them suck at all for a day or two, so that they are fed by hand, it becomes hard to get them to suck at all when a new nurse is provided.

Sigmund Freud postulated a number of stages in a child's development during which certain aspects of the environment had particular impact. He described these stages in terms of erogenous zones, where pleasurable sensations were centered. The first stage he called the oral stage, in which the mouth is the erogenous zone. (Any mother can testify to this! Who among us has not longed for a pacifier with a boomerang's ability to replace itself each time baby drops it, or regretted the thumb that she used in its stead. And then comes the tedium of constant surveillance to ensure that the growing glutton doesn't sample hors d'oeuvres from the dog's dish, the sandbox, or the plant pot.) Freud's anal stage comes to the fore during the second and third years of life (perfectly timed, I might add, for potty-training havoc). During this period, the child gets a lot of pleasure out of withholding and expelling her feces. In the fourth and fifth years of life, the phallic stage emerges. Here the child becomes aware of sensations from her sex organs and is attracted to the parent of the opposite sex. Following the phallic period is the latency period when erogenous sensations are eclipsed, while the child concentrates on social and intellectual growth.

Unlike his ideas on femininity and on childhood memories, Freud's developmental scheme has stood the test of time and is still well accepted. Today, there are several theories, built upon Freudian foundations, that postulate personality development as a similar, but modified, series of stages, each of which is related to a particular personality function.

Intellectual capabilities also seem to develop in a predictable sequence of stages, each stage dependent on the child's unique receptivity at the time. The cataloguing of this development has been the life's work of the eminent Swiss psychologist, Jean Piaget. Italian educator and physician Maria Montessori likewise found that children pass through a definite series of sensitive periods. During each of these periods, Montessori believed, the child reveals not only an intense desire, but also a unique capacity for a particular type of learning. Montessori based her progressive educational methods upon these sequential sensitivities, and schools using these methods are still popular today.

There is even, apparently, a sensitive period which influences the selection of a sexual partner. Joseph Shepher of Haifa University conducted a study of premarital sexual activity and marriage patterns in Israeli kibbutzim, and he discovered a most peculiar pattern. Children in a kibbutz are cared for from infancy in small one-age peer groups by child-care specialists. They live together, almost as brother and sister, during the day as well as, in most instances, at night. In early childhood, sexual play is intense and is permitted with little interference from adults. Then at about age ten, natural inhibitions arise in the children and the relations between sexes become restrained. With adolescence, however, these problems disappear and the children develop strong emotional bonds with one another, sharing joys and sorrows in family-like fashion.

In a survey of 2,769 marriages among members of kibbutzim, Shepher found that not one of them involved individuals who had grown up together from infancy within the same peer group. Moreover, not even a single case of heterosexual activity between peers was uncovered. And all this was completely voluntary; no strictures, either of a formal or informal sort, were placed upon such activity. Although there were thirteen apparent marriages between peer members, further investigation revealed that, in every case, there had been an interruption in peer group membership before the age of six. On the basis of this evidence, Shepher suggests that there is a sensitive period between birth and age six during which exposure to other children will "define with whom one will not fall in love." A kind of unconscious taboo exists, one which in a normal family situation has developed perhaps as an evolutionary tack against incest.

A common thread, as you can see, weaves itself through the fabric of human development. A person, as much as a poppy, is prone to periods of special sensitivity. During each, the individual shows particular readiness for particular achievements. It is then that the disposition is innate and the time ripe. For full advantage, the fast-fleeting moment must be seized in haste, its potentialities realized, for one will not pass by this way again.

3

THE FORMATION OF the bond between a mother and her offspring has, like a coin, two faces. There is, on the one side, the developing attachment of mother to her offspring and, on the other, the reciprocal attachment of offspring to mother. Scientists have begun to find remarkable evidence of imprinting on both sides of this biological coin. Having considered some preliminary evidence, we are now ready to turn up the magnification like the biologist with his multi-powered microscope and focus more closely on mother-young bonding, examining first one, then the other side of this intricate process.

It is difficult, of course, to separate these two. As in a solution the ions of different elements are intermingled into transparency, so in the relationship between an infant and his mother there is almost an overwhelming complexity in the interplay of personalities. But the limitations of language make their impositions and so we must try. Let's polarize, then, this solution of interrelationships and collect the ions of information relating, first, to the offspring's side in the bonding process.

A chick and many another bird will, you will recall, imprint on a human caretaker. But they will also follow and imprint upon an amazing variety of artificial parents such as duck decoys, stuffed hens, dolls, milk bottles, boxes, balls, flashing lights, rotating disks, and even toilet floats! Generally, the more conspicuous the object to the human eye, the more effective it is as an imprinting stimulus.

What earthly purpose could be served by such a smorgasbord of possible imprinting stimuli? Some suggest that the answer may be found in considering the diversity of form a mother might present to her young. Her shape, size, and even color might change with distance, lighting conditions, posture, angle of view, and background. To be able to learn to recognize the parent in all such varying conditions requires an initial openness to a wide range of objects. To be too selective, too early, may be to perish. For nature's purpose in imprinting, its selective value, hinges on survival. To learn the parent in detail, to know well the nuances of her every appearance at every time of day, in every setting and circumstance—such means safety, warmth, food, shelter, in short, life to the young bird.

So far I have been speaking only of visual imprinting. But any natural mother is much more than a mere sight to behold, more than a mute silent-movie caricature. And so it is not surprising that imprinting may involve many other sensual modalities. A moorhen, for instance, begs from its mother, obtains warmth from her and follows her avidly once it is a few days old. But it can be artificially imprinted to a different object for each of these responses: it can learn to beg from forceps, to obtain warmth from an infrared lamp, and to follow a wooden box.

Auditory imprinting is also common among birds. Lorenz, as noted, was forced to quack for his mallards. In many species, vocalization between embryos and their parents before and especially during hatching serves to help the young birds learn the sound of their own species. Guillemot chicks are capable of even more subtle distinctions: they can identify the calls not merely of their species, but of their own particular parents. And it is well that they do so. These birds nest in colonies high up on precipitous ledges overhanging the ocean where one wrong step by a chick could chuck it overboard. So the chicks stay put while their parents forage at sea. When a parent returns, it utters a feeding call. Now, if all guillemot chicks raced to be fed, catastrophe could result in a mass tumbling to the sea. But fortunately, the feeding call brings forth but a single chick—the family heir or heiress!

This adaptation to habitat, as seen in the guillemot, is often a key to variations in the mode of imprinting among species. Wild turkeys inhabit mature forests with little understory on Ossabaw Island in Georgia. There, turkey hens lead their poults silently from place to place. Jungle fowl, however, inhabit dense, low-visibility forests in South Carolina. Silence would be insane in such circumstances and so the hen clucks constantly to keep in touch with her young. Follow-up laboratory studies with domestic fowl reinforced these observations: Visual imprinting worked best with turkey poults, while exposure to clucking calls was needed to imprint chicks.

Another variable in imprinting is the timing of the critical period. That tireless researcher, Eckhard H. Hess, having worked with thousands of ducks and chickens, determined their critical period with great precision: It lasts from the time of hatching up to 32 or 36 hours of age, with a peak sensitivity at 13 to 16 hours of age. Another researcher, G. Gottlieb, however, could find no critical period among his Peking ducklings, although more imprinting occurred on the twenty-seventh day after hatching than any other.

While the timing of the critical period may vary among species and even between individuals of the same species, the existence of critical periods is well established. Says John Scott, who has done research on mammalian imprinting: "All highly social animals which have been so far studied show early in life a limited period in which the group of animals with which the individual will form positive social relationships is determined."

Stepping down the evolutionary staircase for a moment, let's take a look at the slave-making ants. These ants raid the nests of other species, stealing their eggs and larvae. The captive ants soon learn to identify with their captors, most likely through scent, and readily assist them in domestic work. So complete becomes their attachment to the slave-makers that they can no longer recognize their own species.

Higher on the evolutionary ladder, among mammals, the presence of olfactory cues during an early stage of life may also result in imprinting. Shrews have been the subject of an interesting study illustrating this. The offspring of certain shrews form caravans with their mother, each young biting and holding on to the rump of either its mother or the littermate in front. Up until the age of six or seven days, they will attach themselves instinctively to each other or even to a rag. But after the eighth day, they will attach themselves only to an object having the odor upon which they were imprinted. If raised among another species, they become imprinted on the specific odor of that species and will ignore even their own mother.

Critical periods for imprinting are also evident in other mammals. The little lamb that followed Mary to school was undoubtedly imprinted to its young charge. Scott's research on domestic sheep gives credence to this old nursery rhyme. If a lamb is taken at birth and bottle-fed by humans, it will prefer to associate with people rather than with sheep.

This same thing can happen to dogs. A close relationship between a female dog and her pups exists for the first three weeks. But lasting social relationships are formed later, between three and eight weeks, when the mother leaves for long periods to feed. The strongest relations are thus between littermates, and these form the basis of the pack organization of adult dogs and wolves. A would-be dog owner, suggests Scott, should take advantage of this critical period to establish a strong bond with his new pet. The ideal time for socialization to humans is when the pup is between six and eight weeks of age. "Removing the animal too early will overemphasize dog-human relationships and delaying the contact until too late emphasizes dog-dog relationships at the expense of human contacts."

All this accumulating evidence of imprinting in so many species up and down the evolutionary scale has led to a wealth of speculation about the likelihood of comparable processes affecting the human animal. Could the infant-mother affectional bond in *Homo sapiens* be formed in a manner similar to that molding the bond between a moorhen and her chick, between a mallard mother and her ducklings, between a lamb and its caretaker, an ant slave and its captor, a female shrew and her young? Based on the universality of imprinting in the animal kingdom, Scott some twenty years ago speculated that there was "every reason" to suspect a similar process in human development. And it is today difficult to escape such a conclusion in the light of exciting new research that has surfaced within the last few years.

Of course the human infant, unlike the chick or gosling or lamb, cannot bodily follow her or his mother until many months after birth. Yet the need to maintain close contact with the mother is as essential as in any other species. Has the mother, then, in a sudden divergence from an evolutionary pattern eons in the making, become the sole initiator of such contact? Or does the infant, despite her relative helplessness, have means of facilitating it as well? Philip Gray in 1958 made the first serious attempt to find evidence of imprinting in human infancy. He proposed that the emergence of the relatively weak, uncoordinated, and immature human baby forced not the elimination of the infant as an active agent in the mother-young bonding process, but the evolution instead of a different system of imprinting.

Our understanding of this system is better than ever before. It begins to operate, as in animals, within the first minutes and hours after birth. During that time, researchers have discovered, both baby and mother seem to be in an unusual state of mutual receptivity. The baby is unusually alert for a full forty-five to sixty minutes in the first hour after birth. (Thereafter, he will fall into a deep sleep for several hours.) If not drugged into drowsiness, the mother herself is at a peak of excitement following childbirth. So attuned to each other are the two that, given the chance, they will interact in an almost dancelike synchrony of movements, facial expressions, and vocalizations. The mother gazes into her infant's eyes for increasingly long periods of time, all the while talking to her infant in a high-pitched voice, somehow instinctively aware that babies are more receptive to higher pitches. The infant, on his part, follows his mother's face and moves in rhythm to her voice—lifting an eyebrow here, lowering a foot there—all in response to the patterns of her speech, the accents, pauses, and inflections. Whether the language is English or Chinese, there is this beautiful interplay between mother and infant.

The ability of the baby to see immediately after birth is a fact which has long been obscured by years of believing otherwise. "At many medical schools in the U.S.," pediatrician T. Berry Brazalton of the Harvard Medical School reports with regret, "students still are being taught that babies don't see anything but blurs until they are four weeks old, that they don't hear because their ears are full of wax, and so on." There has also been the routine use of medication (silver nitrate), which tends to blur a baby's early vision. Necessary as this medication is for the prevention of blindness, it interferes with mother-infant bonding during the important first hour after birth and could be given, just as effectively, at a later time.

Newborns not only can see at birth, they also show an innate preference for the human face. Dr. Carolyn C. Goren of the University of Southern California and Dr. Gerald Stechler of Boston University have separately demonstrated this remarkable fact. Infants a mere nine minutes of age will turn their head and eyes significantly more to follow a proper face pattern than one which is scrambled. And of all aspects of the face, the eyes appeal most to infants. Babies a few weeks old will smile at an experimenter whose nose and mouth are covered, but not at a face in which the eyes are covered. They will even smile at an oval card with a pair of black dots almost as readily as at a human face.

The researcher Kenneth Robson has perhaps best described the infantile fascination for eyes:

> The appeal of the mother's eyes to the child (and of his eyes to her) is facilitated by their stimulus richness. In comparison with other areas of the body surface, the eye has a remarkable array of interesting qualities such as the shininess of the globe, the fact that it is mobile while at the same time fixed in space, the contrasts between the pupil-iris-cornea configuration, the capacity of the pupil to vary in diameter, and the differing effects of variations in the width of the palpebral fissure.

(The palpebral fissure is the almond-shaped outline of the eye produced by the upper and lower lids.) One of the early investigators of human imprinting, J. Ambrose, was first to propose that the eyes of the mother are the human equivalent of what in birds is the "first moving object seen." No doubt by evolutionary design, the distance between the eyes of the mother and infant when the mother is breast-feeding or holding him in her arms is about twelve inches—the distance at which an infant can best focus.

Perhaps even more amazing than the infant's ability to attend and follow her mother's eyes within minutes of birth is the infant's remarkable tendency to mimic behavior at a mere two weeks of age. Babies, in a recent test, were presented with four gestures. Experimenters stuck out their tongues, extended their lips, opened their mouths, or moved their fingers in sequence while the babies watched. Within the first twenty seconds that followed, the infants often responded with similar gestures, significantly more often than could have occurred simply by chance. Obviously, though relatively immobile in comparison to other species, human infants nonetheless have their own unique means of "following." Nature has not left them bereft.

Through following responses, the baby comes to know her or his mother. But besides the visual modality, other sensory cues are also called into play. There is the sound of mother's voice and the soothing tempo of her heartbeat, of which more shall be said later. There is also the smell of her milk, as indicated by a fascinating bit of new research. A group of mothers who breast-fed their babies were asked to wear gauze breast pads for three or four hours. The mother's breast pad along with a sterile one were then presented side by side to the baby. More than three-fourths of the time the babies turned toward their mothers' pads. The infants could also discriminate between the smell of their own mother's breast pad and that of a strange mother. It had taken them a mere eight days of life to accomplish this feat.

In these varied ways, the baby learns the identity of that most important figure in his world—his mother. But he does more than that. As implied earlier, the baby actively, if innately, elicits maternal responses by his various behaviors. In early eye-to-eye contact, not only does the infant learn about his mother, but he attracts her attention as well. Robson was first to suggest that eye-to-eye contact was an innate releaser of maternal caretaking. More recent studies confirm Robson's original conjecture. Mothers of both full-term and premature babies express strong interest in eye-to-eye contact. Three fourths of new mothers, it was learned, will speak of their intense desire to waken their infants to see their eyes open. Some plead with their newborns, "Open your eyes. Oh, come on, open your eyes. If you open your eyes, I'll know you're alive."

Even non-mothers can be aroused by visual contact with an infant. In their recent book, *Maternal-Infant Bonding*, pediatricians Marshall Klaus and John Kennell of Case Western Reserve University's Medical School relate the following experience regarding three researchers who were to assist them in a study of infant behavior:

> We were distressed to hear all three say that they did not particularly like babies, found newborns particularly unappealing, and planned never to have a baby. They grumbled about learning the behavioral assessments. As they carried out the assessment each of the women had her first experience with a baby in an alert state who would follow her eyes with his own, and an amazing change occurred. Suddenly each became enthusiastic about "her" baby, wanted to hold him, and came back later in the day and the next day to visit. At night she would tell her friends about this marvelous baby she had tested. In a few weeks all three decided they would like to have and even breastfeed a baby.

"Such," conclude Klaus and Kennell, "is the compelling attraction of a newborn infant moving his eyes to follow an adult's eyes."

An infant has even more than this in his repertoire, for he can smile too. There is also crying, of course, which can attract the mother from a distance and help ensure that his physiological needs are met. Indeed, the cries of healthy infants actually increase the flow of blood in a mother's breasts, which is likely to induce her to nurse.

But smiling goes beyond the mere physical. It not only draws mother near, but elicits her loving attention. This has actually been documented in a clever way by Professor Lewis Leavitt of the University of Wisconsin. The human heart rate is known to slow when a person is interested in something nearby and speeds up when that person is trying to avoid something unpleasant. So

Leavitt decided to show mothers pictures of crying and smiling babies. Sure enough, the heart rates of the mothers slowed when the smiling baby picture came first. "It seems," says Leavitt, "that a smile is a good way to get attention; an initial cry may turn the mother off."

A unique aspect of imprinting is that it occurs without any conventional reward such as food. A bird, for example, will follow its mother soon after hatching even though it has no real need for food, being able to draw upon its yolk sac for nourishment until its third day of life. The visual following and smiling in human infants, likewise, need no food or physical raison d'être. Rather, their looks and smiles are given simply in return for such psychological satisfactions as holding and hugging, stroking and cooing, and even merely the smiling back by mother.

Ultimately, the infant has but one purpose—to keep close to mother. The young chick will follow the first moving object it sees. If it can reach it and the object holds still, the chick will nestle beneath or beside it, calling at first in pleasure, then sleeping contentedly. Monkeys, too, need maternal contact, as many experiments have proved. On its first day, an infant rhesus may follow a cloth that has been in contact with its face and then drawn away. If such a monkey is placed on its back, it will try to right itself. But, if given the cloth or another object to clasp, it will lie there quietly, making no attempt to right itself.

For a long time, though, psychiatrist and psychoanalyst alike believed in the "cupboard theory" of infant love. A baby's love, they said, began at mother's breast. By alleviating hunger and thirst, mother became the first love, the first drive of her newborn infant. But an infant smiles, as mentioned, not merely for food but for affection. Then, in 1959, in a single well-conceived experiment, a classic of its kind, this long-standing theory was demolished. On the campus of the University of Wisconsin, in Harry Harlow's primate laboratory, two types of surrogate mothers were constructed: one of soft terry cloth, the other of bare wire. Both a wire and cloth "mother" were placed in the individual cages of eight infant monkeys. Four of the infants received milk from the cloth monkey, but not the wire monkey. The plan was reversed for four other infants: They received milk from the wire mother instead of the cloth mother. It was these latter monkeys who, acting completely contrary to "cupboard" expectations, disproved that dusky untested theory once and for all. For, despite the nourishment provided by their lactating wire mothers, these infants came more and more to cling to their cozy cloth mothers. Contact comfort, not epicurean delight, was their heart's desire.

Although contact has been shown to be the primary factor in developing infant affection, it by no means is the only one. A bountiful breast will be preferred by monkey infants, all other things being equal. Rocking surrogate mothers rate higher than stationary ones. Warm mothers, in early infancy, are favored over cool cloth mothers.

The child, like the chick, therefore comes to know and love its mother through a variety of sensory cues. There is the sight and the sound, the warmth and the movement and the feel of mother. There is also the smell of mother's milk and very likely, its taste. Infant affection is founded on this growing physical familiarity, and it develops during a sensitive period that, although estimates of its exact parameters vary, seems to extend to about the sixth month of life. Mother becomes the infant's first love; the sun about whom her world revolves; the person who must always be near, must always be followed—first with eyes, then all fours, and finally on upright limbs. To follow, to be near, to keep close to mother—such is an infant's first passion. Every mother has, at times, both delighted and felt entrapped in the intensity of this infantile devotion. But the infant herself is most vulnerable. What if her world should fall apart? What if mother is no longer around? Or what, on the other hand, if mother was never around?

Such misfortunes can have dire consequences both in monkeys and in humans. A separation from mother can cause such depression in an infant rhesus that it shuffles about, hunched over in grief. Even more poignant are reports by Jane Goodall and others of young chimpanzees who have lost their mothers. Grave depression, bizarre behavior, even death itself, largely from grief, have been the sad aftermath of this traumatic experience.

Much clinical evidence, gathered from data on institutionalized or hospitalized children, prove conclusively the profound effects of such experience for the human child. Separation from mother in the early months or years, or alternately, the inadequate relationship with a mother-figure in those early formative times, can cause a host of problems ranging from apathy to psychopathy. These have been elaborated on in other volumes and are generally well known. Here, I wish only to point out that it was on the basis of such evidence that a sensitive period for bonding between a human mother and her child was first proposed. Estimates for the timing of this sensitive period vary somewhat, as I stated previously, and we cannot humanely attempt to determine precise boundaries by experiment. Yet act upon this knowledge, however limited, we must. And in some instances we have. Institutionalism of children has been greatly reduced. Hospital visitation policies in children's wards have become more flexible. But Doctors Klaus and Kennell have made an additional suggestion. They propose that adoption policies also be modified:

> It is the present custom in this country for adoptions to take place at three to six weeks of age or later. Would the behavioral problems of the adopted child be as great if adoptions occurred at one day or one hour of life? In many societies where there is a high maternal mortality rate, a substitute mother is close at hand and ready to take over immediately following the death of a mother.

It would seem an idea easy to implement, an idea whose time has come. Adoptive mothers are plentiful and are screened even years in advance of the availability of an infant. Why wait those few extra weeks, weeks during which the adoptive infant might get the same early start in learning and loving her mother as do more fortunate infants—weeks which just might be of unknown importance to the infant and her future.

4

Now let's turn to the maternal side of the biological coin of mother-offspring bonding. A growing body of evidence suggests the paramount importance *for the mother* of early intimate contact between her and her newborn, a contact often as predictive of her future maternal behavior as it is of her infant's subsequent social behavior. Today, more and more women are learning about the importance of this bonding and their new awareness may well come to revolutionize childbirth practices in America—despite frequent resistance from the medical establishment.

Breeders of sheep and goats have long known the importance of early contact between a mother and her offspring. If a dam's newborn is removed for a short period for warming in cold weather, the mother may reject it upon return. Nor will any other dam accept the youngster. Naturalist Valerius Geist, who spent some forty months observing mountain sheep, sharing with them the rigors of the Canadian Rockies, tells this poignant tale:

> . . . a young, lamb-leading female broke her hind leg. For days she lay in one spot while her lamb tried in vain to get her up so he could suckle. The little fellow stole short suckles from other ewes while they fed their own lambs and was frequently punished for it with severe butts. . . . Yet the lamb only rose to try again. The female did finally rise and feed, but I soon lost sight of her. Several weeks later I saw her again with her poorly grown bedraggled lamb. She had become little more than skin and bones and limped pitifully, but her leg was well along in healing. I saw her for a few more days and never again thereafter. Nor do I know what happened to her lamb.

Cruel though the ewes' exclusiveness may seem in this case, so fixed a behavioral pattern must necessarily have adaptive value. And one can best begin to understand it by looking into the ways of the gray seal—an animal who, in shunning such exclusiveness, has failed a fair portion of its offspring. Until recently, the gray seal restricted its range to the North Atlantic ice floes, where it bred in pairs or small groups. But the seal has now begun to extend itself to the rocky shores southward, where it breeds in large crowded rookeries. Despite the new living arrangements, the females in these southern reaches have not yet adopted the habit of limiting care to their own pups, a habit characteristic of most other colony-living seals. In the gray seal's small family-type groups in the North, such discrimination is not so essential. But in the well-populated rookeries, the mothers' promiscuous nursing

has rung the death knell for many of the weaker young, who soon
die of starvation.

Among domestic sheep and goats, elaborate measures have
been devised to bring a mother to accept other than her own
offspring. For example, a goat whose kid was stillborn may be
induced to adopt an orphan if it has been rubbed with her own
offspring's placenta or afterbirth. Another technique involves
spraying the orphan with kerosene or with mother's milk. These
methods necessitate careful timing: they must be carried out
within two hours after the mother has given birth and preferably
when the orphan kid is but a few minutes old, if adoption is to
be successful. A dam will also accept an alien kid if she is isolated
in a cubicle with the orphan and prevented from butting it.

Sheep and goats were the subjects of the earliest research on
maternal bonding. In these animals, a critical period for the
bonding process, characteristic of imprinting, was found to have
a duration of about one hour immediately following birth-giving.
If newborn kids, for example, are separated from their mothers
for an hour or more, they will usually be rejected by their mothers
when the two are reunited. In contrast, a number of experiments
have shown that kids will not be rejected by their mothers if the
pair have as little as five minutes of contact before separation,
even if that separation lasts as long as three hours.

Still more surprising is the fact that an *alien* kid will be accepted by a female within those vital first five minutes following
parturition, an acceptance in startling contrast to the total rejection, the butting and refusal to nurse, which occurs not long after
in the natural course of events. As Peter Klopfer, an authority on
maternal behavior in animals, explains,

> Something happens in the space of a few minutes after parturition
> which makes her ready, then and only then, to attach herself to a
> kid. Once she is attached, she displays many of the human signs
> of distress on the removal of the kid. Spared the attachment, the
> removal leaves her as nonchalant as any virgin, despite the fact that
> she may be lactating heavily.

Klopfer believes hormonal changes at the time of parturition cause the temporarily heightened responsiveness to infants.

In rats, attachment between a mother and her pups also takes place within a very brief period of time. Hormones, again, have been implicated. Maternal behavior can be stimulated in virgin rats by a substance present within the blood of a mother rat near the time of birth-giving. After birth-giving the presence of pups seems necessary to maintain maternal behavior. And just as with sheep and goats, separation of mother and young within the first few hours following delivery can have fatal effects upon the mother's acceptance of her young when they are reunited with her. The rat's maternal instincts may be permanently reduced or even completely eliminated as a consequence of such separation. A gradual transition seems to occur, then, from internal hormonal control of maternal behavior to the external stimulation provided by the pups themselves. Significantly, it has been noted that estrogen, the hormone implicated in rat maternalism, also rises in human mothers during the last five weeks of pregnancy.

In monkeys, no less than among other animals, early contact between a mother and her offspring is essential. Monkey mothers separated from their young for more than a day prefer to be near adults rather than their own young. Depriving a monkey mother of tactile contact alone, while still allowing her to see and hear her infant, can also affect her maternal motivation. In some intriguing experiments along this line, researchers found that rhesus monkeys deprived of tactile contact with their young for two weeks rapidly lost interest even in looking at their young.

In another experiment, a rhesus monkey was separated from her own infant and allowed to adopt a young kitten. Despite the species difference, the monkey's initial maternal instinct was so strong that she even began to allow the kitten to nurse. The kitten, however, had "one enormous behavioral flaw," as Harry Harlow put it. Unlike an infant monkey, the kitten failed to cling to its adoptive mother. Finally, after several days of repeatedly retrieving the kitten, the monkey's motherliness atrophied and the kitten was abandoned.

Harlow has found that a monkey mother normally maintains the maximum amount of contact with her infant, either cuddling it closely to its chest or cradling it in a looser, more relaxed position within the confines of her arms and legs. Abnormal monkey mothers however, who neglect or abuse their infants, neither cuddle nor cradle them. From experiments such as these, Harlow has concluded that contact is one of the most important mechanisms that bind a mother monkey to her infant. (Conversely, of course, we've already noted that contact also serves to bind an infant to its mother.) In the same vein, Hinde reports the interesting observation that mother monkeys sometimes carry stillborn babies for days. As he suggests, the infant obviously provides contact stimulation for these mothers, a stimulation they are quite reluctant to give up.

Human mothers also seem to need close contact with their young for maternal feelings to blossom. This is especially evident in data on mothers of premature babies forced into prolonged separation from their infants after giving birth. Pierre Budin, most famous of the early specialists in premature baby care, lamented that "Mothers separated from their young soon lost all interest in those whom they were unable to nurse or cherish." To counteract this problem, Budin urged mothers to breast-feed their premature babies whenever possible.

Martin Couney, one of Budin's students, commercialized the care of premature infants, exhibiting his "child hatchery" technique at the 1933 Chicago World's Fair. The mothers, however, were not allowed to handle their infants in these exhibits; so perhaps it is not surprising that Couney sometimes had difficulty in getting parents to take back their children.

More recent work has also indicated the importance of caretaking and contact in the development of the maternal bond. Researchers at Stanford University report that mothers of premature babies first feel "close" to their infants when they are able to feed them or do something for them. But it is not only mothers of premature infants who need this involvement. As discussed in chapter 2, mothers in the Israeli kibbutz system, where full care of all infants is provided by trained personnel, have demanded to be allowed to participate in the care of their young.

The effect of contact and caretaking became dramatically evident in the heartbreaking Israeli baby mixup that occurred in

1978. Two twenty-one-year-old women gave birth in mid-June of that year at Ramban Hospital in Haifa, Israel. Each mother was given the other's baby, apparently because foreign nurses had difficulty in reading the Hebrew names. To the distress of the mothers, the babies were switched two more times in attempts to correct the original mistake. Finally, blood tests were given that indicated that the babies were still in the wrong hands. But by this time, the mothers had taken the babies home and cared for them for six weeks. Despite the blood tests, each woman refused to part with the baby she had. Said one: "I will always feel that this is my daughter. Even if they prove that she is not mine, I will never be sure. I will feel as if I have two little girls." An expert in immunogenetics, Dr. Chaim Brautbar, was then called in. He tissue-typed the babies and their parents and grandparents. In these tests, bits of cellular material in the babies' blood was matched with those of the adults. The tests established beyond a doubt that the babies were indeed in the wrong homes. Nonetheless, it took the hospital several hours to convince the distraught mothers. "I know you are logically right," said one mother, "but if I talk to you from the bottom of my heart, it's difficult for me to accept what you say." When the final switch was made both mothers wept in anguish and hugged one another and the babies. Through close contact and caretaking, these women had developed strong bonds with the infants they had, even though the infants, as it turned out, were not their own.

Every mother needs to cuddle and care for her infant for full ripening of the maternal bond. She needs to feel and feed him, to hear him and speak to him, to hug him close and to gaze at him fondly. This caretaking and close contact act as the cement that secures the bonding of mother to child. But there are indications that the cement had best be applied as early as possible after a mother gives birth. I have already spoken of the unique intimacy between a mother and her baby within minutes of childbirth. Numerous studies are now confirming the importance of this early contact for maternal bonding. Some of the most interesting of these studies derive from the work of Lee Salk, the well-known child psychologist and younger brother of Jonas Salk, who developed the polio vaccine.

Salk's studies began when he noted that a mother rhesus monkey at New York's Central Park Zoo consistently held her newborn infant on her left side. Forty out of forty-two times, Salk observed this left-sided preference in the rhesus. Salk saw the same thing in human mothers. Of the almost three hundred mothers he observed, four of every five held their baby on the left side of their chest or on their left shoulder. These mothers had all had normal deliveries and early access to their infants.

In reviewing the literature, Salk found that I. Hyman Weiland of the University of Southern California had discovered the same phenomenon among mothers at a well-baby clinic. (A well-baby clinic is one where healthy babies are taken regularly for checkups and inoculations.) To determine whether this left-sided carrying was merely typical human behavior, Weiland watched shoppers carrying packages similar in size to babies. Of the 438 adults Weiland observed, exactly half held the package on the left and half on the right. Babies, unlike packages, obviously had a special emotional effect on the human adult.

Salk was becoming increasingly intrigued and decided to study paintings, sculptures, photographs, and other artistic representations of mothers and infants. True to form, the vast majority portrayed the child being held on the left side. But then Salk chanced to observe maternal behavior that was at variance with these first findings. At a follow-up clinic for premature infants at New York Hospital-Cornell Medical Center, Salk saw that an unusually large number of mothers held their babies on the right side. Of the many possible factors that could cause this atypical behavior, Salk singled out what he thought was the most likely cause—the prolonged separation of the mother from her premature infant.

Salk set out to test his hypothesis with a group of 115 mothers who had been separated from their infants for twenty-four hours or more after birth, comparing them with a group of mothers who had handled their infants within these first twenty-four hours. The results were unequivocal. Nearly 80 percent of the mothers who had early contact with their infants preferred to hold their infants on their left sides. The mothers who were separated from their infants, however, showed no side preference at all—approximately half held their baby on the right side and half on the left. In later experiments, mothers who had been separated from their infants for one to seven days were compared with mothers who had been separated for more than seven days. There was little difference between these two groups. The length of separation mattered little, but its timing was crucial. Only separation during the first twenty-four hours was of consequence. Salk could only conclude that here, indeed, was evidence for a critical period, occurring within the first day after childbirth, during which the stimulus of holding the newborn infant releases a certain maternal response. He noted, also, the resemblance of this phenomenon to that of imprinting found in birds and mammals.

There remained the matter of the biological value of this maternal behavior. In holding an infant on her left side a mother is placing him near her heart. Salk wondered whether this could be related to a need in the infant. Within the uterus, he knew, the most prominent sound to which an infant is exposed is that of the maternal heartbeat. There, in the warmth and security of the womb, the infant is nourished, supplied with oxygen, and shielded from the stress it must deal with after birth. The maternal heartbeat, in this way, may become associated with contentment and well-being. Salk suggests that the infant is imprinted in this prenatal period with his mother's heartbeat. Subsequently, after birth, a baby is more soothed and quieted in the uncomfortable and alien world in which he finds himself when held on a mother's left side close to the wonderfully familiar thump-thumping of her heart.

To verify these ideas, Salk exposed a group of nursery infants to a recording of the normal adult heartbeat. These babies gained more weight and cried far less than other infants not exposed to the heartbeat recording. Other sounds, incidentally, such as a gallop heartbeat rhythm and an abnormally fast heartbeat, caused such an increase in crying and restlessness that they were discontinued for the infants' well-being.

This early imprinting on the maternal heartbeat seems to have long-lasting effect in young children. In a study of twenty-six children between the ages of one and three, Salk found that children fell asleep twice as fast when exposed to the sound of a normal heartbeat, than when exposed to no sound, to the sound of a metronome, or the sound of lullabies. Even in adult life, Salk believes there is evidence of this prenatal imprinting. In almost every culture in the world, people enjoy the rhythms of music and dance. Moreover, says Salk, "From the most primitive tribal drumbeats to the symphonies of Mozart and Beethoven, there is a startling similarity to the rhythm of the human heart." Could such correlation between cultures so diverse be mere coincidence?

Another response to the imprinted stimulus of the heartbeat, Salk suggests, may be found in the use of the word *heart* in poetry, literature, and song, as well as in everyday language. He explains that although a small part of the brain, the hypothalamus, is known to be the seat of emotions in the human being, people everywhere and in all periods of history have persisted in referring, instead, to another part of the anatomy—the heart—in speaking of love and deep emotion: "I am broken-hearted." "My heart is with you." "I love you from the bottom of my heart." Certainly, as Salk has shown with his studies of mothers, the folk expression, "Close to a mother's heart," may be far more than a mere idle remark.

In addition to Salk, other researchers have also found impressive evidence for the value of early mother-child contact. At Duke Hospital, associated with the Duke University School of Medicine in Durham, North Carolina, Dr. Angus McBryde noted significant changes in maternal behavior when rooming-in was made compulsory. Rooming-in is an arrangement in which newborns are kept in a bassinet close to their mother's bed, rather than in a separate nursery. Mothers are given the opportunity to hold and feed and care for their babies right from the start. After rooming-in was instituted at Duke, the number of mothers who breast-fed their babies increased by nearly 25 percent, while phone calls from worried mothers during the first few weeks after departure from the hospital decreased by an astounding 90 percent. In Sweden, likewise, mothers randomly assigned to rooming-in were more confident, felt more competent in care-giving, and were more sensitive to their infant's cues than mothers without rooming-in.

Several studies have dealt with mothers of premature infants, some being allowed early contact, others being permitted only the traditional late contact after a postpartum separation from their infants of twenty to forty hours. Early contact mothers were consistently more "motherly." One study concentrated on such attachment behavior as looking and smiling at the infant, holding the infant close and caressing the infant. Always, the early-contact, non-separated mothers showed the greater attachment behavior. In a second study, the feeding behavior of a group of early- and late-contact mothers was chosen as a measure of maternal performance. When these mothers were observed one month after discharge, the differences between them were again significant. Late-contact mothers held their babies differently, changed position less, burped less, and were not as skillful in feeding as early-contact mothers.

Among mothers of normal full-term infants, success in breast-feeding has been associated with early contact. One of the largest studies of this involved two groups of one hundred women each in a Brazilian maternity hospital. In the early-contact group, each baby was put to breast immediately after birth and remained with its mother throughout hospitalization, sleeping in a cot beside its mother's bed. The late-contact group had normal arrangements —a glimpse after birth and then visits, approximately thirty minutes in length, every three hours, starting at twelve to fourteen hours after birth. The babies of this late-contact group were kept in a separate nursery. The two hundred mothers were surveyed when their infants reached two months of age. In the early-contact group, more than three fourths of the mothers were still successfully breast-feeding, in contrast to only a fourth of the late-contact mothers.

Supporting evidence has also come from Sweden. An investigation of forty mothers was undertaken to determine the effect of skin-to-skin contact between mother and infant during the first thirty minutes of life upon maternal behavior three months later. Interestingly, the late-contact mothers complained of more problems with night feedings, despite the fact that they night-fed only half as long (twenty-four nights) as did the early-contact mothers (forty-eight nights). Moreover, the late-contact mothers had household help for a longer period than the other group. Other significant contrasts between the two sets of mothers emerged during home observations. The mothers who had early contact spent more time with their infants in the *en face* (face-to-face) position and kissed them more frequently. The late-contact mothers, on the other hand, cleaned their infants more often. The differences are striking: one group providing affection; the other, sanitation. All of this seemed to have effect on the infants: Those of early-contact mothers cried less and smiled and laughed significantly more than did infants of the late-contact mothers. Later follow-ups revealed that mothers given early contact breast-fed their babies longer, by about two months, than did the other group. The above findings are all the more impressive when one realizes that *the only difference between the two sets of mothers occurred in the first thirty minutes after childbirth.* All infants, of both sets of mothers, were wrapped and placed in cribs near their mothers' beds from thirty minutes of age to approximately two hours after birth. With evidence such as this, the existence of a "prime time" for human maternal bonding, a critical period within minutes of childbirth, can no longer be casually dismissed.

But perhaps most far-reaching in its implications, most provocative in its conclusions is the research which began in the early 1970's at Case Western Reserve University in Cleveland, Ohio. This research, involving studies of full-term, firstborn infants and their mothers, reveals not only immediate beneficial effects of early mother-child contact, but increasing effects over a time span of five years. Marshall Klaus and his associates conducted the initial study with a group of twenty-eight mothers of lower socio-economic status and their newborn infants. Half of these mothers were allowed routine contact with their infants: a glimpse of the baby shortly after birth, brief contact and identification at six to twelve hours, and then the traditional twenty to thirty minutes every four hours for feeding in the three days after delivery. The other half were permitted extended contact with their infants: In addition to the routine contact, these mothers were given their infants for one hour within the first three hours after birth, plus an extra five hours each afternoon of the three days following delivery. This amounted, then, to sixteen additional hours of contact within the first three days after birth.

Differences between the two sets of mothers were first noted when the infants were one month of age. The mothers who had extended contact with their newborn infants said that they picked up their babies more frequently in response to crying and tended to stay home with them more. Observations also revealed that these mothers were more comforting during stressful office visits and showed more fondling and eye-to-eye contact during feeding.

Later, when the children were one and two years of age, maternal speech patterns were examined by psycholinguist Norma Ringler and her associates at Case Western. The researchers found that mothers in the extended-contact group asked significantly more questions, used more elaborate, varied, and informative speech, and spoke more words per utterance than did the routine-contact mothers.

Finally, at five years of age, children of both sets of mothers were tested for their linguistic and intellectual abilities. The remarkable results compel consideration by every mother, educator, hospital administrator, and doctor, indeed by every citizen in our country. For the children of mothers who had extended contact with their infants in those first three days after birth scored consistently and significantly higher (on a statistical basis) in every test given them. They had higher IQ's, better language comprehension, more advanced vocabularies, and greater expressive ability.

These are the results, of course, of but a single study. The final sampling—ten mother-child pairs—was small. Hopefully, more and larger studies will soon be undertaken to determine whether the findings of Ringler and her associates will hold to be universally true. Nonetheless, these results have multiple ramifications. Like Salk, Ringler suggests that her work may indicate a so-called imprinting time between mother and child in the first few hours after birth. Does "the quality of a mother's attachment to her child affect the way she speaks to him and the effort she makes to adapt her words to his readiness?" Ringler asks. If so, Ringler believes, "her speech may be a very sensitive indicator of their relationship."

However tentative these conclusions may be, certainly Ringler's findings, along with the many others already cited here, must force us to reevaluate the traditional maternity hospital practices that affect the care of mothers and their infants. As Ringler herself says, "Permission for a mother to spend a few additional hours with her newborn infant immediately following delivery may change the linguistic environment which she provides for her child in his first few years of life. This in turn may affect the child's language and learning far into the future."

There it is. A truly astonishing body of research. Unconsciously, without our knowledge or awareness, the bonding between mothers and infants appears to be affected by hospital practices often beyond our control. Can mothers, under more natural arrangements, be imprinted in the first day or hour after childbirth so that they are automatically better mothers? Are we consequently, in the twentieth century, thwarting a marvelous natural mechanism that may have been eons in the making? With strong suggestive evidence already before us, is it a risk worth taking?

5

NOT EVERY WOMAN will want to bear a child. In a recent Virginia Slims American Women's Opinion Poll, only 38 percent of a national quota sample of three thousand respondents considered having children very important to a good marriage. In the Netherlands, the percentage of women (and men) who do not want children has risen from 1.5 to 9 percent in the last ten years. And this is good. For surely one of the most fundamental goals of emancipation is the freedom to choose whether to bear children, knowing that being a parent is only one of the paths to personal fulfillment.

The majority of women, however, do want children and probably always will. Motherhood is too integral a part of the female's biological heritage ever to be completely dismissed. If no longer a cultural imperative, motherhood is still, for many, a source of great satisfaction. Nonetheless, childbirth is becoming a relatively rare event for most American and European women, occurring twice, sometimes three, more rarely four times in a lifetime. Due to the easy availability of birth-control devices, childbirth is now more often a premeditated act, rather than the random, unwelcome dictate of fate it was so often before. Today, wonderfully, more women actually *want* to be mothers when they give birth than ever before. And it is among these women that the traditional ties between mother and infant may well become stronger than in the past. Because of the insights gleaned from the recent research on mother-infant bonding, these women will be able to maximize their maternal experience. For other, less fortunate, mothers—mothers of unwanted children or mothers whose wanted children inadvertently, through disease, deformity, or behavioral difficulties, turn out to be less than they wanted—for these mothers, the new insights may indeed prove critical, a subject we will pursue more thoroughly in Chapter 7.

Based both on their research and their clinical experience, pediatricians Klaus and Kennell have made a number of innovative proposals designed to enhance the process of bonding between a mother and her infant. Of fundamental importance, they maintain, is the treatment of pregnancy as a normal and natural process, not as a disease requiring elaborate medical interference. Some European countries seem much more cognizant of this fact. In Denmark, a healthy pregnant woman is usually seen regularly by a midwife, is examined several times by a doctor, and then gives birth in a maternity clinic attended by her midwife. Though lacking some of the emergency equipment, such as blood banks, usually found in a hospital, these clinics have a warm, homelike atmosphere, where mothers and newborns seem to thrive in early and intimate contact. If however, pregnant women have diabetes, toxemia, premature labor, or other complications of pregnancy, they are seen by an obstetrician and deliver in a hospital. In Holland, when a mother gives birth at home, a mother-helper takes over the care of the family and helps the midwife in delivering the baby.

In the United States, it is often quite different. Feminist and sociologist Alice S. Rossi has eloquently protested our obstetrical system. Addressing the medical and nursing professions, she asks in bitterness,

How dare you strap us down on a delivery room table? How dare you claim you "deliver" us when you cheat us of the knowledge and the experience of actively giving birth to our own child? Why are we moved from a relatively cozy setting at the end of the first stage of labor to a blindingly lit delivery room, cut off from our supportive men, while you try to anaesthetize us in second-stage labor just when we have reached the point where we can do something? . . . The whole paraphernalia of medicine—anaesthesia, the abyss below the delivery table—serve the function of retaining the dominant status of the attending physician, and thus prevent women from seeing that a physician is her "aide" in giving birth, and not her lordly "deliverer."

Rossi predicts that while in the past feminists have been more concerned with issues of contraception and abortion, they will also come to concern themselves with "the right to actively enjoy pregnancy and control the childbirth experience."

Other groups are already at work trying to bring about changes. Spearheading this movement is the International Childbirth Education Association, which seeks to change childbirth from an "illness" to an exciting and rewarding experience in which both parents actively participate. Doctors Klaus and Kennell share this philosophy and their proposals would delight Rossi. Some, at least, in the medical profession seem to have listened. To begin with, these pediatricians recommend group sessions for prospective parents that provide information on all the varied physical and emotional aspects of labor and birth, together with the demonstration of special preparatory exercises. Such classes are especially helpful today when childbirth is so rare an event in the average family setting that little forehand knowledge is had by most young adults. More important, it allows a woman to become an active participant rather than a passive "victim" of her new experiences.

My husband and I found such a class extremely valuable. But I did resent, as did others, I later found, the implication that my delivery would be painless if I did regular exercises and breathed as directed during labor. Although others have found it helpful, in my fast and intense labors, special breathing was no use at all. But mostly I was disappointed, with myself perhaps, at the pain.

Now, too late, I read that "The really painless delivery occurs one per 1000 or less, and as such is an exception to the rule." Klaus and Kennell, too, speak frankly of the intense, if brief, pain associated with natural childbirth. I had always known, of course, of women who had had painful deliveries, but had they exercised and done their required breathing? I should have been told. Natural childbirth has much to offer, but I would echo those others who warn that its advocates best avoid their pie-in-the-sky promise of painlessness. Such an unnecessary euphemism is insulting —women in most cases can handle the truth as well as the pain.

In their choice (or rejection) of pain relief methods, mothers will want to be informed of the effects both on their infants and themselves. Heavy use of anesthetics comes most frequently under attack. The drugged infants born under such circumstances are prone to respiratory problems and brain damage, their responses are dulled, and they need to be treated as post-surgical patients. At the same time, drugged mothers are robbed of consciousness at the moment of birth. They may even be missing orgasmic sensations, for these are frequently reported to occur during natural childbirth. Moreover, the relatively common post-spinal headache may keep a mother on her back and limit her interactions with her infant for up to five days. But of greatest significance to our present discussion of bonding is that both mother and infant will be unable to share those precious moments of heightened perceptions and reciprocity that immediately follow childbirth. They will miss that special sensitive period that can serve to enrich their relationship through the days and months ahead. It is not, of course, that bonding cannot take place if this should occur; the human species is far more adaptable than that. It is only that it will be more costly—and unnecessarily so.

There are other aspects of the childbirth setting that must also be considered. Rossi is properly enraged at the disruption of labor by the unnecessary rush to the unfamiliar isolation of the delivery room. Klaus and Kennell would eliminate this insensitive, tension-producing practice and allow labor and delivery to take place in the same room. In addition they stress the need for some one person, the husband perhaps, or mother or friend or midwife or even nurse or obstetrician, to remain with the mother throughout her labor and birth. It has been shown that the reassurances provided by this person make labor easier, and that the easier the labor and delivery, the more readily the mother will accept her newborn infant. I like the flexibility of their suggestion—that the presence of any of a number of people can be valuable. So often only the husband is recommended. I myself didn't want my husband to be present. For me, it would have been one more thing to be worried about—worried that I would be worrying him —and I just didn't want to have to think about that. It is often not realized that it can be very difficult to watch a delivery. To each her own, of course; many women, for reasons as valid as mine, prefer their husbands' presence.

While I do not regret that my husband was not with me in the delivery room, I ache with regret that my infants were not with me after my deliveries. I was awake; I would have liked that. It was an opportunity forever lost, an experience missed amid the modern sterility of the standard hospital delivery. Without doubt, hospitals are nice places if you are in need of emergency care, but relatively speaking, there are few births which require such care. Women and their babies have probably lost far more than they have gained in hospitals. Jimmy Carter, I recently heard, is the first United States President to be born in a hospital. Is this a mark of progress or a sign of our ignorance? I myself am not sure. Klaus and Kennell, like most doctors, certainly do not advocate home births. Rather they prefer to change hospital policies, providing in so doing the best of two worlds—the best of medical care and, at the same time, many of the amenities of a home birth, but within the hospital setting. The concept is great, but with institutions as stagnant and incorrigible as they so often are, Utopia may, for most of us, be long in coming.

Klaus and Kennell have recently begun to study home births using video tape recordings and films, and drawing on the wide experience of midwives such as Raven Lang, who has herself written a book on the subject. In contrast to women who deliver in hospitals, women giving birth at home appear to be in control during labor and, after giving birth, are in an exuberant, ecstatic state, as are the onlookers. The new mother picks up her baby immediately and within minutes puts him to breast. Just how universal this pattern for the home birth will prove to be needs more investigation. A woman wanting a home birth may be more maternally inclined to begin with. There might be other factors, too, as pediatrician T. Berry Brazelton's perceptive comments indicate:

> In many other cultures the first 30 minutes after birth are devoted to the mother herself. She seems to need and prefer a recovery period of her own before she becomes interested in the infant. This makes a good deal of sense and I think the ecstasies we see may in larger part be related to her relief at having finally made it to the other end of labor. This euphoria can certainly be mobilized to attach to the infant, and in American culture, where so many roadblocks have been institutionalized, mothers who are experiencing home births may be demonstrating behaviors that are signs of relief at having their autonomy intact.

There may, however, be more to it than that. All animals show excitement at parturition. Cats, for example, become very active just before giving birth—they roll about, lick themselves and make rapid circling movements—all of which indicate a high level of excitement, say researchers. Once the kittens are delivered, the mother noses and licks them, and characteristically encircles them between her legs. Even birds appear to be excited when their eggs hatch. The parent bird may sit on the nest's rim to watch as hatching proceeds. At times, the parent may call to its youngsters in low, encouraging notes. A female gray-cheeked thrush sang continuously as one of her eggs hatched—"evidently an emotional response to the event" says famed ornithologist Alexander Skutch. Rather than an anomaly, ecstasy during birth may well be our heritage denied us by the trappings of culture.

No matter what the setting, home or hospital, the precious importance of early intimacy between the mother and her infant is now well documented. Nor should fathers be excluded. Although most studies of this sensitive period have dealt solely with the mother and her infant, fathers are beginning at last to receive some attention. In a recent study, fathers became far more actively engaged in care-giving during their infants' first three months when asked to undress their infants twice and to establish eye-to-eye contact with them during the first three days of life. The male of the species has, perhaps as much as the female, been caged in superimposed roles not of his own choosing. Listen to Margaret Mead's intriguing commentary:

> No developing society that needs men to leave home and do their thing for society ever allows young men in to handle or touch their newborns. There's always a taboo against it. For they know somewhere that, if they did, the new fathers would become so "hooked" that they would never get out and do their "thing" properly.

I'm sure, in the days ahead, we will hear much more about the expanding role of fathers. Their time, too, is coming. While women are beginning to share the challenges of the marketplace with men, men in turn are beginning to share more fully in the equally challenging tasks of parenting.

Klaus and Kennell make several additional recommendations regarding the immediate post-delivery period. To enhance the important eye-to-eye contact between infant and mother, they would delay eye medication until after the mother has had an extended period of time with her infant in the first hour after birth.

They also suggest a period of privacy for the mother, father, and infant as soon as the placenta is delivered and the episiotomy, if performed, is sutured—all of which can be done within fifteen minutes at most. (Regarding episiotomies, it is Rossi's opinion that foot stirrups cause the perineal tissue to be stretched, thereby giving physicians their justification for performing the routine episiotomies, which would not otherwise be necessary. Klaus and Kennell question the effect of episiotomies on the "comfort, mobility, and ability of the mother to care for her baby.") In their own practice, pediatricians Klaus and Kennell place a heat panel over the infant and instruct the mother not to cover him. She is also encouraged to hold him against her bare chest. During this time of intimacy, lasting perhaps thirty to forty-five minutes, the new family unit can be formed, encompassing the long-awaited infant. In the days ahead, continued close contact between mother and infant is made possible through rooming-in arrangements, and liberal visitation policies allow father and siblings to maintain close relations with the mother.

It does not take much perception to note that most of these recommendations are simply aimed at the restoration of a natural arrangement of immense wisdom—an arrangement whose value was not even envisioned by us until recently, despite all our technology and affluence and sophistication. We should have known, of course, for it is of most ancient lineage, as old perhaps as the first Archaeopteryx with its brand-new feathers skimming over the tropical lagoons of long-ago Bavaria, as old probably as the first small mammals scurrying beneath the feet of dinosaurs. Of imprinting in birds and mammals, we have long been aware. But, as if we are still unconsciously at odds with Darwin's nineteenth-century discoveries, we fail to take note that these are our own ancient bloodlines.

There is even, when you stop to think about it, a much greater need for close bonding between the human infant and mother than in most other mammalian species. Our infants are, after all, exceedingly immature in so many ways. This has been partially due to our evolutionary switch to an upright posture and the increase in our infants' brain size without a corresponding increase in our pelvic capacity and our birth canal elasticity. It is consequently, as Rossi has commented, "more critical to the survival of the human infant than to any other species to provide for prolonged infant care through intense attachment of the mother and infant."

Taking such an evolutionary view, one is saddened at the current demoralization of motherhood. Mothering has reached its pinnacle of development in the human species, largely as a result of our marked intellectual capacities, and yet it is so frequently dismissed as demeaning by radical feminists. One wonders whether women are not, some of them, taking on the very male mentality they so often criticize.

Males, it must be remembered, are limited to only one form of interpersonal reproductive behavior—sexual intercourse, while females have at least three—sexual intercourse, birth-giving, and nursing. Of these three, however, the female's role in intercourse has received most attention, perhaps because of its significance to adult men. Consider one very obvious example of this—the female breast, with its dual function in both maternal and sexual contexts. It is currently far more acceptable to display the breast sexually than to display it in the maternal act of nursing. Have we not let masculine interests interfere with our priorities? (Changes on this score are hopefully in the offing. Topless swimsuits are now being worn by women on the beaches of France. The sight of female breasts, as a result, may soon become so commonplace, so respectable, so natural that women will feel free to use them as nature intended.)

And what of our patterns of parenting? The male prerogative has been to emphasize his work, relegating home and family to secondary status. Must women do likewise to be fulfilled? Alice Rossi has wondered. "It is not at all clear," she states, "what the gains will be either for women or children in this version of human liberation."

It takes a good deal of ability and assertiveness for a woman to achieve her rightful equality in the marketplace. But she needs comparable skills to maximize her reproductive experience. Studies have shown the interrelatedness of good sexual adjustment, enjoyment of pregnancy, low incidence of nausea during pregnancy, short and easy labor, desire for and success in breast-feeding, and the preference for little or no drugs during childbirth. This composite of characteristics does not fit the stereotype of the traditional submissive woman. On the contrary, it takes much independence and assertiveness for today's woman to achieve sexual and maternal fulfillment. Impediments, both masculine and medical, have too often stood in the way.

Such women, desirous of maternal as well as sexual and intellectual fulfillment, have not yet emerged sufficiently in the feminist movement. But when they do, the movement will achieve the balance it needs to be truly representative of the full gamut of female interests. And its ranks, doubtless, will swell accordingly.

(7) A Question of Balance

There is no animal more invincible than a woman, nor fire either, nor any wildcat so ruthless.

Aristophanes

1

ONCE, IN A Malaysian jungle, zoologist George Schaller and his guide came upon a female orangutan and her large infant feeding on green fruit high in the forest canopy. Plainly unhappy with the intrusion, the ape mother leaned over, snatched up her infant, and fled from tree to tree. When the men still followed, she grew extremely agitated and kissed the knuckles of her hands loudly and made burping and gulping sounds several times in succession. "Then," Schaller says, "she peered down at us from a height of 100 feet, a shaggy almost grotesque creature, black against the evening sky. Over a period of fifteen minutes, she ripped off twigs and branches and hurled them at us. Several times she swung a branch like a large pendulum and at the peak of the arc closest to me she released it . . . with the branches crashing down around me I had to jump nimbly at times to escape being hit."

That a primate mother, or any other, will defend her young

with all the ferocity and strength and cunning at her disposal is, of course, hardly a revolutionary discovery. The literature of animal lore is filled with such tales. And even had I not heard of them, I would have known. For I too am a mother and I too at times feel a fierce protectiveness akin to Schaller's orangutan. No, I have not faced any potentially murder-minded predator. The dangers of civilization are usually far subtler, and so are a mother's modes of defense. For me, in years past, there were cars and medicines and paints and tools and knives and sharp-edged furniture—seemingly all of the endless paraphernalia of modern life from which to protect my witless, uncoordinated and uninhibited youngsters. That they survived past age five still seems to me one of life's minor miracles. And the animal mother's bout with an occasional predator, while momentarily more violent, seems in the long run infinitely easier. My children are growing now and so are my concerns. How will I protect them from drugs and venereal disease and sexual deviants and auto accidents and alcohol? How will I ever, in the inflationary havoc of our times, put them through college so they won't have to go it alone as I once did? I want everything for my children. Everything I didn't have and more. And I know without doubt that I would beg, borrow, or steal, as well as lie, cheat, and even prostitute myself if sufficiently driven for the needs of my children. Wouldn't most any mother?

Interestingly, women who are extremely passive-dependent show aggression *only* in defense of their children. Some communes, especially those associated with the drug culture, have attracted women who are unusually passive and dependent. These young women, as described in one study of an East Coast urban commune, "drifted in a passive way into a dependent relationship with a boy," and were "remarkably undemanding, seemingly unresentful, and tractable to their partners' whims." But motherhood brought remarkable behavioral changes: "Though these girls could not demand for themselves, they could demand for their children." One of the young mothers, Maryann, was a case in point. "Only once, when it appeared that Edsel might have abused the baby did we see Maryann become enraged and protective of her infant." Then there was Carla:

Warm but firm with the babies and at the same time fiercely
protective of them, Carla could and did suppress her rage with
Eric's inadequacies as provider and partner; in fact a row culminating in the necessity for five stitches in her scalp found her accepting
even this, but his inability to provide the necessary immunizations
roused her to an abusive rage. Her sense of responsibility for the
children was the prime motivating factor in her leaving Eric
. . .

The sharing of children in communes can also create emotional
difficulties for many mothers. Often, these mothers come to reserve for themselves the right to protect and punish their youngsters. Studies of urban middle class communes indicate that only
rarely will a mother allow a male communal member to discipline
her children and then only with her express permission.

Mothers have always been fiercely protective of their young.
The human mother and her orangutan counterpart are one in
this, and one with a multiplicity of species. The hen, the elephant
matriarch, the cow moose, as well as mothers among monkeys and
mice, among grizzlies and voles, among elk and elands, rats and
rhinos, gazelles and zebras—all of us will defend our youngsters
to the death if need be. And this has happened.

In Ontario, a biologist reported finding the fresh carcass of a
female wolf near her den of pups. Eleven of her ribs had been
broken, as were two of her neck vertebrae. The culprit was most
likely a black bear, since hairs from this species were found near
the den entrance. Hans Kruuk once saw a wildebeest cow killed
while she tried to defend her calf against a pack of twenty-one
wild dogs. And this is an animal which only very rarely acts in its
own personal defense. Like the commune mother, a wildebeest
female is regularly aggressive only on behalf of her babies.

Although sometimes killed, mothers often seem endowed with
invincible strength and extraordinary savagery in fending off enemies from their young. With ears laid back and eyes rolling, a cow
moose will attack any intruder, even a big bull moose, and will
pursue the culprit for long distances. Margaret Altmann saw a
cow moose swim after a bypassing horse who was headed toward
the island on which she grazed with her calf. In the water battle

which followed, the horse was seriously beaten and only with great effort did it manage, finally, to stagger ashore. Another enraged cow moose attacked a bear who was carrying off her calf. Pouncing upon the bear with her front hooves, the cow moose wounded it severely and was able to retrieve her youngster.

Among some races of rabbits, a mother will fearlessly assault any lab attendant. She will lay back her ears, stamp her feet, and viciously bite and kick, despite the overwhelming size differential between her and the offender. Female mice, several days before birth, may be so aggressive that they will kill any males unable to escape their savage attacks. After the birth of litters in laboratory situations, these females often ferociously attack forceps placed close to their nests. The most aggressive will cling so firmly with their teeth to the forceps that they can be lifted from the nest by picking up the forceps. Others, of a different subspecies, seem relatively nonchalant about forceps, but become "unrelenting tigresses" toward strange males. They continue their attacks even after the males show complete submission, and the males, soon finding their submissive postures totally ineffective, leap wildly about, doing their best to dodge the females' vicious onslaughts.

Female voles, rodents related to mice, will attack any animals that come near the nest, including individuals that were previously dominant. The prairie dog, a colonial rodent, usually lives in communal burrows housing up to two males and five females with their offspring. But during the breeding season, a mother with young pups will seal off part of a burrow and defend it against all comers.

A female rat will attack any alien male entering her nesting area and will invariably succeed in driving him away. She is just as aggressive, however, in other contexts. Although rats of both sexes are normally nonviolent, under unnatural lab set-ups, they can become barbarous. In one study, strange rats from different areas were introduced into one enclosure. The rats soon started to settle in and establish territories; simultaneously, female-male pair formation took place. In the warring which ensued, the females of the species became especially cunning and ruthless, such that Konrad Lorenz referred to them as "veritable murder specialists." These female rats would stealthily slink up to a victim and then suddenly pounce upon it in a deadly attack, often severing an artery in its neck. In seconds, the fight was over and the victim soon died of massive internal hemorrhaging. Here, of course, was no maternal aggression; no youngster was present. But the establishment of territory was certainly a prerequisite for motherhood. Eventually, after one rat pair had eliminated all other rivals, they set about building a family with equal energy. And the "family spirit" of this growing rat pack, marked by great tenderness and tolerance, stood in incredible contrast to its ruthless prelude.

Among species in which maternal aggression is particularly well developed, the grizzly bear is one animal so powerful and unpredictable that it scares almost everyone. Any visitor to our western mountains is warned of this fearsome carnivore and, of all grizzlies, a sow with cubs is most dangerous. She is, in fact, responsible for a full 82 percent of all bear attacks on hikers and campers in the national parks of Canada and the United States. Come between her and her young ones, and your life is at stake.

For her size, a hen or a goose is probably just as aggressive as the grizzly, attacking anything that comes too near her chicks or goslings. Many other birds, however, more vulnerable perhaps than these hardy souls, have developed subtler means of dealing with danger. Rachel Carson tells of Silverbar, a young hen sanderling, who cleverly diverted a polar fox from finding her nest of newly hatched chicks. Silverbar flew first to willows up in a ravine away from her nest. When the fox started up the ravine,

> the sanderling fluttered toward him, tumbling to the ground as though hurt, flapping her wings, creeping over the gravel. All the while she uttered a high-pitched note like the cry of her own young. The fox rushed at her. Silverbar rose rapidly into the air and flew over the crest of the ridge, only to reappear from another quarter, tantalizing the fox into following her. So by degrees she led him over the ridge and southward into a marshy bottom fed by the overflow of upland streams.

In a similar way, a lapwing was seen to decoy a weasel four hundred yards away from her young and a female stone curlew was able to successfully lure a retriever from her nest.

I myself have often watched a killdeer use such diversionary tactics. Shrieking, beating the earth with her wings, flashing her tawny rump, the killdeer dramatically feigns injury in her attempts to lead you farther and farther from her nest. The common nighthawk also puts on a broken-wing act. Flushing at the approach of an intruder, she settles in a spot away from the nest. There, she limps along, rocking from side to side, with drooping, quivering wings. If the enemy fails to follow, says one naturalist, "she may fall across the top of a low stump or rock and lie there as if at her last gasp with head down and one wing hanging as if broken, meantime uttering doleful cries, while the young lie flat and motionless." Around hatching time, however, the nighthawk is far bolder and she will rush, hissing, at an intruder, her great mouth wide open and conspicuous with its pink-to-red lining.

Distraction behavior is also found among mammalian species. It was in this way, as you may recall, that the macaque mothers, Red Witch and Old Female–1, protected their sons from dominant males. The mother gazelle will try to distract the hyenas' attention from her fawn by running between the two, often very close to the hyenas, keeping just out of reach of their fangs. If an elk mother is disturbed, she creates a distraction by breaking noisily into flight away from the calf's hiding place.

Along with diversions like these, mammalian mothers often group together for defense. Hans Kruuk has seen up to four female gazelles try to distract the attention of hyenas from the same fawn. In an elk nursery group, the lead cow noisily breaks into flight and then turns toward the intruder, while other females quickly and quietly lead the calves to safety. Vervet mothers, as we've seen, join together to attack males who frighten their infants, and elephant females form phalanxes about their youngsters in the face of predators. Phyllis Jay reports that if a male langur scares an infant, "the mother instantly threatens, chases, and often slaps the male. Other adult females near the infant may join the mother and chase the male as far as 25 yards." Female langurs will also battle together, although seldom successfully, against an invading male intent on infanticide. Eland cows cooperate in defense of their calves. Kruuk reports that, upon seeing a calf chased by hyenas, "female eland came running up . . . from all directions, attacking the hyenas and chasing them in all directions and over long distances."

I could go on. Maternal aggression is commonly found, as well, in chimpanzees and baboons, in squirrels and snowshoe hares, in sheep, weasels, cats and many other animals. It is a passionate, poignant phenomenon found abundantly throughout the natural world. Harry F. Harlow once said, "The aggressiveness of any male could not surpass maternal aggression when the life or safety of her young is threatened. Such behavior is adaptive for the survival of both the individual and the species." He was speaking primarily of the monkeys he has so long studied, but it could equally be said of many a species.

Sometimes, however, this same wonderful, essential, adaptive instinct goes awry and its seething energy becomes appallingly misdirected. A mouse will eat her litter; a gorilla will murder its newborn; a human mother will abuse her helpless infant. Why?

<h1 style="text-align:center">2</h1>

WE DON'T KNOW all the reasons for maternal malfunctioning. Sometimes we don't know any, for certain. Amazingly, we don't even know about mice, among whom mothers will not infrequently kill and cannibalize their young. Yet these hapless creatures have been shocked, injected, traumatized, isolated, trained, domesticated, bred, and observed perhaps more than any other test animal. You'd think we would know everything about these mothers. In one laboratory, however, 93 of 278 litters were killed and eaten—and no one is sure why. There is some reason to believe that such cannibalism is genetic; some, that it is induced by an abnormal balance of hormones. But still scientists are not certain.

Among wild deermice, under natural conditions, there is almost no evidence of such maternal aberrations. Under laboratory confinement, however, with its day-to-day disturbances of cleaning cages, feeding, inspecting the litters, and experimental testing, deermice can, like other lab mice, be driven to desertion and cannibalism. Often, too, young deermice are found with sores and scabs caused by the mother's teeth as she holds them in her mouth and jumps about the cage. Seen especially when the young are frequently removed from the mother, this behavior is thought to result from a desire to relocate her litter. These observations suggest, of course, the dangers of tinkering with natural ways worked out through long, long years of evolutionary trial and error. It has been bad for mice and, as I have already intimated in the last chapter and shall show even more clearly in the course of this one, it has been bad for us.

In some circumstances, scientists are pretty sure that cannibalism among caged rodents is simply a mistake. At the birth of her young, a mammalian mother usually bites off the umbilical cord, eats the placenta and licks her offspring. When disturbed, however, a rodent mother may eat her babies, too, by accident. "This," says zoologist Cloudsley-Thompson, "is the explanation of the domestic tragedies that sometimes occur with tame rats or hamsters."

The cause of cannibalism in tree shrews is also well known— the mother simply can't stand the smell of her infants' urine. In the wild, a female tree shrew leaves her infants alone for the most part, helpless in the nest, and comes back only for a quick few minutes of nursing every forty-eight hours. If however she is forced to stay too close to those smelly babes of hers, she will kill and eat them.

Among several bird species, food problems can cause cannibalism. When mice are scarce, the tawny owl will eat her young, starting with the smallest. This obviously has adaptive value, for the eldest nestling is thus more likely to survive. Buzzards, bullfinches, and kestrels are also inclined to cannibalism when food supplies run low.

Turkeys taught us something important about maternal aggression. A turkey hen, while brooding her eggs, is highly irritable and will attack almost everything that moves. And the nearer the approach to her nest, the more belligerent she becomes. As her chicks are about to hatch, her aggression soars to boiling point. Yet her chicks, which are also living, moving creatures, are not attacked by the turkey hen. What stops her? Experiments with deaf hens have given us the answer in a dramatic and unexpected way. Deaf turkey hens peck their chicks to death as soon as they hatch. Unable to hear the distinctive crying of their chicks, the hens do not recognize them and consequently, the hens attack these "strange" moving objects as they would anything else. Further experiments with normal-hearing turkey hens have confirmed this, for they will peck natural-looking but silent model chicks as furiously as will the deaf turkeys. But if the model chick also cries like a live turkey chick, the hen will immediately begin to utter call notes and will take it under her wing as if it were her own. Looks matter little to the hen. The polecat, which resembles a weasel, is a natural predator of the turkey and its presence normally would invoke furious attack. But build a model of this animal and equip it so that it cheeps like a turkey chick, and the turkey hen will be instantly solicitous, her aggression immediately inhibited.

The turkey hen walks an emotional tightrope. She must be always alert, edgy, full of nervous deadly energy, ready any and every moment to murderously attack nest enemies. Yet at the same time she must not harm her own. And nature, in superb simplicity, has endowed the turkey hen with the wherewithal to perform this tightrope act with the greatest of ease. Along with her goodly capacity for aggression has developed a mechanism for its inhibition, triggered solely by the chirping of her chicks. And it is an ingenious mechanism of no mean accomplishment, for it works under the vast majority of circumstances in which a mother turkey might find herself.

Obviously, the fact that a mother does not usually attack her young is not to be taken for granted. As Konrad Lorenz has said, this "has to be ensured in every single species by a special inhibition such as the one we have learned about in the turkey hen." Young mice, like turkey chicks, make sounds—ultrasonic calls that we ourselves cannot hear—and their sounds serve to "prime" the maternal behavior of the mother and may be equally effective in inhibiting her aggression. Slight disturbances, unfortunately, can sometimes break down such inhibiting mechanisms. Konrad Lorenz tells of the tragedy which occurred when an airplane flew low over a silver-fox farm, causing all the mother vixens to devour their young.

Many species are more visually oriented than turkeys and mice, and their young are protected in colorful ways, literally, from adult aggression. In the water rail, baby birds sport red caps that inhibit chick-biting in their elders. Kittiwake nestlings, in turning their beaks away to appease strange adults, reveal a characteristic color pattern on their necks. Against the white background is a distinctive dark marking, the total effect of which prevents adults from attacking. Juvenile night herons wear a striped plumage that elicits much less aggression from adults than does the plumage of a mature bird.

Babyish behavior also serves to protect the young in many species. The young heron begs and flaps its wings and tries to "milk" the beak of any territorial adults that come near. As long as the youngster continues to act in this infantile manner, it is absolutely safe from attack. Similarly, an eagle nestling must be able to beg for food, if it is to escape being harmed by the parent bird. If too weak or too hungry to do so, the young eagle may be ignored and trampled, or worse, it will be considered as prey and be promptly eaten.

Herring gull chicks must learn to duck their heads to avoid threatening their parents, who can otherwise easily mistake their young for other adults. Young dogs, as Lorenz points out, utilize a comparable gesture. Approached by a threatening adult, a puppy will throw himself on his back, exposing his hairless baby belly—a sure sign that he is too young to be a rival. At the same time, for good measure, he trickles out a few drops of urine, which further assures the adult that he's merely a youngster.

Often pet dogs and cats can be as indulgent toward human toddlers as they are toward youngsters of their own species. My sister's one-year-old Jenny could pull the tail of the family cat, jostle him about, and aggravate him in any number of ways, without so much as a nip or a scratch. If put upon too much, the cat would simply run off and hide. Adults, on the other hand, were never allowed to perpetrate such indignities. The cat, my sister was convinced, somehow realized that little Jenny was just a baby.

Infantile behavior, special coloration, distinctive vocalizations —all these can serve to protect a young animal from attack. Nature also works in more subtle ways and infants often simply look so appealing that parents (and other adults as well) just can't resist them. Usually such infantile attractiveness is designed primarily to elicit care-taking behavior on the part of parents. But, of course, in doing so, it simultaneously precludes parental aggression. Among many bird species, nestlings have gaudy mouth linings and when they gape, their parents are irresistibly compelled to regurgitate food for them. As always, there are a few species that have taken nature's hint and gone to the hilt with it. The desert horned lark, for instance, has jet-black blotches and bars on its tongue in Halloween contrast to the vivid orange of its palate. The young crested coua of Madagascar has two raised "bull's eyes" on the roof of its mouth ringed in circles of vivid red and glistening white. Here certainly is a mouth no mother could miss! The palate of a young bearded tit resembles some neon-light extravaganza: a brilliant carnelian-red is accentuated by rows of glistening white conical processes. Nestlings of one of the oriental parrot finches, the Gouldian finch, literally light the way for their parents. In addition to characteristic black markings on tongue and palate, these young birds boast what are called "reflection pearls" in the angles at the sides of their beaks. These pearls, in brilliantly opalescent greens and blues, glow like little lamps and help to guide parents in the gloom of the covered nest. All these lavish colors and structures are designed solely to impress the parent bird—for in the economy of nature, they disappear entirely when the youngsters reach maturity.

Among many primates, infants have characteristic colors that adults find adorable. Baboons, brown as adults, have black babies with pink faces and ears. This infantile coloration stirs strong maternal feelings in females, as well as fiercely protective reactions in males. Later, as the baby's face darkens and its coat changes from black to brown, the mother's interest gradually wanes, although adult males remain strongly protective. Finally, at ten months, the baboon has the coloring of an adult, leaves its mother, and makes its own way among its peers. A baby rhesus is dull brown just like adults of the species, except for a special pink parting to its hair which females seem to find most attractive. A baby langur is born with a dark-brown coat of hair, distinctively different from the light gray of adults, and immediately upon birth becomes the focus of interest for all the older females in the troop. Intensely curious, they gather around the mother and line up, eagerly awaiting a chance to hold it. But the infant's moment of glory is as short-lived as its brown coloration. During its fourth and fifth months, as the youngster slowly assumes the gray coat of adulthood, it likewise gradually loses its special appeal to adult females. Infantile coloration is similarly distinctive among many other primate species. The black-and-white colobus has white babies, the light-gray vervet has black babies, while the dark-skinned chimpanzee has fair-complexioned infants.

Babies are usually shaped differently, too, than adults. As Konrad Lorenz has noted, they have relatively large heads, big eyes, chubby cheeks, small noses and chins, and short legs—all of

(After K. Lorenz. *Studies in Animal and Human Behaviour.*)

which give them a loveable, cuddly appearance. This is true of human infants, as well as baby monkeys, baby birds, baby fish, baby dogs, and even artificially babified dogs like the Pekinese. And they all look especially cute to us humans. Indeed, the "cute response" serves to elicit parental care responses in humans and probably in other vertebrates as well.

Beatrice T. Gardner and Lise Wallach became interested in this so-called cute response. They knew that there are a number of seabirds and shorebirds that prefer certain exaggerated, larger-than-life models over otherwise comparable natural objects. Many such birds, for example, will choose to incubate an oversized artificial egg rather than their own more moderately proportioned productions. Or they will choose artificial eggs with larger, darker spots rather than those of more modest natural coloration. Or again, they will choose a clutch with more eggs rather than one of more limited natural numbers. Similarly, a herring gull chick will prefer to peck at a larger redder beak than its parent could possibly possess.

The experimenters wondered if we humans might respond similarly to the babyish look we find so appealing. They made silhouettes of baby heads, ranging from those of real babies to those they called "super babies," which had even larger foreheads and smaller chins. They also made a similar series of silhouettes of adult heads, exaggerating, in the "super adult," the tendency toward a receding forehead and a protuberant chin found in the mature human being. The researchers presented these silhouettes to college women and men, asking them to choose which ones looked most babyish. The students, especially the women, consistently chose a super baby head over that of a normal baby, as well as over any of the adult heads.

Like the seabird drawn to an egg of unreal size, we humans are drawn to an exaggerated caricature of an infant, finding it more cute, more babyish, more real than reality itself. We may be more than birds, more than monkeys, but we have added on and built upon; we have not rebuilt from scratch. We may have lost tails and outsize canines and most of our hair, and along with these, certain behavioral patterns as well. But we are not isolated products of some "special creation." We share, rather, a bit of all that went before us from algae and ants to gulls and gibbons. And among the things we share is this special attraction for our own offspring, though it is an attraction nonetheless unique for each of us, each species. While the lark and the coua may be mesmerized by the gaudy gape of their offspring, while monkeys may be moved by the charming coloration of their little ones, we ourselves are touched by the cute and cuddly shape of our infants. And there is also, for us, the magnetism of eye-to-eye contact, as mentioned in an earlier chapter.

The importance of these visual attractions between the human infant and parent becomes especially evident in their absence. A blind mother, unable to see her infant, must learn to substitute other sensual modes, commonly the auditory, in her interactions with her infant. That she can do this is due, of course, to the great flexibility and easy adaptability of our species. In this, we have progressed further than deaf turkeys, who have no alternative but to peck away at their seemingly silent chicks. Happily, we are not programmed so tightly, so predictably as that. And it is this very lack of ultra-specialized, immutable responses, together with our unmatched ability to learn and adapt to new circumstances, new climates, new foods, new ways of thinking and living and loving, that have constituted the genius of humankind and have allowed us to become the most dominant and widespread mammalian species the earth has ever known.

Our blind, fortunately, can learn in novel ways to respond to their infants. But there is another side to this. Just as our mode of maternalism is not irrevocably programmed, neither is our aggression completely controlled. When the puppy rolls over, the adult dog simply cannot strike. But we humans can and do abuse our infants. Their lovable looks and fragile vulnerability are not always enough to stay us.

3

AT A RECENT conference, Dr. C. Henry Kempe, a pioneer researcher in the field of child abuse, stated that there are 380 cases of reported child abuse per million people in the United States each year. And at least two thousand of the children concerned die each year as a result of their injuries. Whether such abuse is actually increasing, or increasingly reported, is debatable—but either way, children, many of them, are suffering.

And who are the abusers? They are more often mothers than fathers, which is not surprising since the care of children still falls overwhelmingly on women. The most severe injuries, in fact, are inflicted by women, especially young single women. None of us, however, is immune to the feelings that lead these desperate women to batter their youngsters. Even so civilized a woman as Margaret Mead recalled that,

> . . . once when she (an infant daughter) raged, I found myself stamping my foot in the kind of blind responsive rage a mother can feel when her child screams unappeased. I caught it, realized what it was. Experienced only once, it was enough to make me recognize what lies back of the desperation of a young mother, innocent of all knowledge of babies, who feels that she will never be able to cope with her baby and goes into a postpartum depression.

Among those especially vulnerable to such destructive feelings are mothers who were separated from their newborn infants. As described earlier, these mothers are often less affectionate, less communicative, less confident, and less successful than other mothers. Now I must report a far grimmer side to the story. According to Dr. Kempe, early separation due to the illness of either the infant or mother can lead to abuse. Infant prematurity is another common reason for early separation and, sadly, a disproportionately high number of prematures are found among both battered children and among children with the failure-to-thrive syndrome. (According to Drs. Klaus and Kennell: "Failure to thrive without organic disease is a syndrome in which the infant does not grow, gain weight, or develop behaviorally at a normal rate during the first few months at home. Such infants show rapid gains in all aspects of development when given only routine hospital care.") Although only about seven to eight percent of live births are premature each year, between 23 and 31 percent of battered infants are prematures, as are 25 to 41 percent of those infants who fail to thrive. Unconsciousness during delivery also seems to take its toll. A tenfold increase in child abuse has been reported after delivery by Caesarian section as compared with normal deliveries.

Even relatively short-lived and mild illnesses in the newborn appear to affect the relationship between a mother and infant. Typical minor problems include mild jaundice, slow feeding, and mild respiratory illnesses requiring incubator care during the infant's first twenty-four hours. The mother's behavior in such cases is often disturbed for an incredibly long period of time—an entire year and even longer—despite the fact that her baby's condition is completely cleared up before discharge. Here again is impressive evidence for the importance of close contact in the first few hours after childbirth.

In Russia, child battering is completely denied, but then so is wife battering, which is known to exist. Russian physicians, however, believe they have good reason to doubt the former. Russian women, they explain, are permitted unlimited abortions. Moreover, if a woman does not want her infant, she can place him in an infant house, where he is cared for until his third year. These mothers usually visit their babies once or twice a week. Marshall Klaus looked into the admission rates for full-term and premature infants in several of these infant houses. As might be suspected from all that is now known of maternal bonding, Klaus found that premature infants were represented in numbers out of proportion to their distribution in the total infant population. The percentage of prematures in these infant houses was eight to ten times greater than the percentage of infants delivered prematurely. Once a child is three years old, a Russian mother must decide either to put him up for adoption or to take the child home. Again, predictably, mothers of prematures opt for adoption twice as often as mothers of full-term infants. Dr. Klaus came to the conclusion that the "Russians also have problems with maternal attachment when infants are born prematurely."

There is another aspect of maternal bonding that has special import for mothers of twins. Often, the larger of a set of twins will be discharged from the hospital nursery earlier than the smaller one, who is left there to grow. Follow-up studies suggest that mothers have a much more difficult time adjusting to this second infant than to the first. In Lausanne, Switzerland, three sets of mothers with twins were observed for a short period. In each case, the larger twin was discharged before the smaller. Within three months, two of the smaller twins were returned: one had been battered, the other failed to thrive. The mother of one of these unlucky children felt that her larger twin was hers, but not the smaller one. Drs. Klaus and Kennell discovered similar problems among mothers of twins with whom they worked. The doctors believe that these observations illustrate a basic principle of maternal bonding—that a mother can become closely attached to only one infant at a time. Interestingly, this may explain why mothers of twins tend to dress the two children alike.

Monotropy, as this principle has been labeled, is seen also among nurses who work with infants. In premature nurseries at Case Western Reserve's University Hospital, each nurse has been found to have a favorite infant. Although she usually likes other babies, at any one time she is especially attached to only one and will feel a real loss for several days after this infant leaves the nursery with its mother. At Madera, a large adoption home in Greece, nurses live on the grounds with infants who will be placed in adoptive homes at the age of four to five months. Here, too, each nurse becomes closely attached to a favorite and her grieving after the infant is adopted is even more prolonged, lasting from four to six months, and is similar to mourning responses that follow the death of a close relative. Although three thousand infants have been raised at Madera, no nurse has ever become attached to more than one infant at a time.

It hardly seems necessary to spell out the obvious implications of our new knowledge of maternal bonding upon the problems of child abuse. Insofar as it is possible, twins should be dismissed together to minimize the problems that can result from a mother's preference of one over the other. Regarding premature infants, more liberal visitation policies must be permitted in hospital nurseries so that parents, particularly mothers, do not suffer from the complex problems of early separation. Klaus and Kennell report great strides in the medical treatment of the premature infant that should permit this on an ever wider scale. Moreover, they refer to a recent "burst of studies of infant stimulation" that show the importance of mothering to the well-being of the baby. If the premature infant is stimulated by being cuddled, touched, rocked, or fondled daily during his stay in the hospital nursery, he has fewer breathing problems, gains more weight, and advances faster in certain other areas. Even more important, if his mother is allowed to nurture him each day in this manner, she is bound to become more deeply attached to him and less prone to abuse him.

It is good that at long last we are learning some of the biological bases of our behavior. But it is also frightening to me, frightening that it took so long. I have two children and never did it cross my mind that it might have been beneficial, especially for me, to hold them in their first hours. Never did it occur to me that I might have had more patience with them, and more joy, more affection, more empathy with them—or would have had more with less effort, less strain—had I been able merely to cuddle them in those precious early hours.

What else do we not know? What remains to be discovered, lying yet hidden behind the facade of our modern sophistication? Are we missing something, something else yet? Are we today trampling over our essential biological selves, just as we are trampling our endangered plants and wasting our last whales and elephants and eagles?

4

ABUSED CHILDREN ARE likely to become abusive parents. This is widely acknowledged by doctors, sociologists, and abusive parents themselves.

Among rhesus monkeys, brutally reared youngsters also become hyper-aggressive in maturity. This is true not only of rhesus youngsters raised by mothers whose cruelty was due to early isolation (of which more will be said later), but also of youngsters whose wild-caught mothers were abusive for unknown reasons. During their first year, these young rhesus are extremely hostile with their peers. In adolescence and adulthood, they proceed to become ever more violent, even to the extent of murder.

Gary D. Mitchell, at one time a student of primatologist Harry F. Harlow, recorded the above observations on the rhesus. Besides the brutally reared rhesus, Mitchell also studied normally reared rhesus as "controls" by which he could make legitimate comparisons regarding the effects of the two styles of upbringing. In the end, Mitchell came up with a quite astonishing similarity between the two groups: *The total amount of hostile behavior in each group was nearly the same.* Nonetheless, there was one big difference and it lay in the way the two groups expressed their hostility. The normals were able to redirect their anger. Rather than hurt each other, they harassed the experimenter, shook their cages, or simply yawned away their negative feelings, as monkeys will do. The brutally reared group, however, were far more prone to attack one another, seemingly oblivious to the subtleties of redirection.

Past experience is important in the lives of many animals, as it is important in the lives of humans. Although instinctual predilections and imprinting mechanisms may play important roles, experience too, at least among mammals, is an ever-present, ever-prominent factor affecting behavior. And it has great bearing on how we, mouse or monkey, ape or human, care for our youngsters. Monkeys isolated in their early months from all other members of their species grow up to be out-and-out psychotics. They clutch themselves and rock back and forth in the corners of their cages, exhibiting behavior similar to that of human mental defectives. Sexually, these isolates are all but hopeless. The males try to mount from impossible angles, while the females refuse to be mounted in any manner.

But despite the lack of cooperation shown by such abnormal females, a considerable number can eventually be mated by very patient and persistent normal males. For the other abnormal females, experimenters sometimes arrange that they be more or less raped. The consequence of all this is the creation, as Harlow put it, of a "new kind of animal—the monkey motherless mother." Most of these mothers are supremely indifferent to their offspring; others are violently abusive. They will hesitate not at all to crush their infant's face to the floor, or chew off its feet and fingers, or, in one case, crush the infant's head like an eggshell between the teeth.

A few infants willing to endure incredible physical punishment manage to succeed in nursing, but it is unnerving to watch their desperate attempts to make contact with an abnormal mother. Here is how Harlow describes it:

> She would beat them and knock them down; they would come back and make contact; the mothers would rub their face into the floor; they would wriggle free and again attempt contact. The power, insistence, and demandingness of the infant to make contact and the punishment the infant would accept would make strong men reach the point that they could hardly bear to observe this unmaternal behavior.

Many infants, for their own safety and survival, must be removed from such brutal, insensitive mothers.

Some unmothered mothers, however, do show a limited amount of maternal behavior and a few also groom their infants a bit. Not much to speak of surely, and yet it is rather remarkable —for the isolation to which these mothers are subject as youngsters is far more extreme than would ever be permitted among humans. Variously arranged, such isolation often involves months, even a year of lonely living for the monkeys. But amazingly, despite this immense deprivation as infants, despite the fact that they never knew a living, loving mother of their own, these motherless monkeys are able to learn from their new experiences as adults. And with the arrival of the second and succeeding babies, their mothering becomes much improved.

Motherless chimpanzees are even more capable of changing their ways, even after several years of initial isolation. Behaviorally, chimps are more flexible than rhesus monkeys and as such, are better equipped to overcome the severe effects of early deprivation.

These early isolates are not the only ones to have a more difficult time with their first infants. A great many inexperienced, first-time animal mothers are not very good mothers and will ignore or even attack their newborns. Deermice, for instance, lose many more of their first litters than they do later ones. A deermouse mother will deal with an intruder in one of three ways. She may attack it, nose or groom it, or simply ignore it. Researchers found that mothers who either attack or ignore the intruder are significantly more likely to lose their first litter. The aggression of an attacking mother, it seems, may become directed mistakenly toward her own offspring. The passive mother, on the other hand, who ignores the intruder, may lose her own litter through neglect. Like the turkey we spoke of ealier, the deermouse mother must strike a delicate balance between the aggression she needs to protect her offspring and the gentleness she needs to mother them. Apparently, with later litters, deermice learn the trick, for no matter what their mode of dealing with an intruder, the loss of a litter becomes relatively rare.

In primates as in deermice, mothering takes know-how, and problems tend to occur especially among first-time captive mothers unfamiliar with infants and infant care. In the gibbon, the chimpanzee, and the gorilla, naive females are sometimes frightened by the very appearance of their own infants. When Achilles, a female gorilla at the zoo in Basel, Switzerland, gave birth to her first infant, she conscientiously tried to care for it. But because of her inexperience, she made no attempt to help the hungry infant find her nipple and the infant soon had to be removed to save its life. The second time around, Achilles was obviously less nervous and things went much better. Within a day, her newborn was nursing and Jambo, as the baby was named, continued to thrive in the months ahead, becoming the first gorilla infant to be successfully raised with its mother in captivity.

The animal psychologist Hediger once related the interesting case of a female chimpanzee who gave birth in captivity, but hadn't the least notion of how a baby should be carried. Instead of having the youngster sit on her back facing forward, she placed him facing her rump. It was awkward and apparently, she sensed something was wrong, but did nothing. Then, by chance, she happened to see another chimpanzee female who carried an infant in the correct manner, and immediately she switched her infant around in imitation.

Wild chimpanzees, while not quite so ignorant about mothering as captive ones, also improve with practice. Jane Goodall found that the infants of new mothers got into more "scrapes" than did youngsters of experienced mothers. Goblin was the firstborn of the young female chimpanzee, Melissa, and he was always finding himself in the thick of things. Once Goblin tottered into the path of a displaying male who dragged him like a branch along the ground. Melissa heroically rescued her infant, but was severely beaten for her interference. On another occasion, a fight broke out near Goblin, and Melissa rushed in to get him out of the line of battle, but she inadvertently grabbed the wrong infant. Fortunately for Goblin, a male chimpanzee came to his aid and protected him from attack.

For the most part, however, primates reared in the wild are quite competent at caring for their firstborn. The reason, it appears, is that they practice *before* they become mothers themselves, as "aunts" to the infants in their troop. (There are "uncles" too, incidentally, although they are not as common.) And there is evidence that they do, indeed, need the practice. Phyllis Jay saw seven female langurs drop infants through awkwardness. All of these females were young; at least four had not yet borne infants of their own. Similarly, female vervets seen carrying infants upside down or in other bizarre positions are inevitably immature "aunts." Among squirrel monkeys, juveniles may leave an infant dangling on a branch at the approach of danger, whereupon the mother will rush over to retrieve it.

The human female, no more than the monkey female, automatically grows up to be a supermom. She needs know-how and experience. But as families grow smaller, few teenage girls (or boys) will have a chance to learn to care for infants and young children at home. Moreover, our constant mobility, along with the demise of the extended family, lessens the opportunity for the passing down of family lore. To fill the void, we are inundated with multitudes of how-to books, books written by strangers to replace our lost traditions. Dr. Spock, of course, was one of the first of these and today, there are literally hundreds of child-care books written each year. In addition to these books, more courses on child care are offered today than ever before.

Lanie Carter of La Jolla, California, teaches such a course to expectant parents. She is a professional grandmother on the staff of a pediatric clinic. In addition to her classes, Carter visits each mother in the hospital the day after her child is born and again at home to answer any questions about feeding or bathing the infant. Later, parents may telephone her whenever they have questions on toilet training, on sibling rivalry, or on any of the many concerns new parents have.

Dr. Sarita Eastman, one of the La Jolla pediatricians, explains why she hired Mrs. Carter in this way:

> I started the service three years ago because I found that so many parents of newborns were tense and nervous. Although well educated, many of the couples had little knowledge of child care because they had never been around young children. They had lots of questions but were reluctant to "bother" us doctors because they didn't want to appear stupid. In the past, they would have gone to grandmother for answers, but in mobile California it seems that nobody has an extended family living nearby.

Other doctors have directed their energies toward helping the battering parent. Doctors Henry Kempe and Ray Helfer believe that since many such parents were beaten themselves as children, they most likely missed the mothering they needed to develop into loving and sympathetic parents. Dr. Helfer is convinced that it is not too late to make up for this past deprivation and he provides substitute "mothers" for parents in the Child Abuse Program at the University of Colorado Medical Center in Denver. These "mothers" are available at all times—for advice, for sympathy, and even for actual relief at times when the parent feels she or he can cope no longer.

Child abusers have also joined forces to help themselves. Parents Anonymous, based on the model of Alcoholics Anonymous, was started by a self-confessed child abuser in California. In addition, telephone hot lines have been set up in several metropolitan areas to help parents in emotional emergencies.

Books, courses, professional grandmothers, surrogate mothers, hotlines, Parents Anonymous—all are vitally needed by today's parents. For we humans cannot, like monkeys and mice, practice on our firstborn children in hopes that we'll do better the next time around. We cannot afford to neglect, physically abuse, or psychologically maim our youngsters and bank on improving our performance with time. Today, after all, most of us have but two children and there is little room for error.

And above all, let's not forget the chimpanzee. If chimps, our closest relatives in apedom, have a fighting chance to recuperate from two or three traumatic years of total isolation, we humans —even more flexible, more resilient, more adaptable than they— should be able likewise to overcome past problems with help and effort. Though we may be mightily influenced by our early experiences, still we are not totally determined by them.

We are, ultimately, far freer than birds and mice and monkeys. We are not so stereotyped as the turkey who can know her chick only by its cheeps. And we are not so hapless as deermice who unavoidably must lose many of their first litters through inexperience. And we are not so set in our ways as the rhesus monkey, or even the chimpanzee. We can change and compensate and learn, early or late in our lives, more easily than any other species —and there are times when we must.

5

THE BIRTH OF a chimpanzee is a special event for its entire troop. When a mother first appears with her newborn, all gather around to get a glimpse of the infant. The baboon baby and its mother likewise become the center of attention for their group. The two immediately move into the heart of the troop where they, along with as many as twenty other mothers and newborns, are encircled by protective males. From birth on, langur infants and their mothers are also star attractions, catered to by all the adult and subadult females in the troop, though the males, like Victorian fathers, stay well away from the maternity scene.

A new mother-young set is not always the social magnet of their group as in the above species, but among social animals everywhere, they are, at the very least, surrounded always by others of their kind. The social primates enjoy the intimacy of their troops, purple martins relish the camaraderie of their crowded apartment houses, dolphins and sperm whales cavort congenially in their nursery schools, weaverbirds thrive in their thatch-roofed community centers, wallabies keep company in their mobs, sea lions chum about in pods, walruses hobnob in herds, penguins consort in colonies, herons have their rookeries, elephants fraternize in family groups, lions live in prides, and dogs and wolves congregate in packs.

But for humans it is, at least lately, quite different. We have so oddly arranged our affairs that a new mother and her infant, once home from the hospital, are isolated as if they were members, not of the most sociable of species, but of some solitary type like the moose or bear or tiger whose general intolerance of togetherness is dulled just often enough to keep their kind going.

Alice S. Rossi and other researchers have suggested that this unhealthy isolation may be a reason for the postpartum depression that affects so many modern mothers. Such isolation, as Rossi points out, is a

> radical departure from the experience of the species in our long history. In earlier stages of human history, mothers moved in a world crowded with supportive kin who supplemented their care of infants, a situation in sharp contrast to the experience of most American women today. Not only is the natural process interfered with through medical distortion of spontaneous birth, the mother separated from the baby for most of the critical first days of life, the infant fed on a rigid hospital schedule, and kept in a brightly lit and noisy nursery, but then the mother is sent home with her infant to cope as well as she can totally on her own. If she breaks down under this strange regimen, she is regarded as incompetent to handle "normal" female responsibilities.

If there is a single reason that most interferes with the enjoyment of motherhood today, I think it is this isolation. Among mothers I know who have chosen to stay home with their youngsters, nearly every single one has emphasized that she missed her past job not so much in itself but in the daily companionship it offered her. It is the loneliness, the boredom, the monotony of motherhood that bothers mothers most.

Worst of all, this unnatural isolation can create a potentially dangerous situation. Alexander Mitscherlick, author of *Society*

Without Father describes the typical home setting as a "confined, relatively isolated cell-like space" where a mother and her children are penned up together more closely than in the past. While mothers are cut off from adult stimulation and rewards, the children too must cope with a hothouse environment, often without easy access to children of their own age. Sibling rivalry then becomes all the more intense, with a "top dog" oldest child lording it over the younger, smaller, weaker ones.

Konrad Lorenz has written of his aunt's reactions in a similarly claustrophobic situation. The aunt employed a series of housemaids, keeping each no longer than eight to ten months. At the start of each girl's employment, the aunt was immensely pleased with her newfound "pearl." But she soon began finding more and more fault with the maid, until in a final row the aunt would fire the unfortunate girl, refusing even a reference. This same event occurred repeatedly, predictably, and each time, after his aunt's damned-up aggression had erupted, she was restored once more to her amiable, reasonable self and found another "perfect angel" in her next employee.

Lorenz personally experienced the same phenomenon as a prisoner of war. Sometimes called "polar malady," it also affects members of expeditions and crews of small boats—any very small group of people completely isolated and totally dependent on one another. Unable to argue with strangers or outsiders of any kind, pent-up aggression builds up until it erupts over the most minor irritations—"in a way," Lorenz says, "that would normally be adequate only if one had been hit by a drunkard." These ridiculous explosions typically occur, according to Lorenz, over small mannerisms in friends, like the way they cough or clear their throats or a peculiar manner of speaking.

I don't think the average homebound mother has to take off on an expedition to the North Pole to become acquainted with this malady. It's one she has probably experienced many a time, but never knew by name. And it's undoubtedly one of the main reasons for her rush off to office and factory, now that her employment opportunities are at long last improving.

The isolation of the home, for the woman without sufficient

outside interests or without sufficient funds for those interests, is not good for her or for her children. In the stifling, restrictive atmosphere which results, says Mitscherlick, "the whole ambivalent emotional tension of the child is predominantly concentrated on the mother who often feels overburdened by this and feels more ambivalently towards the child in consequence . . . To a greater or lesser extent the child becomes the object on which she discharges her unpleasure tensions."

Tom Annunzia, a social worker in the Midwest, has described the situation in more down-to-earth terms: "I've seen women who have a lot of potential for trouble. They're alone all day . . . They get 'cabin fever.' They get marital problems. Inevitably they take it out on the kids."

In Japan, infanticide began to increase in 1958 after a ten-year decline—this despite the fact that contraceptives are widely used and abortions are easily obtained. The Japanese lay the blame on increasing urbanization and the resultant trend away from the traditional extended family toward the modern nuclear family. One of their studies shows that infanticide is more likely to occur in families where the mother spends a great deal of time alone with her infant.

In our country, the worst abusers are also socially isolated, reports social worker Leontine Young in her book *Wednesday's Children.* They belong to no club, no church, no organization of any kind, nor even any informal group as among neighbors or friends. Their isolation serves not only to hide their severe disturbance, but aggravates it as well.

Women who frequently abuse their children have told Dr. Ray Helfer of their dreadful loneliness. Said one mother: "I never had anyone."

Some provocative new research out of Yerkes Regional Primate Research Center in Atlanta, Georgia, shows loneliness is hard on gorillas, too. "When they are caged alone with their babies, abuse by gorilla mothers seems to be the norm," says Ronald Nadler, a psychologist at the center. Paki, the first gorilla to give birth at Yerkes, was a classic example of this. Caged alone with her new daughter, Paki ignored or pushed the infant or dragged her along the concrete floor. When Paki's snarling toward her daughter grew more intense, the infant was finally removed and raised by human caretakers. Nadler was quite concerned because gorilla reproduction—which is still rare in captivity—had been given high priority at the center. Investigating further, Nadler found that of thirty first-time gorilla mothers, twenty had abused, killed, or ignored their babies. Most of the remaining ten had lived in groups or with a male companion. So the next time Paki gave birth, in 1974, she was not left alone. Another female gorilla, Paki's old cagemate, was moved into the cage with the new mother and her infant. The companionship worked miracles. Paki soon stopped snarling at her baby and was able to raise it without problems.

Nadler then experimented with an even more natural setting —a small number of gorillas, male and female, in a grassy outdoor enclosure. "We wanted to give these gregarious animals a family setting, and the same type of companionship they might enjoy in the wild. We figured it was our best chance of putting an end to the child abuse and our best chance to learn what we could from these advanced animals about the health and welfare of human beings."

Three female gorillas soon gave birth and, though each a first-time mother, there was no child abuse. When one nervous young mother first fumbled with her newborn, the cooing of the other gorillas seemed to give her confidence and soon she had the infant suckling contentedly. Another inexperienced new mother ignored her infant at first and then held it upside down. But she quickly improved her performance, possibly by watching and learning from the other young mothers.

The relevance of this gorilla research to our own human situation is striking. Unfortunately, the loneliness of young human mothers is more prevalent today than ever before. Says psychologist Roy Kern of Georgia State University,

> In years past, a human's family situation was like that of wild gorillas. Folks stuck together and there was always a grandma or an older sister to help when things got rough. Now the trend is to go it alone, out in the suburbs maybe, where the young mother is stranded all day with no company except that of her wailing child.

No wonder she gets confused and depressed. She's like a captive gorilla in an isolation cage.

Our "polar malady" confronts us. Today's mothers have come a long way—the wrong way. Yet we humans cannot readily return to the extended family of old nor to the earlier intimacy of primate troop life. Evolution pursues its relentless course and we must, willy-nilly, go on. But as our evolution in this has been primarily cultural, so also will be our solutions.

We have tried baby-sitting, but as invaluable as it has proved to be, it is usually insufficient. We have tried communal living, but as lofty as our ideals might be, it has seldom worked well. We have tried nursery school and it is an excellent choice—for those who can afford it. And we have tried day care, our latest solution, and we don't, in truth, know the full answer yet, especially in regard to infants. But certainly it holds great promise as a shift toward a more natural way of life for mothers and children, enabling both to interact within a broader social milieu. We are, after all, a social species.

And so our biology haunts us. We are humans last, not first. We have needs and problems, desires and dictates in common with many another species and, for our own good, we must take cognizance of them.

The miner's canary flutters, then falls, and the miner knows. Gas is spreading—odorless, insidious, deadly. And the miner hastily takes his leave. Like the canary, the female gorilla in the cruelty of her loneliness also warns us. And we must go just as quickly.

Too long, mothers and their children have led lives of desperate isolation, cooped up together within the caverns of our modern making. Too often, infants have been taken from their mothers in the first critical moments after birth, then handed over too late, and mothers head home, let down and lonely. In these things, we have wandered too far from the ways which once were ours. It has not been good for us, and it has not been good for our children.

(8) What's a Mother to Do?

The theory of group selection . . . predicts ambivalence as a way of life in social behavior . . . the individual is forced to make imperfect choices based on irreconcilable loyalties—between the "rights" and "duties" of self and those of family, tribe, and other units of selection, each of which evolves its own code of honor.

EDWARD O. WILSON

1

WE ARE. YOU are. I am. And our being derives from the evolutionary success of our ancestors. No dodos, no dinosaurs in our line. No, our forebears played their hands right. They swung with the eons, floated with the continents, rose with the mountains, fell with the seas, shifted with the sands, survived Pliocene drought and Pleistocene ice. And so, here we are. And everything should be hunky-dory. As parents, we will be single-minded in our evolutionary devotions—attending to our children, passing to them our long-honed shrewdness in the game called life, and they will be eager to learn, eager to play the next hand. All of us will be wonderfully united by a common goal—the continuing success of our kind. Our children's interests will be our interests, and ours, theirs. And mother's interests will be father's interests, and father's, mother's. God's in His heaven. All's right with the world. Any flaw, any conflict, any antagonism, all such unnecessary friction between kin can only be attributed, as in one of those soul-stirring TV sagas, to a less than perfect world.

That is one view of things and, overdrawn as it is, it has some merit. Certainly, parental love and filial love and the love between a mother and father truly exist and all are a part of evolution's strategem to ensure the preservation of the species. But the view is a shortsighted one and when we turn in our rose-colored Pollyanna glasses, we will see, just as the popular song predicts, that even in the best of all circumstances life is no garden of roses.

Basically, it is because we differ. Sex has had its say and in consequence, each of us boasts a unique set of genes—different, individual, idiosyncratic. And since our genes are not identical, neither are our interests. There is always and inevitably a division, a cleavage, between like and unlike, between self and other, between parent and child, mother and father, individual and group. And with the cleavage comes conflict, as natural as morning dew and the nighttime moon, a built-in feature of our biology. Its absence is the aberration, as unnatural and sterile as the sheared, unending sameness of golf-course grass.

This chapter is about conflict, especially as it concerns the female of the species in her role as mother. It concerns conflicts with the kids, about how to raise them, about who will raise them. What's a mother to do?

Robert L. Trivers, a theorist at the cutting edge of sociobiology's expanding frontiers, has worked out an intriguing theory of parent-offspring conflict, and it seems to fit the facts better than any of the older theories.

2

AT THE CORE of Trivers's model is the idea that a child, in self-interest, seeks to get more than her or his fair share of parental resources. Parents, on the other hand, have an equal genetic interest in each of their children and consequently, are preoccupied with sharing their total parental investment of time and energy and resources among them. As the second of seven children, Trivers concedes that his theory evolved from the conflicts he himself experienced in growing up in a large family and in the

arguments he had with his father. But there is much good ethological evidence for it, too, some of which had not been explained
as well before.

Conflict during weaning, for instance, is common in mammals.
When a growing youngster becomes capable of feeding itself, a
mother would be better off to stop nursing and to give her energies over to bearing and later nursing another offspring, if she is
to maximize her own reproductive efforts. But the youngster,
interested primarily in its own well-being, still wants to continue
nursing. This clash between interests can be terribly traumatic for
youngsters, and most difficult for mothers. In baboons, for instance, weaning takes several months, during which a mother and
infant have daily confrontations. When a mother rejects her
infant by pushing it off her back or holding it away from her breast
or slapping it, the infant cries out in fear and frustration. A
rejection at dusk, when infants ordinarily return to the warmth
and security of their mother's bosom, can be agonizing for the
young baboon. Frantic in the growing darkness, the youngster
may run from one adult to another, crying pathetically—and this
in a species among whom vocalizations are held to a minimum.

Weaning is hard on chimpanzee infants, too, and they often
become extremely depressed during the process. They lose their
appetites; they sit huddled for long periods of time; they have
little zest for playing, little interest in their surroundings. Their
depression may last for months, for some, even a year or longer.
And it is not that their mothers are heartless. In fact, chimpanzee
mothers are remarkably sensitive and tolerant, almost always re-
buffing their infants' attempts to suckle in a firm but quite gentle
manner. Among the chimpanzees at Gombe National Park in
Tanzania, only one mother was observed to use any physical
aggression during weaning.

It is hard to know whether weaning is worse on mothers or on
their infants. After the early months of weaning, a langur mother
becomes increasingly tense and irritable at the incessant approaches of her infant, and at the screaming and the slapping and
the jumping on her which often follows her rejections. Sometimes, she will groom her infant to placate him, but not even this
always helps. A still-angry infant may slap his mother and she may

return the slap, or simply grimace and slap the ground. "What's a mother to do?" she herself may be wondering in some nonverbal langur way.

Problems in weaning are also known to occur in rats, cats, dogs, and a variety of other mammals. Very similar are the conflicts over parental feeding sometimes seen in birds at the time of fledging. Another kind of parent-young confrontation is evident among some mammals when new young are about to be born. At calving time, elk and moose cows and the does of many species of deer (white-tailed, mule, and roe deer) will chase off their yearlings. Youngsters may also be ousted for territorial reasons. Beaver kits are driven out at two years; chipmunks within two weeks after they leave the nest. A single territory, after all, can only support so many animals.

But what if an older mother knew that a youngster was her last? Why shouldn't she continue to nurse and coddle him indefinitely? Biologists have shed a new light on this and on the whole puzzling phenomenon of menopause. Genes, again, may be at the bottom of things. While a woman shares half her genes with each of her children, she also shares genes, although half again as many, with each of her grandchildren. There may well come a point when she will do more to ensure her gene survival by helping with her grandchildren than by raising youngsters of her own. Due to hazards associated with a mother's increasing age, for example, her own offspring are likely to suffer from a higher mortality rate. In humans, we know, birth defects become increasingly common after the mother reaches thirty-five years of age and, eventually, reproduction stops completely with the onset of menopause.

Slowed or discontinued reproduction in later years has also been observed in several nonhuman primates. At Gombe, the two oldest chimpanzees (one of them was old Flo) appeared to have passed through menopause during the last few years of life, since sexual swellings were no longer observed. Among langurs, older females have less than half as many infants as their younger counterparts.

With the decline in their reproductive potential, older females often take on new and different roles. One of these is the defense of the troop, in which old langur females are particularly active.

They have less to lose from such risk-taking, in terms of future reproduction, than do younger troop members. Among mountain sheep, an old female may become the favorite "aunty" for the yearlings while their mothers are off lambing. Margaret Altmann has described an aging bison cow who similarly acted as an aunt or guardian for the calves of other herd members and, in addition, became involved in herd leadership and safety activities. Among bottle-nosed dolphins, older nonpregnant females ally themselves with pregnant females and help care for newborn calves by swimming at their sides. Sometimes, these old females have been seen lifting a stillborn calf to the surface, apparently as a rescue attempt. In humans, of course, grandmothers are traditionally enthusiastic about helping with their grandchildren.

And what of men, whose fertility declines more gradually than women's? The new thinking suggests that this may be due to the fact that men invest considerably less in each individual child. No large egg, no months-long pregnancy, no nursing after birth is required of the male of the species. He simply produces his sperm and that is it—not too taxing a proposition even for an older body. And so, aging men may yet sire viable offspring by mating with younger women. Consequently, it may always pay for a male to invest in children rather than grandchildren.

But let us return, once more, to the main topic at hand—the ever-present, ever-exasperating and inevitable conflict between parents and their young. During weaning, parent-offspring conflict crescendos, but such conflict is never completely out of the picture. An infant monkey under twenty weeks of age is constantly trying to get away from its mother to explore and its mother must unendingly pull it back by tail or foot. (This may roughly correspond to the "terrible twos" of human children and, as Alison Jolly suggests, a tail for pulling our disaster-prone youngsters out of trouble at that age would be quite an asset!) After this period, however, a monkey mother becomes less protective and allows her infant more freedom. Paradoxically, although her infant is more active and independent that ever before, it is now the infant who more often approaches the mother to maintain contact. As Trivers explains, when the interests of mother and infant begin to diverge, the infant must take more initiative to induce continued parental investment on her part.

Parents usually have an edge in any such conflict of interests. After all, says Trivers, "An offspring cannot fling its mother to the ground at will and nurse." Being smaller, weaker, and less experienced than its parents, a youngster resorts, instead, to psychological tactics to get what it wants. Well-fed fledgling birds, for example, sometimes scream in exaggerated hunger to induce their parents to continue feeding them. During weaning, young Gombe chimpanzees may work their whimpers into screams and tantrums as a ploy to gain nipple access. Puppies have been known to withhold tail-wagging until given more food. Human children, similarly, may refuse to smile until they get their own way.

Natural selection would, of course, favor a youngster's efforts to communicate its own interests. "The child," as Trivers points out, "is not just an empty vessel to be filled by the parents but a sophisticated organism capable of acting in its own self-interest from early on." This view of the child, as an active and self-directed participant in its development, has become well accepted among psychologists. The old *tabula rasa* concept—that the child is born a blank and is thereafter shaped entirely by environmental forces—is a concept as decrepit as creationism.

A parent having prior experience with children should be better able to see through some of their psychological ploys. At Gombe, old Flo was the only chimpanzee mother who had previously weaned an infant and it was she who most consistently refused to give in to her youngster's whims. Yet even she often wound up with him riding on her like a baby after he was old enough to walk on his own. Reverting to infantile behavior is a favorite tactic of young animals. Naturally, parents are strongly selected to respond readily to younger, more helpless and vulnerable offspring, and older offspring often seem to take advantage of this. Psychologists have long been aware of the same phenomenon in humans and refer to it as regression.

Trivers has also used his theory to explain sibling rivalry. Parents, being equally interested in each of their children, may be expected to discourage them from harming one another. The children, on the other hand, will be more inclined to act selfishly. (There will be a limit to this, however, as the children will have

some genes in common and therefore, some mutual interest.)
Parents will also tend to encourage their children to act altruisti-
cally toward cousins and other more distant relatives and even
toward nonrelatives where the long-term indirect effects of reciprocal altruism are involved. Children, typically, will tend to resist
such exhortations.

Does it sound a bit like home? The great appeal of Trivers's
view is that it seems to explain so many of the things, little and
large, that go on in families. Parents' appeals to their children to
help with the chores and to study hard; their valiant attempts to
impart such virtues as honesty, decency, responsibility, generosity,
thoughtfulness, and self-sacrifice; their admonishments against
fighting and their insistence on sharing and cooperation—all
these can be seen as being designed to promote altruism, either
at present or in preparation for future living. Even that all-too-
common hassle over when to go to bed can be readily explained
as a conflict over the preferred amount of parental investment.
Parents, since time immemorial, have favored an early bedtime.
Not only does it save them time and energy at night, but it
reduces the offspring's demands on them during the following
day. Children unfortunately never see it that way.

I personally find the theory of parent-offspring conflict
strangely comforting. That my children and I so often fail to see
eye to eye; that I must tell them and tell them, and they so seldom
seem to listen; that I give to them generously, but it is never
enough; that I encourage them to dress warmly, but they prefer
freezing; that I insist on vegetables and milk, while they beg for
soda and candy; that they tease and torment one another constantly, while I demand peace and apologies—all this is only
natural. Nothing wrong here. That's just the way things are. And
I am comforted. I sigh in relief.

Parenting problems, after all, crop up everywhere among species of every kind. More than half of all bald eagle infants die
during their first year—many are pecked to death by their
stronger siblings. Wood storks must contend, like us, with "juvenile delinquents." Immature, unmated juvenile birds roam
through the colony, like a gang of young thugs, driving parents
from their nests, breaking the eggs, and killing the nestlings.

Mountain goat mothers must chase away the rambunctious "teen-agers" in their group; even in play the sharp horns of the yearlings can injure or kill a baby goat. Young grizzlies are not always attentive to their mother's lessons on berry hunting and squirrel digging, and a smack will be forthcoming if they do not shape up. A mother elephant is known to growl at her youngster when it tries to push its way to the water hole she has just dug.

Primates of every persuasion must also deal with their children's squabbles. To break up fighting between rhesus monkey siblings, a parent may wind up cuffing one or the other to stop the nonsense. As among our own youngsters, play fighting merges all too soon into real fighting in young primates. I have before me descriptions to that effect for rhesus monkeys, for baboons, and for chimpanzees. No doubt it is universal in the primate world. Jane Goodall describes how the chimpanzee Flo broke up such a squabble, and it is easy to empathize with her rage: "Flo rushed over at once, her hair on end. She flew at Evered [a young chimpanzee] and rolled him over and over until he managed to escape and run off screaming loudly."

I know just how mad a mother can get! With my sons, play begun in fun and laughter invariably seems to deteriorate—as if on some predestined schedule—into a chaos of hurt bones and feelings. Some days you begin to feel like an ogre—wary, expect-ant, rankling at the first sound of laughter. You've heard *that* before!

It is comforting, at least, to know that such problems are not unique to us, to some peculiar perversity of our human species, or to our complex human culture, but are rather just part and parcel of being primate. Let TV stick to its glib happy endings, let pediatricians and family psychologists promise their pie-in-the-sky perfection if you follow their prescriptions. I know better. My children and I are genes apart, and we can't possibly exist in some never-never land of heavenly harmony.

It is comforting, too, to learn that some of our other problems may likewise only be natural. Take toilet training, for instance. We are bound to have difficulties, if you look to our primate heritage. Dogs and cats are relatively easy to train, but a monkey is something else again. And it's no wonder, since, in their natural habitat, monkeys defecate wherever they are. Always on the move, with no permanent den, they have no further contact with their fecal matter anyway and so there would be no adaptive value in doing otherwise. We humans, in contrast, happen to be the only primates to have taken up a permanent residence, and, like many of the burrowing rodents, we now have certain areas reserved for defecation. But our youngsters remain unbelievably slow in catching on to this fact, which suggests that it has not yet become part of our natural repertoire.

There is also another of our primate penchants that can cause difficulty for parents. The damage animals do, says Lorenz, is directly proportional to their intelligence, monkeys of course being the worst offenders on this score. Lorenz's pet Gloria, a "magnificent" capuchin monkey, was a magnificent example of this. After cleverly escaping her cage one day while Lorenz was out, Gloria shredded two volumes of medical books, tossed the remains into a saltwater aquarium, and dumped in a lamp to boot. Bright little dickens that they are, pet monkeys obviously can spell financial disaster for their owners. And our own children are smarter, yet! If I knew then what I know now, if I had looked at things with this evolutionary perspective, would it have helped when I found that my kids had painted the bathroom with lipstick and rouge, when they had dumped over my prize aralia and broke off its main stem, when they had tried out their new Cub Scout saw on a desk?

Whatever the problems of parenting, though, and whatever the inherent conflicts within the family—the jealousies and rivalries, the irritations and arguments—family life offers, for most of us, immense rewards far surpassing the negative features. While parents differ from their youngsters by half their genes, they share the other half, and between siblings it is the same. Given this sharing, there is a common footing within the family, a mutuality of understanding and concern and interest and affection potentially greater than that found in most other interpersonal relationships. As such, the family can play an important role as a refuge for its members, a place of warmth and renewal, a base from which members can make their daily forays into the less personal world of school and work.

Perhaps this is why, as Margaret Mead once observed, all past revolutionary attempts to abolish the family have failed. Perhaps this is why, too, in a recent Gallup poll, people the world over, regardless of income, said that family life gave them their greatest satisfaction. A realistic appraisal of the family, considering both its many rewards and its very real difficulties (as freshly approached by Trivers), will enable us to find the best ways to strengthen it, our first and most essential institution.

3

As EVOLUTION WORKED out the role of male and female among the various primates, a mosaic emerged, varied in pattern and nuance, yet always admirably adaptive for each species. Aside from the fact that only females are equipped for nursing and, as such, must remain readily available to their infants, little has been standardized in the primate repertoire. Among some species, the differences between male and female roles are minimal and even in appearance the two sexes may be quite similar. In the gibbon, for example, both sexes are much the same both in their body size and in the size of their canines. As might be surmised, female gibbons are highly aggressive and, together with their mates, will vigorously defend their territories against intruders. Jane Lancaster reports that, among her vervet monkeys, females also join the males with gusto to drive off invading neighbors. It is only new mothers who, for the safety of their infants, stay back from the battlefront. But sometimes, when the monkey group mobs a predator like a python or crocodile, even a mother can't resist the action and she'll pull her infant from her chest, plop it beside the nearest "babysitter," and run over to join the attack.

Sexual differences are far more pronounced in the hamadryas baboon, both bodily and behaviorally, than in the above two species. The adult male of this species weighs more than twice as much as the female and the thick mane hung about his neck and shoulders not only protects him, but adds apparent size and strength to his dimensions. Then there are his canines—long, razor-sharp daggers designed for defense, the male's most important function in baboon society. But despite this macho visage, the male baboon is more paternal than might be expected. Adult males, especially the older, more dominant ones, will fondle infants, carry them on their bellies, and, of course, vigilantly protect them from all harm. Males have also been known to "adopt" young weaned juveniles and care for them solicitously.

Among some of the other primates, females are in complete charge of raising the youngsters, and the male has little function other than impregnation. Here, the orangutan is a prime example, the only one of the great apes to adopt such a life-style. Interestingly, the male orangutan, like the baboon, is twice as big as the female, though paternally speaking the two species have little in common.

Certainly, there are no simple correlations to be made between sexual roles and the differences in size between the sexes or in the evolutionary status of the species. The only safe generalization to be made about primates, as George Schaller once observed, is that they have tried everything.

And so, seemingly, have we humans. In her far-flung travels, Margaret Mead found an astonishing variation in the qualities assigned to each sex by different human cultures:

> Now it is boys who are thought of as infinitely vulnerable and in need of special cherishing care, now it is girls. In some societies it is girls for whom parents must collect a dowry or make husband-catching magic, in others the parental worry is over the difficulty of marrying off the boys. Some peoples think of women as too weak to work out of doors, others regard women as the appropriate bearers of heavy burdens, "because their heads are stronger than men's." The periodicities of female reproductive functions have appeared to some peoples as making women the natural sources of magical or religious power, to others as directly antithetical to those powers; some religions, including our European traditional religions, have assigned women an inferior role in the religious hierarchy, others have built their whole symbolic relationship with the supernatural world upon male imitations of the natural functions of women. In some cultures women are regarded as sieves through whom the best-guarded secrets will sift; in others it is the men who are the gossips. Whether we deal with small matters or with large,

with the frivolities of ornament and cosmetics or the sanctities of man's place in the universe, we find this great variety of ways, often flatly contradictory one to the other, in which the roles of the two sexes have been patterned.

Today, in this time of changing sex roles in our own society, it is good to know of the sexual versatility inherent within our species, rooted as it is in our multifaceted primate heritage. Neither male nor female need be pigeonholed by sex, neither, quite clearly, in humans nor in primates. Yet, even as we accept this, change is not always easy. New conflicts confront us; new problems perplex us. This is especially so regarding women's expanding economic horizons.

As we progress toward equal opportunity, still we have not, especially in the United States, covered all our bases, particularly in the area of child care. Our situation is unique to most of human history. In the agricultural and industrial societies of relatively recent times, economic productivity has been largely divorced from the maternal role. But this has not always been so. For over 90 percent of our history, estimates anthropologist S. L. Washburn, we humans lived largely as hunter-gatherers. Some of us, in fact, still do. And among today's remaining hunting and gathering societies, as you will recall, women almost everywhere contribute half to three fourths of the basic food staples needed for subsistence. This is thought to have also been the case among the Pleistocene peoples of Africa, the continent where humankind was born. Women make their enormous contributions as gatherers of vegetable foods, which are far more reliably found than are the game animals their hunter-husbands pursue.

More important to us at the moment, however, is the fact that the gathering of food is eminently compatible with infant care. Women among the 'Kung people of the Kalahari Desert take infants up to two and even three years of age on their foraging trips. Older children—too big to be carried, too small to walk far —stay behind in the village and are watched by adults who are taking the day off from work.

Gathering, as anthropologist Judith K. Brown has pointed out, is easily carried out in the presence of infants since it can be interrupted and readily resumed, does not require rapt concentration, is not dangerous, and can be carried out relatively close to home. Hunting, on the other hand, would be unthinkable with an infant slung on one's back, and so too would most modern occupations. Most of us mothers today, then, unlike mothers through most of human history, are forced to choose between infant care and working outside the home, at least if we wish to work and raise children simultaneously.

It is a new and often agonizing choice to have to make and all we can do is look carefully into the needs of both our infants and ourselves, cope with these needs as best as we can in view of our own circumstances, and make our decision. Anthropologists have made numerous cross-cultural surveys of the way children are reared among different peoples, and they have found that variations abound. Some cultures are extremely authoritarian; others, very permissive. In some societies, children are thought of as little adults who must do their share of the work, while in others, children are pampered and protected, and have only to play until well past puberty. Children, Jane Lancaster concludes, have thrived in a great variety of cultural contexts.

But always in the past, there were essential features common to every style of parenting. Infants always enjoyed a certain minimum of intimate contact with their mothers, as there was no substitute for breast-feeding. Among many hunter-gatherers and traditional societies, moreover, mothers carry their infants about by day and sleep with them by night. In more "advanced" societies today, however, what with bottle-feeding and infant seats, babies may miss a great deal of the cuddling and contact they need.

In the past, too, children always grew up in the presence not only of their parents, but of a great many other familiar and caring kin, including grandparents, aunts, uncles, and other siblings. If a parent died or was inadequate emotionally or simply needed help, there were plenty of substitutes to take her place. I have already decried the contrasting current situation in which an unhealthy isolation is imposed on mothers and their young children. Ideally, day care today can supplement the maternal role as the extended family once did. But the overcrowded, impersonal, and ever-changing milieu typical of some urban day care centers, as Lancaster observes, is hardly comparable to being cared for and cuddled by a group of familiar people in a familiar environment.

This is not, however, to write off day care, for it has worked in other countries. Jane Lancaster attributes the success of day care centers in Israel and China to the fact that the personnel are familiar neighbors or villagers, and there is little staff turnover. Obviously, this kind of day care arrangement closely approximates the care-taking once shared within an extended family. In our own urban conglomerations, however, a previous familiarity between children and day care personnel rarely if ever occurs. And as long as the poor pay and prestige of day care work prevails in our country, we may never be able to attract sufficient numbers of long-term, dedicated day care personnel. Nonetheless, our day care services might be immensely improved if we could, perhaps through neighborhood or church-affiliated centers, provide our children with more stable and familiar care-givers.

There is also age to consider. Infants have quite different needs than do older children. In eastern Europe, reports sociologist Alice S. Rossi, there has been a trend away from group day care for children under three years old. Researchers in Czechoslovakia suggest that the noise and commotion of group living is too much for the under-three child. After a great deal of national debate on the problem, the Czechs are now opting for private foster care for younger children, as well as long-leave policies for working mothers. A recently published study of day care facilities in New York City, based on research spanning seven years, also recommends private care for the youngest age group—in this case, children under two years of age. Such private care is officially labeled "family day care" and is provided in a licensed private home or apartment with less than six children of various ages, in the charge of one caretaker. "On the basis of the study," asserts Dr. Margaret Grossi, a co-investigator for the project, "children will not suffer adversely from their experience in day care settings in New York City."

Even those who claim to be "solidly against day care for kids under three," as is Harvard's Burton L. White, would probably not object to family day care. White, who has studied child development for over eighteen years, believes that if a mother must work full time, she should hire someone else who is good at raising children, rather than avail herself of group day care services. Ideally, White would like to see more half- or three-fourth-time jobs for both parents so that they could share in child care. "Why," says White, "should the woman have all the fun?"

Quality group care for infants can be quite successful, however, another Harvard psychologist contends. In a study completed in 1976, Jerome Kagan and fellow researchers followed sixty-four children from three months to two and one half years of age. Half of the children were in day care, while the other half were cared for at home, and youngsters in each group were matched in ethnic and family background. Both sets of youngsters developed at the same social and intellectual pace. In both sets, moreover, parent-child bonds were strong and the home had the greatest impact on development. Similarly, child care researcher Bettye Caldwell and her colleagues found that, by two years of age, children in group day care were as attached to their mothers as children brought up at home. However, some differences did emerge as the children entered nursery school. Those small groups of children who had spent their infancy together in a day care center became very close to one another and developed more intense and exclusive interrelationships than did other children their age. Teachers also found the day care children to be less compliant than their classmates. As you will recall, Israeli kibbutz children also form fast friendships with their peers and are closely attached to their mothers.

By and large, these studies suggest that both home care and day care, especially private or "family" type day care, may be equally valid alternatives for children. But one may also ask—and it is a question which is too frequently forgotten—what is best for mothers? It is not an easy thing, after all, for a mother to leave her infant with a substitute caretaker. Whether women are working out of financial necessity or to achieve a more comfortable economic status, whether women are establishing a professional career or seeking the diversions and companionship of a job, women are, in doing so, relinquishing a time-honored, daylong intimacy with their infants. Elizabeth Friar Williams, in her

thought-provoking *Notes of a Feminist Therapist,* addresses herself to the same dilemma: ". . . while the modern woman is
certainly entitled to free choice of role changes and of new identities, she should also realize that not choosing a once-valued role
in the service of a new ideology may also bring her pain." Williams herself chose to work primarily through her home so that
she could remain close to her children.

It is not, of course, that the bond between a mother and her
infant will be hopelessly damaged if a mother works. Numerous
studies, as we have seen, prove otherwise. But what does a mother
miss? What are the costs? Pediatrician T. Berry Brazelton is
concerned about the suffering a mother goes through when she
leaves her infant in the care of others. He likens this suffering to
grieving, "grieving for having to share the nurturing role." While
many women are not aware of this grieving, it can nonetheless
affect them in many ways. Here is how Brazelton describes it:

> . . . one of the most important ways of coping with grief is to
> distance oneself from the beloved object so that the grief won't be
> revived. Hence, it doesn't surprise me that when a mother comes
> to get her baby at the caregiver's house or the day-care center at
> the end of a working day and the infant begins to disintegrate and
> cry, she blames herself for having left the child and she imagines
> that the baby and the secondary caregiver also blame her. Then she
> becomes angry at having to blame herself and eventually she pulls
> herself away from the infant's protests. Inevitably she begins to
> think that the baby is "better off" at the caregiver's house or the
> day-care center and that she herself is not a fit mother anyway.

Babies will typically cry when their mothers pick them up at
the end of the day. Brazelton believes this is all part of a period
of intense communication. Babies appear to save up all their
important feelings of the day, both their frustrations and joys, for
their mothers. And after the crying, there comes a beautiful, calm
time for sharing the more positive messages. Mothers who understand this, says Brazelton, can cope better with their grieving and
do not draw away from their infants.

Working mothers must also beware of the "superwoman syndrome." All too often, women attempt to be all things to all people. Theirs is the classic tug of war, as described so well in this chapter's opening quote, a tug of war between the rights and duties of self and those of others. This conflict and the ambivalence it breeds are common, of course, to individuals within any social species; but in our own species, I think, the female is most taken up in the struggle. For she, especially, now juggles old roles and new, traditional longings plus modern strivings, ancient if outmoded mores side-by-side with new and challenging opportunities. It is exciting, but it can also be overwhelming. One woman, for example, a patient of clinical psychologist Jacqueline Larcombe Doyle, got only four hours of sleep a night. In order to meet the demands of her husband, her children, her profession, and her need for a little privacy, she just kept cutting down on her sleep. Obviously, this woman needed to learn to be more selfish, "to put a priority on her own needs," as Doyle explained. "I like to think of that kind of selfishness," says Doyle, "as educated and informed, something that goes with the understanding that women have the right to think of their own needs without guilt."

On the other hand, such a woman may find great personal satisfaction in each of her roles, and may consequently choose to work part time so that she doesn't "miss" her motherhood. I myself have always felt that this would be the ideal situation and had there been better child-care opportunities when my children were young, I would have done so. As it is, I was a "full-time" mother for some seven years, years during which I could leisurely enjoy my children's growing physical and intellectual prowess and years during which I also had the opportunity to develop interests I might never have had the chance to do otherwise. I became expert at making pressed flower pictures, many of which still decorate my home. I involved myself in environmental causes, gave my first public speech, wrote my first published article, and took several interesting courses in the natural sciences. I look back with great fondness on those busy—but not too busy—years.

Not long ago, Jean Lipman-Blumen, a sociologist then working at the Radcliffe Institute in Cambridge, Massachusetts, carried out an extensive survey of the life-style and life plans of over one thousand married women who had attended college. The year was 1968—before the women's liberation movement had had its major impact. Although women have often been said to act on the basis of feelings and emotions, Lipman-Blumen found instead that the women in her survey chose their roles on the basis of certain ideologies, powerful sets of beliefs that shaped their behavior often without their being consciously aware of it.

Although the women's ideologies regarding the role of the female ranged over a wide continuum, they could be grouped into two main categories: traditional and contemporary. In the traditional view, of course, a woman's primary responsibility is home-making and child-rearing, while a man's is financial support for his family. In the contemporary view, all responsibilities—domestic, financial, parental—are shared, on an egalitarian basis, between husband and wife.

Both sets of women were found to be equally happy in their present lives and equally self-confident as mothers and wives, as students and employees and citizens. Lipman-Blumen concluded, "The traditional and contemporary sex-role viewpoints lead to two distinct life patterns, but *within each ideological position, women are able to find fulfillment and meaning in their life* (my emphasis)."

Nor is motherhood itself essential to one's happiness. In her recent study, Kathy Welds of New York Hospital's Payne Whitney Clinic discovered the same sense of fulfillment among professional women who voluntarily remained childless as among women who became mothers.

Happiness, in conclusion, can come in an artist's palette of colors, and each woman can paint her own picture, pattern her own life, create her own priorities. Our social institutions are more flexible, more accommodating to a variety of modes of motherhood and of womanhood than ever before. But whatever a woman's life-style, if she chooses to have children, she must do all possible to assure that their age-old needs be met, if not by her personal efforts then through quality care by others. In addition to day care services, one of women's greatest assists in this will come from a long overlooked source—their children's fathers. As

Shana Alexander has said, "Some of the most motherly people I know are fathers."

4

TOOL-USING WAS once regarded as a human prerogative, a fitting testament to the uniqueness of our species. Today, we know better. The sea otter uses stones to crack open mussels. The archer fish downs insects by spitting at them with drops of water. The Egyptian vulture hurls rocks at ostrich eggs to break the shells open. The challengers to our past conceit are a diverse and far-flung lot. There are, in addition, certain wasps and ant lions, finches and nuthatches, buzzards, jays, and cockatoos, plus a handful of primates, who have found tools to their liking. But it is the chimpanzee who is champ among animal tool-users. She fishes for termites by poking twigs into their nests; she employs leaves as sponges and wash rags; she uses sticks for a multitude of things—for levers, whips, clubs, missiles, nutcrackers, and toothbrushes. And humanity's erstwhile uniqueness fades in a blush of belated recognition.

Not long ago, paternal care was likewise regarded as a human prerogative. More specifically, its occurrence was cited as a clear-cut distinction between human and nonhuman societies. But this view, too, has fallen by the way with new and more thorough animal studies. Human paternal care, these studies show, has its immediate precursors among the sociable primates; has parallels among the group-hunting carnivores; has roots remote, primitive, encompassing even some insects.

Among the latter, for example, is the male giant water bug who, ready or not, often takes on the role of egg-sitter. In a number of species, you see, the female needs no lessons in assertiveness. When she is ready to lay her eggs, she simply sneaks up to a male as he is surfacing, wraps her legs about him, and glues her eggs onto his back. Literally stuck with the job, the male will carry and aerate the eggs until the youngsters hatch and take off on their own.

Then there are the burying beetles, those minute gravediggers of the animal world. Working usually as a mated pair, these remarkable insects can quickly inter a carcass many times their size. A bird or a mouse or other small animal is typical fare. Once their booty is buried, copulation takes place. But still the male usually stays on, and together both parents perform a rather macabre, but admirably purposeful ritual. First, they free the carcass of fur or feathers and work it into a ball within the little burial chamber they have prepared. This done, the female constructs a small side chamber above the carrion and there lays her eggs. Back to the carrion again, she claws and eats away at the upper surface, forming a tiny craterlike depression. Both parent beetles now eat and regurgitate partially digested tissue into this depression. A pool of pabulum is eventually created—food for the maggotlike midgets which will soon emerge from the eggs. The parents will feed and care for the youngsters throughout their larval stage. Sometimes, adults will even excavate a passageway where the fully grown larvae can pupate. It is only then, when nothing more can be done for their brood, that the parent beetles take their leave and fly off. Of all beetles, varied as they are, the burying beetles are remarkable in the extent to which both paternal and maternal behavior have been developed.

Paternal care, however, is not uncommon among insects, nor is it uncommon among the bony fishes. We have long known of its occurrence in both these groups. But why this similarity between groups otherwise so disparate? External fertilization appears to be the key factor. Eggs are laid first and fertilized second. Consequently, the task of caring for the young, if done at all, often falls upon the parent who sees the eggs last—the father.

The male stickleback offers a classic example of fatherly devotion among fishes. He builds a tunnel of love into which he lures several females, each of which will deposit some fifty eggs. Chasing each female off in her turn, the male fertilizes the eggs and guards them solicitously. Even after the young fish hatch, the father hovers about them protectively. Should they wander too far afield, he sucks them up into his mouth and puts them back in place.

Sea horses go a step farther, for the males actually give birth to their babies. It all starts when the female squirts her six-hundred-odd eggs into the male's belly pouch and then deserts him on the spot. Unperturbed, the male will fertilize the eggs and obligingly take on a nearly two-month-long pregnancy. Giving birth to a herd of sea horses, however, is no picnic. Kenneth Schoenrock, curator of fish at the Milwaukee Zoo, was recently a firsthand observer at the scene and described it like this: "He [the male sea horse] bent forward and backward in such a way that I almost found myself straining with him to get the babies out. At first, they came out one at a time, rapidly, and then 10 or 20 arrived in one big burst." After an ordeal like this, Dad's had it. Famished, he promptly chucks his paternal goodwill for cannibalism—and his babies best watch out!

Parental care by either sex is relatively rare among amphibians and reptiles. But when it does occur, males may be involved almost as often as females. The male arrow-poison frog of Central and South America, for example, carries his youngsters both as eggs and as tadpoles in piggyback fashion, releasing them eventually in water when they become sufficiently mature. The male Nile crocodile (like the female) will defend his young hatchlings from other crocodiles and from predators of other species. More remarkable, if given the opportunity, the male will take on the entire maternal repertoire during hatching time. He, instead of the female, will gently remove the newly hatched youngsters, one by one, from their sandy nest, collecting them in his mouth. Once the entire brood has been rounded up, he will carry them down to water and release them in the shallows. The male, like the female, will also sometimes help break the eggs to free the hatchlings. Taking an egg in his mouth, the male rolls it back and forth between tongue and palate ever so carefully, a masterly feat of control and sensitivity. The same jaws that can crush the bones of the Cape buffalo can tenderly massage an egg without harming its occupant!

But of all the vertebrates, it is among birds that paternal behavior is most widespread. By and large, in fact, parenting is an "equal rights" proposition in the avian world, with both sexes sharing responsibilities on nearly equal terms, according to noted authority Samuel C. Kendeigh. This has evolved for the most practical of reasons—each male and each female, in most cases, will leave the most descendants if they share in raising a brood.

In nature's usual thoroughness, the entire life-style of birds re-volves around this fact, including their sex life. In the vast major-ity of birds, pair-bonding occurs and the couple lives monoga-mously, at least for a brood or a breeding season. Not only does this serve to intimately unite the two parents in their joint ven-ture, but it also explains the males' heightened interest in their progeny. For unlike females, who undoubtedly lay their *own* eggs (or mammalian mothers who undoubtedly give birth to their *own* youngsters), males cannot know their own issue with certainty if promiscuity prevails. For who, then, fertilizes the egg? Who then is father if free love is the rule? With monogamy, in contrast, there is little question and so fathers, knowing their young, are more disposed to care for them.

Although the total parental input of male and female birds is nearly equal, their individual contributions may vary greatly in kind. Among species lower in the evolutionary scheme of things, such as killdeer, chimney swifts, and flickers, both sexes simply share such duties as incubating and caring for the young. But in some of the more advanced species, like cedar waxwings, yellow warblers, and goldfinches, the male does his part not by taking his turn at incubating the eggs, but by bringing food to the female so that she seldom needs to leave the nest herself. Commonly in these species, both parents will help to feed the youngsters after they have hatched.

Among many other bird species, however, the female spends more of her time brooding the delicate young than in feeding them, while the male devotes himself to the latter. In snowy owls, the separation of roles is complete—the females do all the brood-ing, the males all the feeding when the young are small. Many doves, on the other hand, take shifts: The males feed from mid-morning to late afternoon, and the females take charge for the remainder of the day. European coots divide their broods in two: Each parent cares for its own group of young. Then there are some species, like the English robin and the house wren, in which the female may desert her young to start a second brood, leaving the male to finish raising the first brood.

There are, of course, a number of species in which only one parent takes on the role of caretaker. It may be the female as in ducks, domestic fowl, and the ring-necked pheasant. Or it may be the male as in phalaropes and kiwis. New Zealand's national bird, the kiwi, is a bird of considerable distinction over and above the fact that its name appears on tins of a certain brand of shoe polish. Flightless, nocturnal, with a body resembling a hedgehog's and a beak with a nose at its tip, the kiwi holds the world record for relative egg size. The kiwi hen, I presume, has little energy left after laying her huge eggs, which can weigh a pound or more— up to one fourth of her weight. The male, at any rate, prepares the nest and sits on the eggs for all of eighty days, so dedicated to his duty that he may not leave the nest, even to eat, for up to a week at a time. Among phalaropes, as I've mentioned, the female is larger, more handsome, and more vivacious than her mate. And naturally enough, she's the one who does the courting and defending of the territory, while the male, gentle soul that he is, attends to nest-keeping and baby-sitting.

Things are somewhat less variable among mammals, where the female often preempts the major parental role, largely because she has a monopoly on nursing. Why this ability has never evolved in males is a mystery, a rather unexpected one at that. For if there is one rule of thumb in the natural sciences, it is that almost always, there is an exception to every rule or theory or generalization. But here is the exception to the exception—no mammalian male has ever had the ability to lactate.

Male mammals, of course, are capable of all other kinds of parental care-taking, as is evident in a variety of species. Male rats will lick newborns and retrieve them to the nest as skillfully as mother rats, though it will take them a little longer to get started. In other rodents such as mice, males also may show parental behavior similar to that of females. But the two groups that show the greatest amount of paternal solicitude are precisely the two groups which ethologist Tinbergen has cited as most likely to give us insights into our own evolution and existence—the primates and the social carnivores.

As cooperative hunters and as group devotees the social carnivores, particularly wolves and wild dogs, have organized themselves in a manner convergent with that of early humans. Such convergence occurs when two or more species, not closely related, nonetheless find similar means to adapt to similar environmental demands. The bat and the bee, though unrelated, have both developed wings for flying. The whale and the fish have developed, respectively, flippers and fins for swimming—very similar appendages for a similar contingency, although the animals themselves are most dissimilar in ancestry. Like needs breed like adaptations, be they physical or behavioral in form. As such, we may learn something of our own past and potential from species who, like us, evolved a group-living, group-hunting way of life.

Affectionate bonds abound among wolves and wild dogs, bonds between pack members, as well as pair-bonds between mates. In addition, cooperation and altruism, as described earlier, are highly developed in wolves; nearly unmatched in wild dogs. While only one or two pairs will mate each season, all pack members, males and females alike, help to feed and care for the pups. Males, moreover, can do it alone if they must. On one occasion, a litter of nine wild dog pups was orphaned at four weeks of age and subsequently reared by the remaining members of the pack—all of whom were male. Pair-bonding and parental care by both sexes is also characteristic of the fox, who lives in a family unit, rather than in a pack. After the pups are born, the male fox will bring food to the vixen for the first few days. Later, both parents hunt for food for the young.

Among several of the social carnivores, it is true, we will find little paternal behavior. Male lions and hyenas are more apt to cannibalize than care for their young. But then, among these species, male altruism is rare and male-female bonding, absent. In each of these respects, lions and hyenas differ substantially from wolves and dogs—and from humans, too. Obviously, neither the king of the jungle nor the laughing hyena will offer enlightenment on the evolution of fatherly affection.

As for primates, paternal behavior ranges from nonexistent to exemplary. Amid the diversity, however, certain patterns emerge, patterns which, like a confluence of waters, join together in the evolution of humankind. The close association of pair-bonding and paternal care is one of these, a pattern already observed in birds and carnivores. It is among the pair-bonded, monogamous primates that males are most likely to lavish paternal attention on their youngsters. The New World monkeys are particularly keen on monogamy and most males, true to form, actively help to raise the young. Male night monkeys and titi monkeys carry their infants virtually at all times except when they are being nursed. The male marmoset does likewise for his twins—until together their weight equals his own. The tamarin is also the father of twins and he plays the major role in bringing them up.

Siamangs, apes of the tropical forests of Sumatra, are as monogamous as their New World relations and males are as devoted to their youngsters. The father sleeps with the juvenile at night, while the mother sleeps with the infant. Then, during the day, the father takes charge of the infant and carries him about. Gibbons, apes of the nearby Malayan peninsula, are closely related to siamangs and are also monogamous. While there is only one report to my knowledge of a male carrying an infant through much of the day, males of this species will commonly groom, guard, and play with their youngsters.

There is a second important pattern that emerges in a study of primate paternal behavior. Jane Lancaster has made special note of it. Among the Old World primates, those of Africa and Asia, males of the more ground-living species are "very much attracted to, tolerant and protective of young infants." Outside of a few exceptions such as the monogamous gibbons and siamangs, this is in sharp contrast to many of the more tree-living primates of the Old World, who tend to be rather aloof from their offspring. In these arboreal species, the male's role is often minimal— involving little more than impregnation of the females along with occasional protection against predators. By and large, in fact, males in these species exist only as peripheral members of their group, not even missed much should they die or disappear.

Among the more paternal ground-living species is the baboon. As mentioned earlier, male baboons, despite their ferocious facades, can be the gentlest of fathers. Chimpanzees are also largely terrestrial and males show "almost unlimited tolerance" to their youngsters, Jane Goodall has said. Orphaned infants have been adopted by males among both species. Interestingly, both these primates will occasionally hunt for meat. Many other terrestrial or semi-terrestrial primates, as well as some of the arboreal species, like high-protein foods such as eggs, grubs, insects, small birds, and lizards. But only baboons and chimps will hunt cooperatively for larger prey such as rabbits, pigs, young antelope, and other monkeys. Often, these hunters will share some of their catch with other members of their group. This hunting and sharing, though very limited in extent, reveal behavior potentials that came to full fruition in the first hominids to emerge on the African savannah. Undoubtedly, the provisioning of meat became an important aspect of the human male's paternal caretaking behavior.

Like baboons and chimpanzees, Japanese monkeys also have strong terrestrial tendencies, and males are, similarly, very paternal. Junichirô Itani of Kyoto University was first to discover what he called the "phenomenon of paternal care" in this monkey. He published his important paper on the subject in the journal *Primates*. Itani found that males hugged infants, carried them, walked with them, kept them from wandering about, took them to their bosom when sitting, groomed them, and sometimes played with them for hours. In fact, except for the males' inability to suckle the young, Itani concluded, "there exists no great difference between their behavior toward the infants and the behavior of a mother toward her infant."

Japanese monkeys live in large groups in which mating is promiscuous. Consequently, there can be no recognition of bloodlines between father and child. Nonetheless, relationships between one male and a "special child" often develop. Sometimes, if the mother dies, such a child might even be adopted by the male. Certain males, on the other hand, seem to love interacting with groups of youngsters. Itani describes Monk, an adult male who gathered up ten infants and played with them. Together, they all enjoyed a wrestling session during which some of the infants would jump at Monk and attack him in fun. Another male so frequently fed and supervised and played with groups of infants that he was dubbed the "Kindergarten Teacher."

The rhesus monkey is a close relative of the Japanese monkey, but male rhesus under natural conditions show little interest in family affairs. Nonetheless even they have extraordinary paternal potential, as Harry Harlow and his late wife, Margaret, discovered in the Primate Laboratory of the University of Wisconsin. Pairs of male and female monkeys were housed with their youngsters in "blissful monogamy," as the Harlows put it, and the rhesus fathers, despite their reputation in the wild, were excellent fathers. They would not allow abuse or neglect of their infants, they conscientiously guarded against predators (the experimenters), they played with their youngsters far more than did mothers, and they good-naturedly ignored their offsprings' biting and pinching and pulling, behaviors adult males never tolerate in adolescents or adults. Most provocative of all was the effect of this paternal input on the young monkeys themselves. They became "the most self-confident, self-assured, and fearless animals" the Harlows had ever seen.

We human beings are, of course, even more terrestrial than monkeys and chimpanzees. We are also, basically, monogamous —at least serially monogamous—which is, after all, not a very different situation from that among the many animals who pair, not for life, but for a season or so. No other primate has so thoroughly integrated these two modalities into its life-style. And as both modalities, both monogamy and terrestrialness, are separately associated with increased male interest in the young, together they suggest an unsurpassed—and largely untapped—paternal potential in the human male.

Too often in the recent past, however, the male of our species has had little opportunity to develop this potential. He has been kept from the delivery room and nursery; he has been forced to work long hours, leaving him little time for his offspring; and psychologically, he has been victimized by a masculine mystique, as powerful as the feminine mystique, which has placed little value on a man's paternal warmth and nurturance and, at the same time, excessive value on his monetary worth and marketplace expertise.

Margaret Mead has said that in cultures where males are expected to do the hunting or gathering, they are never permitted to imprint on their infants during the first month. By explicit taboos, they are pushed out of the way. Taboos or not, it has been very much the same in our own culture. Men must not be distracted from their work. My father, for example, was nearly a stranger in our house. A grocer, he worked six and a half days a week, all but Sundays from dawn to dusk. How many other fathers must repeatedly work long hours overtime or travel for days and weeks—or if not, lose their jobs?

But things are changing. While we women are now demanding an equal share in the economic security and power that once was the male domain, men are beginning to demand the time and the freedom to be equal participants in parenting. Not surprisingly, Sweden has been at the forefront of this move. Paternity leaves, still relatively rare in the United States, are increasingly common in Sweden, where both parents, mother and father, may share as they like a total of nine months' leave to deliver and care for a newborn baby. In 1977, more than 10 percent of eligible fathers took advantage of the program, including such well-known men as weightlifter Hoa Dahlgren, popular singer Janne Carlsson, and labor economist Per-Olf Edin. These paternity leaves averaged about forty-two days in length.

In our own country, studies have shown that where fathers have a chance to interact with their infants soon after birth, they play an exceptionally active role in nurturance and care-giving. Fathers, in fact, tend to be far more responsive toward infants than our American culture has acknowledged, say some researchers. Pediatrician T. Berry Brazelton customarily sees prospective parents in his office before they deliver their first baby. Ten years ago, about 50 percent of the men came with their wives for the interview, but today the figure is closer to 85 percent. He is also seeing more fathers who demand time off from their jobs to help share in the care of their infants and more fathers who bring their children in for check-ups and know all about their physical development. Fathers, says Brazelton, are beginning to say with pride, "It's a new day for men. We too can do two things at once—be active in our professions and participate in a meaningful home life as well."

This growing involvement of fathers with their children may also come to be at least a partial solution to the problem of isolation, described in the last chapter, that faces so many young mothers today. I know of an engineer, for example, who worked shorter hours during his child's first three years. Not only did this give him more time to enjoy his fatherhood, but his musician wife was able to take on several students each day and so maintain her professional career. I also know of a husband and wife, both writers, who shared equally in the care of their infant, each writing for half the day, while the other baby-sat. In a suburb near mine, two police officers, husband and wife, have made essentially the same arrangement. Working different shifts, they take turns caring for their infant in their off-hours. In addition to these, there are countless fathers who care for their children on weekends and evenings so Mom can work part time, attend classes, or simply enjoy time out from motherhood.

Children will also benefit from this kind of duo-parenting. Each parent, of course, will be less strained, more attentive, and more loving than one who has continual twenty-four-hour-a-day, fifty-two-week-a-year responsibility. Equally important, children will enjoy a more balanced upbringing. Margaret Mead touched upon this in her engrossing autobiography *Blackberry Winter*. If close contact between a father and his child is postponed, says Mead, if an intimate bond between the two fails to develop, then the father's relationship with his child will be "drastically different" from the mother's and "the experience of the children of the two sexes also will be forever different."

Without such a common experiential background, equal rights and opportunity may never become fully realizable. In *The Managerial Woman*, authors Margaret Hennig and Anne Jardim describe the childhood of twenty-five women who rose to the top echelons of management. Each, as a young girl, enjoyed a very special relationship with her father, sharing with him many interests such as sports, fishing, and finance, interests ordinarily restricted to fathers and sons. Another study revealed the same thing: All the women enrolled in the masters program at Harvard Business School in the year 1963–4 had also been extremely close to their fathers and had, since early youth, participated in a wide variety of traditionally masculine activities. All these women absorbed from their fathers skills and attitudes that helped them in their climb to success in the male-dominated business world— they learned the necessity for teamwork, the confidence to take risks, the enjoyment of competition, and the satisfaction of high aspirations and achievement. Girls certainly stand to gain much from their fathers' increased interest and attention.

Boys, too, of course, would benefit greatly from more paternal imput into their early lives. In a past chapter, I described how all infants, male and female, are immersed in their first months in their mother's femaleness and femininity. A girl, without harm, can continue to identify with her mother; to do so, in fact, will enhance her own femininity. But a boy has the more difficult task of separating himself from his mother before he can begin to realize his own masculinity. Were his father, however, to play an integral part in his early development, a boy might be spared this added burden. Equally important, he would grow up realizing that men can be as nurturing and as loving as women.

5

EVOLUTION MARCHES ON, trailing behind it fragments of the old, blazing before it banners of the new. Always, there is this mixture of past nostalgia and future promise, a mixture to be reckoned with as we examine the possibilities of the present, as we ask today our title question, "What's a mother to do?" We have discussed the conflict that occurs between parent and offspring, a conflict that, like death and taxes, will no doubt always be with us. It is a conflict as long-lived and natural as its more respectable alter ego, familial love and camaraderie.

Changing rapidly, however, are the roles of mother and father, of female and male. As more and more mothers work outside the home, children will need supplemental care—by day care personnel, by other mothers, or, best of all, by fathers. The paternal potential is there, evolved over the eons, in certain insects and fish, in birds and carnivores and many primates. The human male, in fact, far surpasses most other social animals in his fatherly care and concern, so much so that for a long time, as we have noted, he was considered unique in this among social animals. No doubt about it, the human father can be superb when given the opportunity or the necessity for child care, as he is more and more today. And our children, female and male, will be the better for it—and so will their fathers.

Conclusion

MANY A RECENT book on the human female has been devastatingly depressing. If the reader is a woman, as she reads she must choke back years of sexual discrimination and bias and rape and violence. Not that these books aren't important. They are and vitally so. Bias must be exposed before it can be eliminated.

Bias has also been prevalent in the natural sciences,—the role of the female has been neglected, distorted, and demeaned. But happily, the natural order itself could not be tampered with. And so the females of the various species—no matter what men wrote and sometimes still write—live lives of worth and prominence within their animal societies. The female is frequently leader and head of her genealogy and wielder of power both through personal influence and through group coalition. She is nature's original and most durable model. She and her young are the focal point within most animal communities. And she can, on occasion, live and reproduce entirely on her own—without male assistance.

In the long run, on an evolutionary scale, the female has a proud and inspiring heritage. It's fine to be female in the natural world.

Bibliography

Alexander, Shana. *Talking Woman.* New York: Delacorte Press, 1976.

Altmann, Stuart A. *Social Communication Among Primates.* Chicago: The University of Chicago Press, 1967.

Ardrey, Robert. *The Territorial Imperative.* New York: Atheneum, 1966.

Avers, Charlotte J. *Evolution.* New York: Harper & Row, 1974.

Barash, David P. *Sociobiology and Behavior.* New York: Elsevier, 1977.

Bastock, Margaret. *Courtship, An Ethological Study.* Chicago: Aldine Publishing Company, 1967.

Bateson, P. P. G. and R. A. Hinde, eds. *Growing Points in Ethology.* New York: Cambridge University Press, 1976.

Bermant, Gordon and Julian M. Davidson. *Biological Bases of Sexual Behavior.* New York: Harper & Row, 1974.

Bernhard, Jessie. *The Future of Motherhood.* New York: Dial Press, 1974.

Blair, Blair, Bordkorb, Cagle, Moore. *Vertebrates of the U.S.* Second Edition. New York: McGraw-Hill, Inc., 1968.

Brownmiller, Susan. *Against Our Will.* New York: Simon and Schuster, 1975.

Campbell, Bernard, ed. *Sexual Selection and the Descent of Man.* Chicago: Aldine Publishing Company, 1972.

Carson, Rachel. *The Edge of the Sea.* Boston: Houghton Mifflin Co., 1955.

Carson, Rachel. *Under the Sea Wind.* New York: Oxford University Press, 1941.

Chase, Naomi F. *A Child Is Being Beaten.* New York: Holt, Rinehart and Winston, Inc., 1975.

Chevalier-Skolnikoff, Suzanne and Frank E. Poirier, eds. *Primate Bio-Social Development.* New York: Garland Publishing, 1977.

Ciba Foundation. *Parent-Infant Interaction.* Amsterdam: Elsevier, 1975.

Clapham, W. B., Jr., *Natural Ecosystems.* New York: The Macmillan Co., 1973.

Cloudsley-Thompson, J. L. *Animal Conflict and Adaptation.* Chester Springs, Pennsylvania: Dufour Editions, 1965.

Darling, F. Fraser. *A Herd of Red Deer.* London: Oxford University Press, 1937.

Darwin, Charles. *The Descent of Man and Selection in Relation to Sex.* 1871. (*The Works of Charles Darwin,* Vol. 9, New York: Ames Press, 1972).

Dawkins, Richard. *The Selfish Gene.* New York: Oxford University Press, 1976.

De Vore, I. *Primate Behavior.* New York: Holt, 1965.

De Vries, Hugo. *Species and Varieties.* Chicago: Open Court Publishing Co., 1905.

Douglas-Hamilton, Iain and Oria. *Among the Elephants.* New York: The Viking Press, 1975.

Downs, James F. *The Navajo.* New York: Holt, Rinehart and Winston, Inc., 1972.

Droscher, Vitus B. *They Love and Kill.* New York: E.P. Dutton and Co., Inc., 1976.

Eimerl, Sarel and Irven De Vore. *The Primates.* New York: Time-Life Books, 1965.

Erikson, Erik. *Childhood and Society.* Second Edition. New York: Norton, 1963.

Flavell, John H. *The Developmental Psychology of Piaget.* Princeton, New Jersey: Van Nostrand, 1963.

Forbush, Edward H. *A Natural History of American Birds of Eastern and Central North America.* New York: Bramhill House, 1955.

Foss, B. M. *Determinants of Infant Behavior,* Vol. 2. New York: John Wiley and Sons, Inc., 1963.

Foss, B. M. *Determinants of Infant Behavior,* Vol. 3. London: Methuen, 1965.

Freedman, A. M., H. I. Kaplan, and B. J. Sadock, eds. *Comprehensive Textbook of Psychiatry.* Baltimore: Williams and Wilkins Co, 1975.

Freud, Sigmund. Dissolution of the Oedipus Complex. *Standard Edition of the Complete Works of Sigmund Freud.* Vol. 19. London: The Hogarth Press and the Institute of Psycho-Analysis.

Freud, Sigmund. Female Sexuality. *Standard Edition of the Complete Works of*

Sigmund Freud. Vol. 21. London: The Hogarth Press and the Institute of Psycho-Analysis.

Freud, Sigmund. Femininity. *Standard Edition of the Complete Works of Sigmund Freud.* Vol. 22. London: The Hogarth Press and the Institute of Psycho-Analysis.

Freud, Sigmund. Some Psychological Consequences of the Anatomical Distinction Between the Sexes. *Standard Edition of the Complete Works of Sigmund Freud.* Vol. 19. London: The Hogarth Press and the Institute of Psycho-Analysis.

Freud, Sigmund. "Three Essays on the Theory of Sexuality." *Standard Edition of the Complete Works of Sigmund Freud.* Vol. 7. The Hogarth Press and the Institute of Psycho-Analysis.

Friedan, Betty. *The Feminine Mystique.* New York: Penguin Books, 1965.

Friedman, Richard C., Ralph M. Richart, Raymond L. Vande Wiele, and Lenore O. Stern, eds. *Sex Differences in Behavior.* New York: John Wiley and Sons, 1974.

Geist, Valerius. *Mountain Sheep and Man in the Northern Wilds.* Ithaca, New York: Cornell University Press, 1975.

Geist, Valerius. *Mountain Sheep: A Study in Behavior and Evolution.* Chicago: University of Chicago Press, 1971.

Goodall, Jane. *See* Lawick-Goodall, Jane van.

Grzimek, Bernhard, ed. *Grzimek's Animal Life Encyclopedia.* New York: Van Nostrand Reinhold Co., 1975.

Guggisberg, C. A. W. *Wild Cats of the World.* New York: Taplinger Publishing Company, 1975.

Harden, Garrett. *Biology, Its Principles and Implications.* San Francisco: W. H. Freeman and Company, 1966.

Harlow, Harry F. *Learning to Love.* Second Edition. New York: Ballantine Books, Inc., 1971.

Hennig, Margaret and Anne Jardim. *The Managerial Woman.* Garden City, New York: Anchor Press/Doubleday, 1977.

Henslin, James M., ed. *Studies in the Sociobiology of Sex.* New York: Appleton-Century-Crofts, 1971.

Hess, Eckhard H. *Imprinting, Early Experience and the Developmental Psychobiology of Attachment.* New York: Van Nostrand Reinhold Company, 1973.

Hickman, C. P., Sr., C. P. Hickman, Jr., and F. M. Hickman. *Integrated Principles of Zoology.* St. Louis: The C.V. Mosby Company, 1974.

Hinde, Robert. *Biological Bases of Human Social Behavior.* New York: McGraw-Hill Book Company, 1974.

Hirsch, S. Carl. *He and She.* New York: J.B. Lippincott Company, 1975.

Hite, Shere. *The Hite Report: A Nationwide Study of Female Sexuality.* New York: Macmillan Publishing Co., Inc., 1976.

Hrdy, Sarah B. *The Langurs of Abu.* Cambridge, Massachusetts: Harvard University Press, 1977.

Jackson, Hartley. *Mammals of Wisconsin.* Madison, Wisconsin: The University of Wisconsin Press, 1961.

James, William. *The Principles of Psychology.* New York: Holt, 1890.

Jay, Phyllis C., ed. *Primates, Studies in Adaptation and Variability.* New York: Holt, Rinehart and Winston, Inc., 1968.

Jolly, Alison. *The Evolution Of Primate Behavior.* New York: Macmillan Publishing Co., Inc., 1972.

Jolly, Alison. *Lemur Behavior.* Chicago: The University of Chicago Press, 1966.

Kaestner, Alfred. *Invertebrate Zoology.* New York: Interscience Publications, 1970.

Kempe, C. Henry and Ray E. Helfer. *Helping the Battered Child and His Family.* Philadelphia: J.P. Lippincott Co., 1972.

Kendeigh, Samuel C. *Parental Care and Its Evolution in Birds.* Urbana: The University of Illinois Press, 1952.

Klagsbrun, Francine, ed. *Free to Be You and Me.* New York: McGraw-Hill Book Company, 1974.

Klaus, Marshall H. and John H. Kennell. *Maternal-Infant Bonding.* St. Louis: The C.V. Mosby Company, 1976.

Kluckhohn, Clyde and Dorothea Leighton. *The Navaho.* Cambridge, Massachusetts: Harvard University Press, 1974.

Kortlandt, A. *Aspects and Prospects of the Concept of Instinct.* Leyden: Brill, 1955.

Kruuk, Hans. *Hyaena.* London: Oxford University Press, 1975.

Kummer, Hans. *Social Organization of Hamadryas Baboons.* Chicago: The University of Chicago Press, 1968.

Lack, D. *Ecological Adaptations for Breeding in Birds.* London: Methuen and Company, Ltd., 1968.

Lack, D. *The Life of the Robin.* Witherby, London, 1946.

Lang, R. *Birth Book.* Ben Lomond, California: Genesis Press, 1972.

Lawick-Goodall, Jane van. *In the Shadow of Man.* New York: Dell Publishing Company, Inc., 1971.

Lee, Richard B. and Irven De Vore, eds. *Kalahari Hunter-Gatherers.* Cambridge, Massachusetts: Harvard University Press, 1976.

Lehrman, Daniel S., Robert A. Hinde, and Evelyn Shaw, eds. *Advances in the Study of Behavior,* Vol. 2, New York: Academic Press, 1969.

Livingstone, David. *Missionary Travels and Researches in South Africa.* London: John Murray, 1857.

Lorenz, Konrad. *King Solomon's Ring.* New York: Crowell, 1952.

Lorenz, Konrad. *On Aggression.* New York: Harcourt, Brace, and World, 1966.

Lorenz, Konrad. *Studies in Animal and Human Behavior.* Cambridge, Massachusetts: Harvard University Press, 1971.

Malinowski, Bronislaw. *The Sexual Life of Savages.* New York: Halcyon House, 1929.

Martin, M. Kay and Barbara Voorhies. *Female of the Species.* New York: Columbia University Press, 1975.

Masters, W. H. and Johnson, V. E. *Human Sexual Response.* Boston: Little, Brown and Co., 1966.

Mead, Margaret. *Blackberry Winter.* New York: William Morrow & Company, 1972.

Mead, Margaret. *From the South Seas.* New York: William Morrow & Company, 1939.

Mead, Margaret. *Male and Female.* New York: William Morrow and Company, 1949.

Mech, L. David. *The Wolf.* Garden City, New York: The Natural History Press, 1970.

Metz, Charles B. and Alberto Monroy, eds. *Fertilization.* New York: Academic Press, 1967.

Millett, Kate. *Sexual Politics.* New York: Doubleday, 1970.

Milne, Lorus J. and Margery J. *The Mating Instinct.* Boston: Little, Brown and Co., 1954.

Mitscherlich, Alexander. *Society Without Father.* New York: Harcourt, Brace and World, Inc., 1969.

Money, John and Anke A. Ehrhardt. *Man and Woman, Boy and Girl.* Baltimore: The John Hopkins University Press, 1972.

Money, John and Herman Musaph, eds. *Handbook of Sexology.* New York: Excerpta Medica, 1977.

Money, John and Patricia Tucker. *Sexual Signatures.* Boston: Little, Brown and Company, 1975.

Montagu, Ashley. *The Natural Superiority of Women.* New York: The Macmillan Company, 1968.

Montessori, Maria. *The Secret of Childhood.* Transl. by B. B. Carter. New York: Longmans, Green, 1936.

More, Sir Thomas. *Utopia.* Transl. by P. K. Marshall. New York: Washington Square Press, 1965.

Morgan, Elaine. *The Descent of Woman.* New York: Stein and Day, 1972.

Morris, Desmond. *Patterns of Reproductive Behavior.* New York: McGraw-Hill Book Company, 1970.

Moynihan, Martin. *The New World Primates.* Princeton, New Jersey: Princeton University Press, 1976.

Murdock, George P. *Africa, Its People and Their Culture History.* New York: McGraw-Hill Book Company, 1959.

Najarian, Haig H. *Sex Lives of Animals Without Backbones.* New York: Charles Scribner's Sons, 1976.

Newton, Grant and Seymour Levine, eds. *Early Experience and Behavior.* Springfield, Illinois: Charles C. Thomas, 1968.

Ommanney, F. D. *The Fishes.* New York: Time-Life Books, 1969.

Rabin, Albert I. *Kibbutz Studies.* Michigan State University Press, 1971.

Rheingold, H. L., ed. *Maternal Behavior in Mammals.* New York: Wiley and Sons, 1963.

Rudnai, Judith. *The Social Life of the Lion.* Wallingford, Pennsylvania: Washington Square East, Publishers, 1973.

Scarf, Maggie. *Body, Mind, Behavior.* Washington, D.C.: The New Republic Book Company, Inc., 1976.

Schaffer, H. R., ed. *The Origins of Human Social Relations.* New York: Academic, 1971.

Schaller, George. *The Mountain Gorilla.* Chicago: The University of Chicago Press, 1963.

Schaller, George. *The Year of the Gorilla.* Chicago: University of Chicago Press, 1963.

Schmitt, Francis O. and Frederic G. Worden, editors in chief. *The Neurosciences, Third Study Program.* Cambridge, Massachusetts: The Massachusetts Institute of Technology, 1974.

Seward, G. H. and R. C. Williamson, eds. *Sex Roles in Changing Society.* New York: Random House, 1970.

Sikes, Sylvia K. *The Natural History of the African Elephant.* New York: American Elsevier Publishing Co., Inc., 1971.

Speck, Ross V. and others. *The New Families, Youth Communes and the Politics of Drugs.* Basic Books, 1972.

Stebbins, G. Ledyard. *Chromosomal Evolution in Higher Plants.* Reading, Massachusetts: Addison-Wesley Publishing Co., 1971.

Steiner, Shari. *The Female Factor.* New York: G.P. Putnam's Sons, 1977.

Stoller, Robert J. *Sex and Gender.* New York: Jason Aronson, 1974.

Stone, Merlin. *When God Was a Woman.* New York: The Dial Press, 1976.

Teitelbaum, Michael S., ed. *Sex Differences.* Garden City, New York: Anchor Books, 1976.

Thorpe, W. H. and O. S. Zangwill, eds. *Current Problems Of Animal Behavior.* Cambridge, Massachusetts: Harvard University Press, 1961.

Thwaites, R. G., ed. *The Jesuit Relations and Allied Documents.* Seventy-one volumes. Cleveland: Burrows Brothers, 1906.

Tiger, Lionel. *Men in Groups.* New York: Random House, 1969.

Tiger, Lionel, and Robin Fox. *The Imperial Animal.* New York: Holt, Rinehart and Winston, Inc., 1971.

Tinbergen, Nikolass. *Social Behavior in Animals.* New York: Wiley, 1953.

Welty, Joel C. *The Life of Birds.* Second Edition. Philadelphia: W. B. Saunders Co., 1975.

White, Michael J. D. *Animal Cytology and Evolution.* Third Edition. New York: Cambridge University Press, 1973.

Wickler, Wolfgang. *The Sexual Code.* New York: Doubleday and Company, 1972.

Wilkins, L. *The Diagnosis and Treatment of Endocrine Disorders in Childhood and Adolescence.* Springfield, Illinois: Charles C. Thomas, Publisher, 1950.

Williams, Elizabeth Friar. *Notes of a Feminist Therapist.* New York: Praeger Publishers, Inc., 1976.

Williams, Leonard. *Man and Monkey.* London: Andre Deutsch Limited, 1967.

Wilson, Carl L., Walter E. Loomis and Taylor A. Steeves. *Botany.* Fifth Edition. New York: Holt, Rinehart and Winston, Inc., 1971.

Wilson, Edward O. *Sociobiology, the New Synthesis.* Cambridge, Massachusettes: The Belknap Press of Harvard University Press, 1975.

Young, Leontine. *Wednesday's Children.* New York: McGraw-Hill Book Co., Inc., 1964.

Zajonc, Robert B., ed. *Animal Social Psychology.* New York: John Wiley and Sons, Inc., 1969.

Zubin, Joseph and John Money, eds. *Contemporary Sexual Behavior.* Baltimore: The John Hopkins University Press, 1973.

In addition to the books listed above, I have used many professional journals in the course of my research.

Index

255